D1346359

# SPINNER'S YARN

*By the Same Author*

HOW TO BOWL
TALKING OF CRICKET
THE ASHES 1954/5
BATTER'S CASTLE
BOWLER'S TURN
THE FIGHT FOR THE ASHES 1958/9
THE TEST MATCH GROUNDS
STRAIGHT FROM THE SHOULDER
FRANK WOOLLEY, PRIDE OF KENT
PAT HENDREN
DENIS COMPTON

*With Diana Rait-Kerr*
LORD'S 1946-1970

*Ian Peebles*

# SPINNER'S YARN

FOREWORD BY LORD COBHAM, PAST PRESIDENT OF MCC
AND
GOVERNOR-GENERAL OF NEW ZEALAND 1957-62

**COLLINS**
St James's Place, London
1977

William Collins Sons & Co. Ltd
London · Glasgow · Sydney · Auckland
Toronto · Johannesburg

First published 1977
© Ian Alexander Ross Peebles

ISBN 0 00 216516 3

Set in Imprint
Made and Printed in Great Britain by
William Collins Sons & Co. Ltd, Glasgow

*To Ursula, who appears infrequently in this book, but who has contributed so much to the happy memories herein.*

# CONTENTS

## ILLUSTRATIONS *and* ACKNOWLEDGEMENTS

I am grateful to Emmwood of the *Daily Mail* for being able
to reprint the cartoon used on the cover and to Mr J. M.
Coldham who compiled the index as well as making a number
of valuable corrections to the text.

Writing in *Punch*, Alan Ross once stated that, 'The division between sport and art is a false one, for anyone who has played a game even tolerably well knows that his pleasure in it is more aesthetic than competitive.' I believe this to be profoundly true, and that games lose something of their very essence when the act of winning is allowed to become paramount.

Of all bowlers the leg-break bowler is undoubtedly the most fascinating, and the most fun to watch. He relies for his success upon arts which need years of practice to bring to fruition, complicated movements of wrist and fingers in conjunction with the need for length and direction, and, if he is to reach the very top, the acquisition of that rare and precious quality known to cricketers as 'flight', the ability to deceive a batsman about where the ball is going to land. 'No great batsman,' declared the late Charles Fry, 'has ever been dismissed by spin alone.' Aspiring slow bowlers should not be misled by the amusing rotundity of this remark into dismissing it lightly; it contains more than the proverbial grain of truth.

The leg-break bowler has to be a true artist, for if he has a slightly larger patch at his disposal than Jane Austin's 'square inch of ivory' it does not amount to much more than eight square feet of turf, say five feet long and eighteen inches wide – and on a wet wicket this area is further reduced. The slow bowler is to the fast what the fly-fisherman is to the harpoonist; the gentle wiles with which he lures batsmen to their doom are poles apart from the envenomed darts hurled at them by his more violent and usually less devious colleagues.

Above all he has to be a philosopher, for he has more than most with which to contend, not only with muddle-headed selection committees and nail-biting captains (push it through a bit, George, for the love of Pete!) but an odd demonology which has somehow infected the cricket world with the conviction that leg-spin bowlers

1) are very expensive, 2) never get out anyone other than the 'tail', and 3) are 'no good in Australia'.

Ian Peebles's Christian fortitude was early tested. The young bowler was tried for Middlesex in 1928. He must have been greatly encouraged to read the 'blurb' in *Wisden* which preceded the account of Middlesex matches for that year. 'Further to prejudice the prospects of Middlesex, the hopes entertained that I. A. R. Peebles would prove a considerable accession to the bowling strength of the side were not realized. Peebles played in two of the first three Middlesex engagements and then was seen no more in the ranks of the county except on the occasion of the match with West Indies.'

A reader of those two sentences might be surprised to learn that in his first match Peebles bowled 1.2 overs in the first innings, taking 1 for 1; in the second, in which Durston took 3-15, Haig 0-27, and Hearne, in 19.5 over, 3-27, Peebles in 15 overs took 3-24; all his wickets were clean-bowled. In his second match Hampshire made a score of 540. Peebles took 2 for 104 in 26 overs; in the same match Reg Bettington, already a leg-breaker of established reputation, took 2 for 155 in 35 overs. In the Middlesex match *v* West Indies Peebles in the first innings took 2 for 51 in 18 overs, clean-bowling Constantine at 86, and 1 for 45 in 11 overs in the second. Thus Ian, top of the Middlesex bowling averages for 1926, 'was seen no more in the ranks of the county'.

More percipient were the MCC selectors, who included three leg-spinners for the South African tour which followed in the following winter – Freeman, Stevens and Peebles. Although the mat is notoriously unfriendly to wrist-spinners and only the experienced 'Tich' Freeman did much in the Tests, Peebles in all matches took 34 wickets for an average of 19.38, Freeman taking 56 at 18.17.

The following summer saw Peebles as an established spinner of top quality; he took 107 wickets for under 20 apiece. It is probable that 1929 and 1930 were his best years as a bowler. The whole range was there – he had a lovely easy action, and if the leg-break was a bit less venomous than that of Walter Robins the top-spinner and 'wrong 'un' turned and bounced fiercely. Above all he had the beautiful looping flight of the great bowler. It is interesting to note that of English bowlers who took more than 50 wickets in that season no fewer than 9 out of the top 16 were spin-bowlers.

Another traumatic experience lay ahead, however: the University Match of 1930. It ill becomes an ardent Cambridge supporter to rub salt into a wound which even after nearly half a century must, like Dr Watson's, cause an occasional pang; suffice it to say that never before can such consistently fine bowling have failed to secure victory, especially on a side that although a bit weak in support for Peebles was very strong in batting. Vital catches were dropped, Oxford allowed Cambridge's last four men to put on a heap of runs, and then in the last innings they started an ill-judged assault on some steady Cambridge bowling in a bid for victory. When this failed and early wickets tumbled they went over to defence but fell victims to some decent but by no means unplayable spin-bowling.

Later on in that same summer Ian was brought into an England team the bowlers of which had so far signally failed to contain an immensely powerful Australian batting side, over which the youthful phenomenon, Don Bradman, ruled supreme and apparently invulnerable. Ian did his job and dismissed the great man for a trifling score, having had him first dropped at slip by – of all people – Walter Hammond. He also picked up the wicket of that fine player S. J. McCabe when he had scored only 4, and in the match took 3 wickets for 150 in 55 overs.

In the fifth Test at the Oval when Australia made the big score of 695 Peebles bowled splendidly, taking 6 wickets for 204 in 71 overs. The established veterans performed more demurely: Larwood 46-6-132-1, Tate 65.1-12-153-1, Wyatt 14-1-58-1, Hammond 42-12-70-1. Peebles's victims included Woodfull, Ponsford and Kippax; three out of the first four Australian batsmen; so much for the current misconception that leg-spinners are 'expensive' and only useful for removing tail-enders!

Eight years later the Oval was the scene of an even more one-sided contest; this time it was Australia's turn to suffer on a wicket heart-breaking for bowlers, and England amassed the monumental total of 903 for 7. O'Reilly, undoubtedly one of the greatest spin-bowler's in cricket's history, took 3 for 178 in 85 overs; the other Australian bowlers had to be content with 3 for 675.

The comparison is not without interest; again the accuracy –

although on this occasion the great man took only half the wickets the cost was by no means excessive in such a total, and his wickets included three out of the first five England batsmen – Hutton, Edrich and Payntor.

Peebles and O'Reilly had much in common as bowlers; neither used that ultimate contortion of wrist and fingers for their leg-breaks which tends to lead to inaccuracy; both employed the more sharply-turning 'wrong 'un', both had a teasing flight and neither was easy to use the feet to, being a bit too quick through the air. In 1930 Peebles had just under three runs an over scored off him; in 1938 O'Reilley conceded just over two. Both these performances must, by any standards, be adjudged great bowling on a pre-war Oval wicket.

Peebles took 100 wickets again in the following year, but after that the shoulder injury began to give increasing trouble. He found himself having to rely more and more on the googly, but he still remained a fine bowler, and his command of flight and length and spin would have gained him a place in most post-war England XIs.

Even the Luftwaffe failed to extinguish either the inborn power of flight or rare and mordant wit, and he was still bowling splendidly and posing all sorts of problems on a Free Foresters tour of Holland after the war.

One day, when cricketers recover their sanity and remember that cricket, even Test cricket, is a gay tournament played between friends (albeit in a spirit of intense rivalry) and not morose studies in skill and endurance, we shall see the spinners of Ian Peebles's quality back on our grounds and those of our opponents; batsmen vigilant to punish severely any vagaries in length and direction, the bowler out to deceive him with subtle variations of spin and flight.

This is cricket at its glorious best, and as man and cricketer Ian Peebles in his day exemplified it. In *Spinner's Yarn* he writes about cricket beautifully and with knowledge, and above all wholly without rancour; Ian is sometimes critical but never unkind. This book is a record of a long life gladly lived, and I believe that it will appeal, not only to those who cherish fine cricket, but to that far wider circle who appreciate elegant and witty prose. This is a book for the connoisseur of both.

COBHAM

# First Steps

If there is any substance in the thought that a man's career starts with a twinkle in the eye of his father my own start was a somewhat unusual one. When my father journeyed to Inverness to ask for my mother's hand in marriage his prospective father-in-law, Alexander Ross, bustled him into a cab and drove him straight to the local lunatic asylum. As his family assiduously spread this story Grandpa Ross was slightly irritated, for he was bound to admit its truth, and then be called upon to explain that he was going there anyway in his professional capacity as an architect.

My father's mission was otherwise successful and, at the turn of the century, he took his bride to the Manse of Kinloss, he being a Minister of the Church of Scotland. My two sisters were born there, and my younger brother and I when the family moved to Aberdeen. If there was nothing spectacular about my arrival my brother did rather better. On the day he was born my father made a hundred on the Aberdeenshire cricket ground, Mannofield – the last ground in Britain, incidentally, upon which Don Bradman made a century.

When I was two years old we moved to Wick in Caithness where my first recollection is of my mother telling us that there was going to be a great war. Thus Wick, a modest fishing town of 10,000 inhabitants, suddenly found itself important, for not only was it a railhead and base for a mine-sweeping flotilla, but it also boasted a wireless station.

As a consequence we were blacked out, and invaded by a number of important naval and military personages. Our first line of defence against the fury of the Kaiser was a Commander Harold Tennyson, a kinsman of Lionel of that ilk, whom I was to know well in future years. The Commander, with that impetuosity so noticeably a family trait, immediately threw himself into his duties. In his first week of office he observed an unshielded light in a nearby house, and forthwith sent an armed guard to arrest the culprit. When his minions returned with a protesting prisoner an embarrassing situation arose. The prisoner turned out to be the provost of the town, and as he forcibly pointed out the light was still burning brightly – in the house next door to his.

My father returned from his duties in France as a chaplain to the forces in 1917, and soon after we moved again, this time to Uddingston, near Glasgow. Here we celebrated the Armistice and, in the following summer, the Uddingston Cricket Club resumed its activities. My brother and I were immediately and fanatically attracted to the game, and became junior members of the club, which turned out three elevens, a junior team, and also a minors' side for the very young.

The first time I actually played cricket was in the gardens adjoining a residential part of Uddingston. The occasion was a party of both sexes rather below the age of ten. The wicket was a tree, and the sum total of our equipment was a size four bat and a cork ball. The general run of the play I cannot remember, but my own innings has ever remained clear in my mind's eye. I was out first ball. A lady, who bowled underarm with a better aim than many of her elder sisters, delivered a high full toss which hit the tree about eight feet up with a resounding 'clonk'. As no agreement had been reached about the height of the wicket I was adjudged to be out. If I 'walked' it was on account of my ignorance of the rules rather than any precocious gallantry.

Despite this discouraging start my enthusiasm knew no bounds, and my brother and I joined a band of boys who played on an open space known as Kyle Park. The one menace on this otherwise agreeable scene was a bigger boy called Sandy. As a fast bowler he still seems, as I look back, to have achieved a ferocity unattained by Larwood, Lindwall or Lillee. As again our equipment did not run to pads or gloves, and the pitch was hard-baked mud and far from plumb, it was a great matter to get picked on his side and not by the opposition.

As Sandy was also a keen batsman, when I bowled him one day with a newly acquired off-break his indignation was considerable, especially as the ball had been a double bouncer. The

retiring batsman automatically became umpire, and I could almost
feel his intense disgust as he stationed himself at my end. When
I took a second wicket he burst forth. 'Peebles,' he said in a terrible
voice, 'you can't bowl breaks.'

'Oh, yes, I can,' I replied, and made to show him my new magic.
However, he cut this demonstration short with a fearsome threat.

'You wait till your second innings,' he said. 'I'll give you *breaks*.'

Since amongst many scars I have not one which I can attribute
to this occasion, I must have escaped injury, but just how I cannot
recall. I do recall, on the other hand, seeing my adversary in an
awkward situation himself a day or two later. Being a powerful lad,
he made a splendid skimming drive which whistled towards a party
of miners who were sitting in a circle playing cards in a corner
of the park. The ball arrived just as one of their number had risen
to his knees and was brandishing an ace, preparatory to slapping
it down and claiming the kitty. It hit him smack on the back of what
(I'd guess) was a fairly thick cranium, and shot back a goodish
way on the path of its arrival. The recipient was knocked flat
on his face in the midst of his intended spoils, and a deadly hush
fell on the cricket match as he staggered to his feet and glared
ferociously about him. His first suspicions seemed to be directed
at his immediate neighbours, but presently he espied the cricket
game and, with a roar of anger, he charged.

Either Sandy was exceptionally brave or, as in my case, events
had proved too much for the nervous reflexes of his legs, for he
was there when this terrible figure arrived within earshot, and
bellowed out the time-honoured question: 'Who done that?' The
culprit was diplomatic as well as apologetic. 'I done it,' he said,
tactfully lapsing into the vernacular, 'but I didn't try it.' We waited
breathlessly as the visitor turned this over in his aching head. At
length, to our immense relief, he issued a very old-fashioned warning as to what would happen in the event of any repetition (an
unlikely prospect), and tottered back to his cronies.

Our summer holidays were spent with our grandparents and
aunts at Inverness, and my brother and I played cricket through
each and every day on the lawn. Sometimes we were Australia
versus England, sometimes more fanciful sides of our own invention.
Occasionally in the evening we would play Uncle Alastair and

Auntie Jane for a bottle of lemonade. That we usually got beaten reflected great credit on Uncle Alastair, for Auntie Jane was the most absent-minded and reluctant cricketer in all my experience.

As for Grandpa Ross, he was a fine old Highland gentleman. He was in his eighties when we first knew him, a massive figure physically, and a power on the Inverness scene. His heart was that of a twenty-year-old. He took us boys to the engine shed where they built locomotives for the Highland Railway, to the slipway where they launched drifters, and to every other scene calculated to capture a boy's interest. He knew little of cricket but would tell us that he had somehow been called upon to field in a match between Inverness and Nairn in the 1860s. A batsman had hit the ball high into the heaven. 'And,' said Grandpa, smacking his great hands together in an unlikely gesture, ' – I *nabbed* him!'

A rather different but constant joy was Polly Ross, an African grey parrot, who had a prodigious vocabulary, all delivered in a musical Highland lilt acquired from Bella the cook. When one day she escaped and took a trip to the neighbouring tree-tops she scarified the respectable Invernesian crows with a piercing invitation to 'kiss me, darling,' at which they left in a body. She was rescued from her lonely predicament by a sailor who, for an old-fashioned bob, climbed up and brought her safely down. He reported that all the way home she had snuggled against his manly bosom, coyly and ceaselessly enquiring, 'Wha wid pit up with the likes of you?'

Sad to relate, her end was hastened by a predilection for strong drink. When she had a cold Auntie Jane cured her with lumps of sugar soaked in whisky. The side-effects of the cure were spectacular. Polly Ross would burst into song, her repertoire ranging from that fine old hymn, 'Oh that'll be joyful' (the last word repeated *ad nauseam*), to 'Highland Laddie', the latter accompanied by a rousing dance and a great flapping of wings. The possibilities were not lost on us naughty boys, who pandered to Polly Ross's thirst for hard liquor until one fine morning when, instead of waking with a slight hangover, she toppled off her perch never to rise again.

Family life was well-ordered and happy rather than exciting. In after years, when I had achieved a degree of publicity, I was constantly pursued by an amiable but eccentric journalist named

Robin Bailey who was determined to interview me. Some instinct warned me to avoid this but in time I weakened, and the writer later sent me a cutting of his work with which he was highly pleased. My parents were not. Apart from taking exception to the opening phrase which read: 'The strange career of this quaint youth . . .', they were much affronted by the heavy emphasis laid on my Spartan upbringing, endured in the 'hardships of a Scottish manse'. Whatever the accuracy of the first gambit, the second picture is far from true. Ministers of the Kirk were not paid extravagant stipends, but we lacked for nothing in comfort and security. All the manses were large and solidly built, and those of Wick and Birnie of much character. When we were young a nurse and a maid were always part of a cosy circle, and when we came to the South our maid, who had never previously ventured far from Wick, came with us.

My father was the son of a prosperous Lanarkshire lawyer but, far the youngest of a sizeable family, he was orphaned when six years old and reared by a devout elder sister who was a member of a strict Anglican order. He grew up to be a large, strongly-built man and a good all-round games player, better than average at golf, tennis and cricket. His early upbringing may have influenced his choice of profession, but he would have done well to follow his father, for he had a splendid head and a retentive memory. As things were, though not without a certain vanity, he lacked ambition and suffered from a lackadaisical streak, said to be prevalent in the Peebles males.

My mother was extremely talented. Until her marriage she was a professional artist, specializing in portraiture in oils and miniatures, but also producing some pleasing work in water colours. She had also a well-trained soprano voice, and played the violin competently and with an accurate ear. Sadly, however, as a minister's wife she found less opportunity and inclination to pursue these talents as time went on.

The manse at Uddingston did not have any suitable space on which to play proper cricket, but my brother and I, and sometimes my father, would play with a small bat, and bowl round or underarm on a partly paved strip of about twelve yards that led to the coal cellar. It was during one of these games that someone hit a ball through a landing window of unpleasing design in red, blue

and frosted glass, shattering a panel of the red. Mr Murray, the
glazier, was summoned and, having surveyed the damage, heaved
a great sigh of relief. 'Och, my, my, my,' he breathed, 'it's a mercy it
was nae the blue glass – I couldna hae replaced that ever.' Such was
his emotion that it was some time before he could ascend his ladder
but, eventually having done so, he turned to the anxious watchers
below with a final 'Och, my,' waving his hammer by way of emphasis in a fine sweeping gesture. There was a pleasant tinkling
sound as it went straight through the precious blue glass.

My father played cricket for a number of Scottish clubs as his
professional moves dictated. He encouraged us to play and, as early
as 1919, took me to Glasgow to see the Australian Imperial Forces
play a Scottish team. The Australians made 745 for 6 wickets and
one of several centurians, Jack Murray, whom I was to meet in
after-years in his native Adelaide, broke four bats in making 150.
The Scots were routed by the fast bowling of Cyril Docker and
Jack Gregory, both of whom I also met in Australia later. Both
died recently, Cyril at the ripe age of 91.

The most memorable day in my young cricketing life was two
years ahead, when Father and I went to see Warwick Armstrong's
1921 Australian team play a West of Scotland team on the Hamilton Crescent ground at Partick. The West was strengthened by
the inclusion of George and John Gunn and of Arthur Carr, all of
Nottingham. On the second morning we saw Jack Gregory add
thirty-odd runs to an already bulging total with some fine thump-
ing strokes. Then came the electrifying moment when he measured
out his run to attack George Gunn, whose partner was C. T.
Mannes, a fine Scottish batsman who did not seem in any way handicapped by a club foot.

In my imagination I can still see Gregory's tempestuous rush
down the slight slope, a great final leap, the glorious high action,
and the bounding follow-through as the ball went whistling on its
way. From the moment of seeing that first over I knew that Gregory
was the greatest cricketer in the world and, fifty years later when
I have seen a thousand cricketers, he is still for me the greatest.

George Gunn advanced down the pitch to meet him, as was his
way with fast bowlers, middled the first four balls and took a
single off the fifth. Mannes pushed the last to mid-off for a single

and a little later, when Gregory over-pitched, he drove him hard and straight to the screen for four, a startling experience for Gregory in that summer of fast wickets. At the other end, with a pleasant enigmatical smile, Arthur Mailey spun the ball like a top, and tied everyone into knots. The opening pair put up a respectable 41 for the first wicket, at which point Mannes was comprehensively yorked by Gregory. Thereafter I tried at all times to imitate that wonderful action – not a bad model for aspiring bowlers of all types.

At the end of the season I had another treat. Notts made a late tour of the West of Scotland, and played a two-day match at Uddingston. This was due to take place after the date of my return to school, but the Fates were kind to me. A number of boys were helping the professional with the heavy roller in the preparation of the pitch upon which the match was to be played, when I got my foot caught under the two-ton monster. As soon as my foot was released it began to swell like a football, and I could not get a shoe on for the next week. I wonder if a psychologist would see any sub-conscious connection between these events? At any rate, I saw George Gunn once more, to say nothing of a young batsman named Whysall who made fifty-odd, and was tipped as a coming England player. The enormous Fred Barratt shattered the local batsmen, and looked to me to be as fast as Gregory, but this was hardly the case. Soon afterwards the late publisher of this book, W. A. R. Collins, struck him thrice into the river at Ayr, no small feat.

In 1923 a great event took place. Leicestershire county cricket team came up to the North for a short tour. The star attraction was Claude Taylor, who had just made a record by scoring a century as a freshman in the first innings of the university match at Lord's. He was regarded as a fine prospect modelled on the lines of his coach and adviser Donald Knight. As the team walked from their hotel to the Northern Meeting Park, where the match was to be played, my brother accosted him, and asked for an autograph. This was duly given, and he walked to the ground with the 'man of the moment'. The meeting led to a firm friendship which, with the passage of time, led to Claude marrying my sister Margaret.

My turn to walk with the gods came the following day, the Sunday after the match. Suspecting that the players would be directed to the Ness Islands as a local beauty spot at a convenient distance for a Sunday morning stroll, I lay in wait and was soon rewarded. A trio had paused at the first bridge, wondering which path to pursue. They seemed quite pleased when I offered my services as guide, and off we went. The trio, whom I knew well by sight, were George Geary, Ewart Astill and Bert Sidwell, the wicket-keeper. They were infinitely patient in answering my torrent of questions and, in the absence of a ball, bowled stones for my edification. In the company of three real live county cricketers I walked in paradise. Four years later I set sail with George and Ewart for South Africa. Six years later at Lord's I was 'LBW b Geary o'. The loudest appellant was Bert Sidwell from behind the stumps.

Both my parents were determined that their children should have full benefit of the opportunities for good education which abounded in Scotland in those days. A large portion of the family budget was devoted to this object, and my two sisters went to boarding school in Edinburgh, and my brother James and I were day-boys at Glasgow Academy. My brother belied the reputation of our male side by working well at school, getting a good degree at Oxford to become a housemaster at Westminster, and finally an able and energetic headmaster of Hereford Cathedral School.

My own academic education was less successful. Looking back on my school and university days I am always reminded of a notorious case in the '30s of a gang of ex-public school boys – whom the press labelled 'The Mayfair Boys' – who assaulted and robbed a jeweller. The harrassed counsel for the defence was left with little to say except that they were well-educated men. Lord Chief Justice Hewart made short work of this, saying, 'Much has been made of the fact that these are educated men. Rather would I say they were afforded such opportunities for education as their station in life could afford. The results,' he added, 'are not impressive.'

So in my case I was afforded splendid opportunities, and my early days at Glasgow Academy were promising in both work and play. I was a bright boy at my books and won several prizes. At about fifteen I got into the school cricket team and played for three seasons. Rugby never roused my enthusiasm, largely because the ground at Anniesland was miles the far side of Glasgow (again this indolence). My only other real sporting passion was for boxing, which was not part of the school curriculum. At Uddingston there were plenty of willing performers, and we would organize our own bouts and read avidly about the champions. To this day I recall the breathless excitement awaiting our Joe Beckett's impending triumph over a Frenchman (spelt 'Carpentier' but, it seemed, pronounced quite differently) on his way to victory over Jack Dempsey and to the world heavyweight championship. There was no radio at that time, and a tense silence fell the morning after the fight as Father searched the paper for the result. It had just made the stop-press of the Scottish edition and, unbelievably, our champ had been routed. In answer to our anguished enquiries Father replied that it only said it had been a very short fight. That was true enough, the whole bout lasting 74 seconds. This, however, was lengthy compared to the return match, which went just 15 seconds, count and all.

The fact that I was a bright pupil undoubtedly contributed to my general decline as a scholar. Able to jog along with an absolute minimum of effort, I gradually degenerated into a state of complete inertia. Masters despaired and exhorted but were not always helpful, for the Scots *dominies* of that era were thorough but not always inspiring.

Father Peebles also despaired and exhorted but, having been raised in the same educational pattern, he was prone to the 'get on with your work' school rather than the modern and subtler method of pointing to the golden prizes (less taxation!) to be gained by a little application and industry. With the added responsibility of a parent he took action. He went to the local Bank of Scotland agent, a splendid Caithnesian, James Cormack, and asked if he would take me as a trainee.

This was duly arranged, but it was soon apparent to all concerned that, apart from a few blots in the ledger, I was not going to make my mark in banking. Mr Cormack was patient and helpful, but I found the routine a bore and the rudiments of finance uninteresting. The weeks passed dully, but I had achieved the 1st Uddingston XI, and this was an absorbing interest. The only plan I had vaguely in mind was that, when my apprenticeship had been completed, I would emigrate to some country where they played first-class cricket – even if I felt my taking an active part in it seemed over-ambitious. In the meantime I had saved up £40 for a holiday in London where I arrived in the August of 1925 with two main objects in view. The first was to visit Lord's, and the second to attend the recently established Faulkner School of Cricket, which I had seen advertised in the *Cricketer*.

Both missions were extremely successful. My first visit to Lord's happened to coincide with Harold Larwood's, and I saw him take a Middlesex wicket, and read in the papers that here was the best prospect yet seen of the fast bowler for whom England had been waiting ever since the destruction of Gregory and McDonald.

The success of my visit to the Faulkner School was not immediately apparent, for I had envisaged a beautifully kept expanse of turf with a number of nets in orderly rows. It turned out to be in an old garage in Petersham Road, Richmond, with one indoor net and a small changing-room. But no matter; I was in the presence of the great, and Faulkner made me very welcome. I changed and joined the other two bowlers in the net, and started in.

Although I was unaware of it at that moment, the next few minutes were to be the most important in my whole life. There is nothing to be gained in undue modesty after fifty years so, in describing them, I will not posture. At seventeen and a half I had grown to my full height of six foot two and, being exceptionally supple, was said to have a perfect action. I had acquired the knack of bowling the leg-break at fast-medium without the orthodox bent wrist, but showing the palm of my hand to the batsman, in the manner of the great Sydney Barnes himself. The fast matting pitch was ideal for this type of bowling and straight away I beat the batsman, and then knocked his stumps down. I was aware that Faulkner was observing me keenly, but supposed he regarded all newcomers with interest. When the batsman was bowled Faulkner came up to me and said, 'Was that a leg-break?' I was surprised, not realizing that by this particular method it was not easy to detect. When I said it was he smiled and seemed very pleased. He was, in fact, delighted, and long afterwards his chief assistant, an Irishman named Downie, told me that Faulkner had, at that point, summoned him from his coffee break, saying, 'Come and see what I've found.'

I was personally unaware of the impression I had made but, a few days later, Faulkner asked if I would like to stop and share his sandwich lunch, which I was pleased to do. After a few general exchanges he said, 'Why don't you come to the South and play some good cricket?' I said I was apprenticed to the Bank of Scotland and could hardly hope to be transferred at that stage. He said, 'If you came to London you could be my secretary.' This was the most intoxicating prospect. 'If I did,' I asked, 'do you think I would ever play for a County?' He looked at me thoughtfully for a moment. 'If you come to me,' he said, 'you'll go a darn sight further than that.'

## TWO

# *Aubrey Faulkner*

From the Faulkner School of Cricket I returned to Scotland in a state of great elation, eager to break the news to my father that I had got a job with every prospect of fame and fortune. He was a great deal less enthusiastic. The bank, he argued, if not guaranteeing fame and fortune, offered much more solid prospects than it seemed did the Faulkner School. Faulkner he knew as a cricketer but, although he had never heard anything against him, he felt that we should make a few enquiries before committing my whole future to him. I was very impatient, and absolutely determined to accept Faulkner's offer. Eventually, after some correspondence, my father yielded and, having attended evening classes in shorthand and typing, I set forth for London early in the New Year of 1926. This was the most important step in my life to date, and Faulkner was one of the most important figures in shaping the course of my future from then on.

Despite the abundance of talent the game has produced in the fifty years since last he played, Faulkner has strong claim to be numbered amongst the six greatest all-rounders the game has yet seen. So bold a claim may not be universally accepted, and calls for supporting evidence – which I believe can be adduced.

To be an effective all-rounder in any class of cricket the candidate must be wholly adequate in one department and at least useful in the other. If he does not measure up in either he is obviously a total loss in both. (For the moment we are concerned with batting and bowling, although fielding could be a deciding factor.) When it comes to the highest class it means that the player must excel at all points. This even puts a question mark against 'W.G.', for it is difficult to believe that he was a bowler of international standard, despite his vast haul of wickets.

The names which come to mind as qualifying at this rarefied level are Giffen, Hirst, Rhodes, Noble, Jackson, Armstrong, Gregory (for a short spell), Hammond, Worrell and, top of the list, Sobers. Jack Crawford is a possible, while Miller was a magnificent fast bowler but too unpredictable a batsman to qualify. Only Sobers would seem to eclipse Faulkner on both counts but even here, except on claims of versatility, the issue is not so clear-cut where bowling is concerned. As a fielder Faulkner stands very high in this company, all of whom were adequate, some brilliant. Possibly I am a biased witness, but the more I study the contenders the more I am convinced that he is well in the van.

Aubrey Faulkner was born in Port Elizabeth in 1881, and died in London in 1930. He was originally notable as a bowler who bowled leg-breaks and had perfected the newly invented googly. These he delivered with a beautiful wheeling action at a sharpish pace, with great accuracy for one of his type. To a generation of batsmen with little experience of this new phenomenon his 'wrong 'un' was practically undetectable, and he had additionally a fast yorker which he fired, without forewarning, consistently at the leg stump.

These talents alone would have been sufficient to ensure his place in the great South African sides of the early years of the century, but he had further ambitions, and the inborn determination to achieve them. Starting with a good eye, a strong physique, and an intelligent understanding of first principles he soon turned himself into a batsman of international calibre. He never sought nor achieved any flowing grace, but he had a sound defence, and a good range of scoring shots. Brought up on the mat, he was a fine cutter and hooker and, seeing him bat in later years, one was impressed by the tremendous power of his back play. With his timing and a great strength of shoulder and wrist, the ball would come off the bat with a crack like a pistol shot. He was criticized by purists for standing a little 'two-eyed', but it certainly did not seem to inhibit his stroke play in any direction. He was, as I have said, a fine fielder in every position.

Faulkner had made his first appearance for South Africa against England in the 1905/6 series, when the Englishmen were routed by the newly perfected googly. In this series he bowled splendidly and batted adequately. In 1907 he and Vogler led the quartette of spinners who throughout England drew and astonished large crowds wherever they played. Given a wet wicket at Leeds he took six wickets for seventeen in the Second Test. In 1909/10 he exerted his full force as an all-rounder against Leveson-Gower's England side, which went down 3-2. In 1910/11 he toured Australia where South Africa were trounced by a powerful home side, but Faulkner batted brilliantly to average 73 in the five Test Matches. At Melbourne in the Second Test he made 204, but was on the losing side. He was still a great force in 1912 when he took part in the Triangular Tournament of that year, a three-sided contest between the major powers sponsored by his fellow South African, Sir Abe Bailey. In this, like his fellows, he found Sydney Barnes an almost impossible proposition on the succession of wet wickets of that year, and in six innings against England he made no more than 46 runs, falling to Barnes five times. On this sad note (despite some bowling successes) his international career really ended, for he only appeared in one other Test, in 1924, when a hard-pressed South African side persuaded him to turn out for the Lord's match. He was then in his 40s and had played no regular first-class cricket since pre-war days, so was scarcely up to concert pitch. He bowled to the leading English batsmen on a most perfect hard wicket and failed to get anyone out in a total of 531 for two declared, and was unlucky in being run out when just settling down in the second innings, having made 12. Despite this and the failure of 1912 his record for South Africa reads: 1754 runs at an average of 40, and 82 wickets at 26 apiece. It is a consistent career, studded with fine performances.

He stayed in Britain after the 1912 series and had a season in Nottingham club cricket where, not unexpectedly, he caused great havoc. When war broke out he became an artillery man and attained the rank of major, winning a DSO. In 1921 he was a prep school master at St Pyrans, where Freddy Brown was one of the pupils, and it was here that he made his last serious and brilliant appearance in first-class cricket.

All that summer Archie MacLaren had been saying that he could pick a side to beat the seemingly invincible Australians led by Warwick Armstrong. He was given an opportunity of making good his promise in August at Eastbourne, and duly announced his side. It turned out to be a judicious blend of youth and maturity, Faulkner being one of the senior members. Nobody took MacLaren's

ambitions very seriously, but all, including the Australians, looked
forward to a nice, seaside entertainment.

This historic match has been so frequently recalled and described
that it is unnecessary to do so again in any detail. All are familiar
with the astonishing changes of fortune which attended the progress of MacLaren's team – the disastrous first innings, the splendid
out-cricket apparently to little point, the heroic second innings recovery, and then the final overthrow of the Colossus. In each stage
Faulkner played a leading part, making 153 in the second innings
and taking six wickets. It was a magnificent performance judged by
any standards, against opposition which, for most of the match,
had appeared to be in a wholly impregnable position. For Faulkner,
40 years old and long out of first-class cricket, it was the seal on
a great all-round career.

Although frequently prompted by myself and others of the staff
he was always reluctant to talk about his own performances, and
was very modest about the major part he took in the Eastbourne
match. He had enjoyed the great duel he had fought with Ted
McDonald, whom he put very high amongst the many fast bowlers
he had seen and played. He had little opportunity of making a first-
hand assessment of Gregory, who was unwell, and much below form
in the little bowling he did.

He recalled a couple of droll sidelights on two of the major
Australian figures. The first was in fact at the turning point of
the match, when he bowled out that superbly confident genius
Charlie Macartney with a beauty which pitched on the leg stump
and hit the off. At the tea interval the 'Governor General', as was
his nickname, spoke to him. 'You got me in two minds,' he said,
'I was going to hit you for six – then I thought four would do.'
This story has been told of more recent cricketers, but here is the
true source, and no jest was intended. The other incident concerned the gigantic Armstrong, who came in to bat when, for the
first time that season, defeat was more than a probability. Aubrey
said that his lips were pursed as though he was whistling in a
nonchalant fashion – but no sound emerged. Well might he be
anxious, for the rumour was that a wealthy Australian had offered
each man £1000 if the side came through the tour unbeaten.

Having, as he thought, ended his active first-class career with this blaze of glory, Faulkner now developed another ambition. During his career as a schoolmaster he had discovered that he had a natural flair for cricket coaching. Whereas the teaching of ordinary educational subjects did not greatly interest him, he found that the moulding of young cricketers was most rewarding, and he was convinced that he could, by his methods, improve the standard of cricketers of all classes and ages. Soon he had conceived the idea of establishing an indoor cricket school. In this he would be a pioneer for, although people had practised in nets under cover before, no one had devoted a permanent building to the teaching of cricket. The financial risks were considerable, and money was very short, but Faulkner was both brave and enthusiastic. In the early months of 1925 he rented an old garage in Petersham Road, Richmond, bought sufficient equipment to lay out one matting pitch and provide a dressing-room, and announced to the public that the Faulkner School of Cricket was ready to receive pupils of all ages. Plum Warner, 'Shrimp' Leveson-Gower and Colonel Phillip Trevor, the *Daily Telegraph* cricket correspondent, lent their names as directors and, to save drawing on the School's limited funds, Faulkner became the cricket correspondent of the old *Westminster Gazette*.

Although the number of clients was severely limited by the restricted premises Faulkner was a strong man and, by dint of working long hours, he developed a profitable business. When I joined him, in January 1926, he was already looking for larger and more central premises. At Richmond there was no room for expansion, as the pitch was situated in a long, tunnel-like structure. The net hung so close to the brick wall that if the ball was struck square it was liable to rebound with redoubled force. Early on I saw a batsman's expression of satisfaction at making a fine hook turn to one of agony, as the ball cannoned off the wall and hit him smack on the end of the nose so that, like the fielder in *Pickwick Papers*, 'his form writhed in anguish and his eyes filled with tears'. There was no natural light, so the net had to be illuminated by a great profusion of electric bulbs, neon tubes not then being available. The fuse box was in the roof, directly above the bowler's head, and the disadvantage of this was made plain when an earnest and ambitious bowler was exhorted to try an occasional quicker ball. His next delivery achieved a more noticeable variation in trajectory than pace as it shot vertically into the box and, after a minor explosion, plunged us all into pitch darkness, to the intense embarrassment of the sender. The changing-room was sparsely furnished, and the office space cramped.

These shortcomings, however, were easily overlooked in the enthusiasm of the pupils under the masterly guidance of Faulkner, who was without doubt the finest coach I have ever seen. He had by this stage analysed every phase of the game, and had evolved a simple but comprehensive method of teaching it. He had a flair for lucid exposition and, although sometimes impatient, was absolutely tireless; when his right arm failed through fatigue he would bowl a respectable left arm. Having spotted a weakness he had the additional merit of being able to bowl the appropriate ball repeatedly until the flaw as eradicated. He would take as much trouble with an elderly village player as he would with a young university cricketer, provided the subject was keen and willing to learn. One of his earliest and most successful students was Tom Killick of St Paul's School and Cambridge University, followed by Middlesex and England. Anyone who saw Killick play saw the whole Faulkner system personified.

In the spring of 1926 the School moved from Richmond to Walham Green and to another garage, where the concrete floor made an excellent base upon which to lay a matting wicket. Faulkner wanted these to resemble turf as closely as possible, so he experimented with a string carpet under which he put layers of felt of various thicknesses until he had got almost exactly the type of pitch he needed. At Walham Green we were able to have four pitches in parallel, each varying slightly in pace and type.

All sorts and conditions of cricketers came to the Faulkner School. Plum Warner came soon after we moved to Walham Green. He was kind and courteous, and to me most encouraging. When Aubrey bowled his fiercely spun leg-breaks and googlies he met them with perfect batsmanship, and seldom have I seen bowling of the highest calibre more beautifully countered by skilful batting technique. Not every first-class player could cope with Aubrey on the mat. Jack MacBryan, who we all hoped would play for England against Australia in the coming season, was for once completely defeated,

and I remember him crying out, 'I can't play this bloody stuff,' and
throwing down his bat in disgust.

K. S. Duleepsinhji – 'Smith' to his friends – had just recovered
from a serious illness, and spent the spring playing himself back
to form in our nets. He was at that stage not only a beautifully
fluent batsman of very good technique, but also a modest and
attentive pupil. Faulkner naturally made no basic alterations to his
play, but put forward several suggestions with a view to strengthen-
ing various strokes and correcting minor faults. It was interesting
to see how eagerly Duleep received such advice and how immediately
he would apply it, with obvious benefit to the stroke concerned.

Some pupils, if not up to Test Match cricket standards, were
distinguished persons in other spheres. Mr Justice Bosanquet was
given to an occasional very unjudicial cross-bat mow, a lapse
from grace he would explain by saying, 'One is very much prey to
one's natural stroke.' All the brothers Harker, the famous theatrical
family, were, with the exception of their brother Gordon, keen
cricketers and would come the whole year round. Sir Rowland
Blades, later Lord Ebbisham, came during his year as Lord Mayor
of London, and the Chinese Ambassador's son hoped that Faulkner's
coaching would gain him a place in the Eton XI. In the Easter
holidays we were booked out by schoolboys and undergraduates,
so that he and I worked from seven o'clock in the morning until late
at night. During this rush time we would recruit assistance in the
shape of prominent cricketers such as Bob Wyatt and Peter Judd,
of Hampshire, who knew Faulkner's system. Stan Squires, later of
Surrey, was on the permanent staff, and everyone was hard worked
keeping all four nets going throughout the long day until later
evening.

The School as such was a great success, and Faulkner was soon
recognized as being the final authority on all matters of coaching
and training. As a business concern, however, it was always precarious. Many people have since found out indoor cricket nets and
dressing-rooms occupy a great amount of space in relation to the
numbers they can accommodate, and rent and rates are consequently
a major problem.

The School charged ten shillings a lesson, which was roughly 20 minutes' batting and 40 minutes' bowling. It is with a fine nostalgia that I can recall Faulkner remarking that he might indeed raise the fees because, he said, 'Some of these fellows will spend anything up to fifteen shillings on a dinner.' But despite this surrounding profligacy he never carried out his threat. Most sporting clubs and institutions have relied largely on the bar takings to keep their finances afloat, but Faulkner was adamant that he would not apply for a licence. A teetotaller himself, he felt that it would attract bar flies and other undesirables. From experience of other, less rigid institutions, I feel he was mistaken in this. Yet the absence of such amenities doubtless helped to frustrate the fulfilment of the founder's ambition that the School would flourish financially, and eventually develop into a full-scale sporting club, catering for a variety of games.

Aubrey Faulkner was an enigmatical character. In his late 40s, he was slightly overweight, but had a strong, well-knit figure, and was a handsome man, dark-haired and brown-eyed. Besides being a teetotaller he was a non-smoker, but was lusty and highly sexed. About his early past he was reticent. I gathered that he had been born of middle-class parents, but that his father had been an alcoholic, with a tendency to violence where his wife was concerned. This may well have accounted for Faulkner's attitude towards drink. Once in a burst of uncharacteristic candour he told me that after one such assault he had lain in wait for his father who returned drunk and truculent. Aubrey had gone for him; 'I nearly killed him,' he added. This background had left its mark, in that he was inclined to be touchy and defensive and, in the four years that I knew him, he had no close friends.

With his good looks he had, when young, had numerous affairs, but his first marriage had failed. When I knew him he was un-attached, but keen to marry a cousin, Sybil de Berry, who was fond of him but did not want to marry him. In later years he married his secretary, a sweet and very pretty girl, many years his junior.

When in good heart he was splendid company, enthralling us with his tales of the great and famous, and making us laugh with his considerable humour. With an observant eye, a retentive memory, and a shrewd critical sense of cricket and cricketers, he had an inexhaustible fund of memories and stories of cricketing men and affairs.

Like everyone who ever knew the man he had a particular admiration and affection for Victor Trumper. One of his favourite tales bore testimony not only to Trumper's pre-eminence as a player but, at the same time, to the uncalculating generosity of his nature. Aubrey had met him during the South African tour of Australia in 1910 whilst Trumper was running a sports shop. In this capacity he was not an ideal executive, for his immediate instinct was to *give* everything away and, in this spirit, he insisted on giving Aubrey a bat. As a gift it turned out to be a sad disappointment for, in Aubrey's hands, it felt as hard as a plank and, when questioned by the donor, he had to admit it was not much to his liking. Trumper was much concerned to hear this, and asked if he might try it out during the match in progress. Aubrey, in the field whilst this exercise took place, hardly recognized it as the same blade as the ball came bounding from it with a sweet mellow sound. Having made a good number of runs Trumper returned it to Aubrey, saying he had 'softened it up a bit', and it now ought to be all right. But away from Trumper's hands it remained the same old plank.

Faulkner was bowling at Trumper once when Warwick Armstrong, the non-striker, knowing of his surprise fast ball, said, 'Give him a yorker – he doesn't like 'em.' Faulkner obliged, and with a sharp chopping stroke Trumper hit the ball to the square leg boundary. Aubrey looked at Warwick's face but was unenlightened. A little later he tried again, a second and a third time, and met with exactly the same result in each case. At this Warwick grinned unashamedly, and Faulkner knew this was no fluke – in modern idiom, he had been conned.

It may be interesting to the cricket historian and technician to hear at first hand of the first impact of the googly (bowled to the standards of the South African quartette) on visiting batsmen. Warner's team of 1905/6 bore the first brunt of this, and were overwhelmed. Warner himself averaged just under 9 in the Test Matches and was completely nonplussed. However, as I have described earlier in this chapter, being a fine intelligent player, he afterwards learnt how to cope with this form of attack as well as or better than most contemporaries. When Leveson-Gower followed with the MCC team of 1909/10 rather more was known about the googly, and he had Hobbs and Rhodes to lead the way.

Faulkner observed the contrasting methods of these two great players in combating the new form of wrist spinners with interest and a certain amount of amusement. Hobbs by speed of foot would get down the wicket to kill the spin of the good length ball, and would be well back for anything short. Pretty soon he learnt to spot the deception with fair consistency. Wilfred characteristically threw everything into the battle, playing from the crease and never budging an inch in presenting an uncompromising defence. This apparently had a somewhat hazardous air for, as his partner ran effortlessly ahead, his opponents would occasionally chaff the rock-like defender, saying, 'You lucky old so-and-so.' They always received the same incontrovertible reply: 'Ah'm still 'ere.'

Later in the year Victor Trumper encountered the South African spinners for the first time. He and Warren Bardsley put up over a hundred for the first wicket in each innings for New South Wales against the touring South Africans at Sydney. Trumper made 70-odd both times and took a close look at Vogler, Faulkner and Schwarz, after which he confided to his colleagues that, although they might be effective in South Africa and on the softer English wickets, they would be ineffective in Australia. In this he was confirming an earlier prediction made by Plum Warner. If both prophets were proved right it should be said that Vogler was so affected by an alcoholic bout as to be quite useless, whilst Faulkner, after some good performances in the State matches, was wholly preoccupied in leading the South African batting. Schwarz, in taking 23 wickets at 26 apiece, alone did well in the Test Matches.

Like most of his generation Faulkner thought Barnes was the greatest bowler of his times, and could not imagine a better in any other era, past or future. He was clearly the loser in their running battle on the soft wickets of 1912, but said that he had one promising session. At the Oval he played Barnes for an hour in which he made only six runs but during which time he reckoned he had seen the whole superb armoury. His eye was well in when to his surprise and fleeting joy he received a rank long-hop. He picked up the bat, and went to take full toll of this unexpected gift, only to find the ball was through him and his wicket before he had set his feet. It had been twice as quick as anything he had hitherto seen, and he cited this as an example of the Machiavellian cunning behind the masterly technique. He was not in South Africa in 1913/14 when Barnes carried all before him on the matting wickets or this might well have been a battle royal for, on his home wickets, Faulkner's defence was unexcelled. It may be remembered that, without this bulwark, the young Herbie Taylor alone succeeded against Barnes.

His wartime experiences also made good telling, and he warmed my heart with his immense admiration for the various Scottish troops he had supported. He told me of one battalion which never batted an eyelid under fire or other trials, but was practically de-moralized when a stray shell hit the cookhouse and blew the morning porridge all over the countryside. To keep me in my place he would tell me that the Scots were too thick-headed to be fright-ened, but I was not deceived.

I stayed almost two and a half years in Faulkner's employment, which included four months' sabbatical leave for a trip to South Africa. As we always had lodgings in the same house, and latterly shared a small flat in Earls Court, we got to know each other fairly well. It could be said that he was a difficult man to work with but, being almost wholly untrained, naïve and slapdash by nature, I was a most lamentable secretary. During my time at the School my salary remained at £3 a week until I finally gave notice, and was promoted to a temporary instructor's status on condition I helped out over the Easter rush.

To draw up an accurate balance sheet of the benefits and liabilities of this period of my life is not easy. From an obscure position in a Scottish bank, with no perceptible prospect of ever playing first-class cricket, I was introduced by Faulkner into the midst of an esoteric band who had much influence in cricket affairs. He had great faith in my capabilities, and did not hesitate to voice his confidence that I would fulfil his early prophecy. He had told me at an early stage that I was the only one he knew who bowled the leg-break with the same method and pace as Sydney Barnes, and obviously had hopes that I would follow in the steps of the master. With all due modesty I may say that there were certain grounds for his belief. When in future years Barnes showed me his technique I realized that I had used the same method of bowling the leg-break which did not involve an exaggerated bend of the wrist and showed rather the palms, not the back of the hand, to the batsman. Indoors I could bowl this accurately at a good quick-medium pace, and was confident that I could defeat all but the best players almost at will.

It was a bitter disillusionment when, after several months of high expectation, I made my first appearance outdoors. My performance was a caricature of its true potential. The pitch looked thirty yards long, the ball felt like a cake of soap, a gentle breeze became a gale, and my timing and rhythm had fallen apart. Nor did my talent ever return. I could bowl seamers, off-spinners and googlies, but the quick leg-break had gone for good. Occasionally I would bowl a few fairly respectable leg-breaks, but without any great life and with no lasting confidence or control. Yet back indoors I would immediately re-start where I had left off, and all our hopes would vainly rise again, to evaporate on my next appearance. It was a phenomenon which Faulkner himself could not explain nor with which he could cope.

One other item on the debit side was that, with the tremendous amount of bowling the staff were called upon to get through, I was already having slight shoulder trouble which was to be disastrous in future years.

Despite his occasional exasperation with my secretarial blunders I think Faulkner was very fond of me; I certainly admired him, and was very conscious of his efforts on my behalf, appreciating his unwavering confidence on the cricket side. We eventually quarrelled seriously and parted coolly, after which I was not to see him again until a couple of years later, on the second day of the Old Trafford Test Match of 1930. Ben Travers, Tom Webster and I had been lucky to get the last one of few available taxis and, as we drove out of the ground, I espied Aubrey Faulkner standing dismally in a long bus queue, and suggested we give him a lift. This was readily agreed, and I ran back and fetched him along. He was obviously as pleased to see me as I was to see him and, on arrival at the Midland Hotel, we went into the bar and talked with much warmth about the old times. We also made all sorts of plans to meet in the future but, sadly, this was the last time we ever saw each other.

When the season of 1930 was over I went home to Uddingston for a short holiday before setting out for a second tour of South Africa. One evening I went out to buy a paper and was mildly startled to see a placard which read TEST MATCH CRICKETER DEAD. Searching rapidly through the paper, I found the announcement, and was dismayed. It was written of Aubrey Faulkner, who had died by his own hand. On returning to London I learnt that his young assistant, Tommy Reddick, later to play for Notts, arrived early one morning to find a brief note reading, 'I am off to another realm via the bat room.' Horrified, he ran out and found a policeman who, not being much older than he, was equally upset, saying that this was his first experience of this kind of thing. Together they returned to the School, and made their way to the store-room where the over-powering smell of gas alone was enough to confirm their fears. If he had no close friends Faulkner had a great circle of acquaintances and admirers, and a wave of deep shock and regret ran through the entire cricket world.

When I went to call on his young widow she told me something which moved me profoundly. When he seemed to lose heart and all taste for life, she said, he had one abiding interest. It was to look in the morning paper to see how many wickets I, his discovery and protégé, had taken the previous day. Reminded of his interest in me, I was keenly aware of what I owed to him. At least I was grateful for our chance meeting in Manchester.

# THREE

# Golden Opportunity

Compared to the dense traffic in touring cricket teams in modern times a Test Match series was a comparatively infrequent event until the close of the 1920s. With only three countries of Test Match status visits to each other took place at roughly four-yearly intervals, with occasionally a longer break. There were lesser MCC and privately sponsored tours, but selection for those to Australia and South Africa were the greatest prizes available to English cricketers. The ambition of most was to tour Australia, where the senior and generally more powerful opposition was to be met. To play against Australia was, and still is, the height of an Englishman's cricket career, whether at home or abroad.

To make a visit 'down under' was then a major undertaking, involving a sea trip of 13,000 miles, which took six weeks by mail steamer. Once there the cricketer was faced with a grand but daunting programme. To cross the country meant travelling on three different railway systems, owing to the varying State gauges, and took a week all told. For the team hospitality would be warm and plentiful, accommodation variable, and the cricket the toughest and most competitive in the world. Success would be universally acclaimed, but failure was always possible and, to anyone who had progressed thus far, dismal.

The MCC tour of South Africa was a gentler exercise. To this the prelude was a sea trip of seventeen days, an ideal time to spend on a most comfortable liner. The schedule was more leisurely and travel easier, as there was but one railway system of standard metre gauge throughout. The cricket, especially in the Test Matches, was played intensely and keenly, but it did not generate the local pressures nor the wider controversies. Success, of course, was still sweet, but not of such consequence, whilst failure, if still unwelcome, was less traumatic. Those cricketers who knew both countries judged their relative merits according to individual taste and temperament, the more ambitious tending to prefer the greater importance and challenge of Australia. To those whose cricketing ability would never quite take them to Australia, the South African circuit was cricket at its best. To be picked for the tour at the age of nineteen without any real experience of first-class cricket, as I was to be, was like something from the realms of popular sporting fiction. When I look back on the events leading up to my selection I can see that I was even more fortunate than I realized at the time.

During my first cricket season in England I played for Hampstead, a large, flourishing club generally regarded as a nursery for Middlesex. That I did so was largely due to Ernest Beaton, father of Sir Cecil, and a mainstay of the club. He and his younger son Reggie were also strong supporters of the Faulkner School and, having perhaps got an exaggerated idea of my powers, were keen that I should join them. The father, a very good wicketkeeper, did not greatly resemble his illustrious son, being sturdy, bandy-legged and bald, with a walrus moustache, but he was a kind, warm-hearted man.

Our first match was at Uxbridge, whence I was driven by Reggie in a 14/40 Sunbeam, a very smart car at that time. However, it was a disillusioning day, for although I got a couple of cheap wickets it was the first indication I had of the dire effect of continuously bowling indoors. Throughout the season I never found my touch with the leg-break, but still bowled and batted well enough to keep my place in the side.

My most successful excursion was a week with Chiswick Park where I bowled quick seamers on their plentiful green grass. Faulkner felt that this offered much more opportunity, and the following season I played regularly at week-ends, getting a good crop of wickets, mostly by bowling in this faster style.

In July I played in the Gentlemen v Players at the Oval, again as the result of efforts of my enthusiastic 'lobby'. This was never a very popular match, as the sides were drawn from the Southern counties resting at that moment, and usually resulted in an appallingly strong professional batting side. Such was the case in our match, when the order went Hobbs, Sandham, Hearne, Hendren, Mead, down to a player as good as Jack Newman of Hants coming in at number ten. They all enjoyed themselves on a plumb Oval wicket after which it rained, and Alec Kennedy, also of Hants, took all ten first innings wickets. We lost by an innings, while I took Andrew Sandham's wicket for 90 runs.

As I struggled to master the difficulties which beset me outdoors I continued to bowl most effectively indoors, and those who saw me there were loud in their praises. My reputation spread, as many good players came to the School and, having seen me at first hand, made all manner of flattering predictions. But with my failure to live up to them such judgments were more an embarrassment than a help. Bowling fast-medium seamers or quick off-spinners I was a good bowler by any standards, but my ambitions were set a great deal higher than being just that.

It was always present in my mind that, before coming to the School, I could bowl on the turf the very ball I did indoors, and had just reached the stage when I was beginning to gain a good control of length and line. Thus, through no fault of my own, I was placed in a wholly false position, a species of bowling schizophrenic. My career at this time was later described by *Wisden* of 1931 when I was selected as one of their 'Five Cricketers of the Year' (the year being, of course, 1930): '. . . It was no secret that at the outset very many people were under the impression that the abilities of Peebles as a leg-break and googly bowler had been over-estimated. Certainly there was nothing in his early performances to justify the eulogies about his bowling which at that time were being expressed in some quarters.' After awarding a cautious approval of my record in South Africa in 1927/8 the writer continues: 'In 1929 he not only justified himself but those two good judges whose names have been mentioned (Messrs Warner and Faulkner) and who stuck to their guns through thick and thin.' Thereafter the author says of the 1930 Peebles: 'Last season he came right to the fore,' and from then on is generous in his views. The reader who perseveres with the story will find that this passage summarizes a period of much complication.

The same year – 1927 – I played under the captaincy of Plum Warner for the first time. The match was against Julien Cahn's team at Nottingham, and was to have a considerable bearing on my future career. Plum was the best captain I had encountered, and has remained so in my experience. He treated each bowler as though he were Sydney Barnes himself and, with such tactful guidance, no one could but give of his very best. The field would be meticulously placed, always (it seemed) in consultation with the bowler, and it was remarkable how often suggestions such as: 'You ought to have your gully a bit squarer for this chap' would be almost immediately justified. So long as the bowler was in action he would be kept aware of his captain's unflagging interest by encouraging asides – 'I think you are going to get a wicket this over,' or, 'This man doesn't like your leg-break.' Under such enlightened direction I blossomed and, given a softish wicket, took eleven wickets in the match against a very respectable batting side.

The opening bowler at the other end was Sir Alec Douglas Home who, then as Lord Dunglass, sent down a lively out-swinger, and had come near to a Blue at Oxford. In later years I heard him say that the final obstacle to his achieving this was that he had been hit for three sixes off successive balls by Pete Perrin of Essex, a great character, and a very good batsman. Some years previously as Lord Dunglass, having just left Eton, he had come to play for Uddingston on the ground his father leased to the Club, and I had bowled at him when he had batted in a net before the match. Whether he benefited from this service I do not know, for he had just played himself in when the rain came to finish the day. It was remarked by the local players that he had half a dozen different caps in his bag, a matter of some astonishment to those who probably wore one and the same cap throughout their entire cricketing days.

This match may well have influenced Plum to suggest that, as an experiment, I might be taken to South Africa with the MCC side going there in the autumn. The idea was warmly supported by Aubrey Faulkner and one or two others who had seen me bowl on the indoor matting, and was mooted in the appropriate quarters. There it was sympathetically received and, having no first-class form, I was officially included as secretary to Ronny Stanyforth who was to captain the side.

Although naturally overjoyed at this prospect I myself harboured doubts about my ability to live up to the claims of my sponsors. Aubrey Faulkner, and other loyal supporters of the School, were convinced that, once on the matting pitches with the rough ball, I would immediately find the form I had always bowled to indoors and everything would solve itself. This was not exactly so but, as things turned out, I justified those who were prepared to experiment – even if I did not achieve stardom overnight.

I myself had little time for abstract speculation, what with the material preparation for a four months' trip. Despite my association with Faulkner I had only a hazy notion about the physical and geographical nature of South Africa, a state of mind fairly prevalent in my generation. All had heard of the Boer War and most of the Zulu war. Goldfields and diamond mines were matters for the City. Outside those who had actually been there, or had direct interests in South Africa, the generally incurious outlook was epitomized by the contemporary story of the lady who mentioned Cecil Rhodes. 'Nay,' said her cricket-loving swain. 'Tha's thinking of Cecil Parkin. It's *Wilfred Rhodes*.' But all knew that it was a great country for sport and this, after all, was the object of our excursion.

One morning in October 1927 Stan Squires, my colleague at the Faulkner School, called at my lodgings in his venerable Rover. Into it and on to it we loaded a cabin trunk, a cricket bag, and various other pieces of luggage, all brightly and freshly banded with MCC touring colours. So I set forth on the first leg of my journey to South Africa.

Our ship was the *Kenilworth Castle*, launched around 1907, and an old-fashioned liner which looked, felt and smelt like a real ship. She was coal-fired, with great quadruple expansion reciprocating engines which could be faintly heard and felt throughout the ship as they turned over at a steady 72 rpm. This carried us along at a cruising speed of about 15 or 16 knots, pausing only to draw breath at Madeira, on the long haul to the Cape.

We were a good and happy company under the guidance of Ronny Stanyforth, a cavalry soldier and a good Yorkshireman. Over the years we became fast friends but, just then, I regarded him with due deference. At first he seemed reserved and almost austere, but this was only a veneer to a strong personality, an equally strong sense of humour and a warm friendly nature. He was greatly respected and liked by his team, and was most fortunate in having Ernest Tyldesley as his head professional. Ernest, like his elder brother Johnny, was a stout Lancastrian of unshakeable integrity and courage, a great adornment to his profession. These two made a well-balanced and firm leadership which was reflected throughout the team. The rest of the side was: Percy Holmes and Herbert Sutcliffe, the Yorkshire opening pair, Wally Hammond, Greville Stevens of Middlesex, Bob Wyatt of Warwickshire, Eddy Dawson, George Geary and Ewart Astill, all of Leicester, Geoffrey Legge and Tich Freeman of Kent, Sam Staples of Notts, Harry Elliott of Derby (our reserve 'keeper) and myself.

This made a very good side on paper, but without Hobbs, Hendren, Tate and Larwood we were far short of being the full strength of England. Put to the test Wyatt was the only one of the amateurs who could cope with the skill of the South African bowlers on their matting wickets. But the major calamity was the breakdown of George Geary after a magnificent performance in the first of the Test Matches. This more than halved our bowling strength. I was much the youngest and least experienced of the side, and an untried force. If I could recapture my form on the mat indoors my success would be assured, but I still suffered from the doubts created by the experiences of the two previous seasons. I failed to produce the quick leg-break consistently, but by adapting to the conditions I eventually justified my selection, and with a little luck might have had good record in the Tests.

Two days out we found the Bay in boisterous mood and the *Kenilworth Castle* creaked and groaned prodigiously, whereat the old sailors nodded sagely and said she was a good sea boat, flexibly built. Very soon I was to learn that, if I had but few attributes as a traveller, I had one most valuable asset – I was immune to sea-sickness. Fifty years later, having weathered a good number of stormy voyages and bumpy flights, I can confirm this blessing which, apparently, does not denote any great physical or spiritual strength, but depends entirely on a small tube in the ear.

After a four hours' call at Madeira we set off on the longer leg of our voyage. My half-section was Bob Wyatt, who, being my senior by a few years, was my guide and mentor in all worldly matters. He was then emerging as one of the leading all-rounders in the country. Like many people of real depth of character he was not at first easy to know, and he never courted popularity, so that his friendships tended to be staunch and lasting rather than widespread.

As our association led to a life-long friendship he will doubtless forgive me for saying that when he was young his features were cast in a manly rather than in a classically beautiful mould. The same could be said of our reserve wicket-keeper Harry Elliott and, largely because of a similarity in build and colouring, it was possible for the one to be casually mistaken for the other. Neither party thought much of this proposition, but it was brought home to them in rather strange circumstances.

Bob, a good and energetic organizer, was appointed chairman of the sports committee and immediately threw himself into his duties. His first problem was a shortage of rope quoits, so he approached the bosun and asked for a couple of dozen, to be duly assured they would be supplied. When after a couple of days none had arrived he made further application, at which the bosun seemed mildly surprised, but said he would deliver. Again nothing happened, so he made yet another request, and this time the bosun gave him a long, hard look before acquiescing. Again, nothing happened.

One morning Bob, still awaiting some response, was sitting on deck with Harry Elliott when the bosun went past. 'You know,' said Harry, 'I think that chap's a bit out of his mind.'

'What makes you think that?' asked Bob.

'Well,' said Harry, 'he comes into my cabin every morning and dumps a couple of dozen rope quoits there. They're up to the ceiling now,' he said. 'I can hardly get in myself.'

Bob and I stayed up all night to see the lights of Cape Town arise over the horizon. This was fine and dramatic but, as it was the first time I had done such a thing, every time I sat down next day I fell fast asleep. At least I stayed awake long enough to appreciate a first glimpse of the Newlands cricket ground which to this day remains the most beautiful cricket site I have ever seen. The temperature was in the 80s and the pines smelt deliciously, blending with the new-mown grass. All around was a beautiful variety of trees and shrubs and, over the whole scene, Table Mountain shimmered in a myriad of colours.

Our first official function was a civic luncheon in Cape Town at which the guest of honour was General Smuts. He was not much interested in cricket, but strongly approved of anything which furthered goodwill within what was then the Empire. The team lined up as he passed along, shaking us all by the hand. At nineteen and extremely impressionable I was enthralled by this magnificent presence; the great head, with a frontal development which would have pleased Professor Moriarty, and the extraordinarily piercing light blue eyes, seemed to me to radiate greatness.

At the end of a splendid lunch our captain rose to reply to the toast of MCC proposed by the Mayor. He was, as I have said, quiet of aspect at first sight, and this was the first major speech we had heard him make. He spoke with a fluency and eloquence which took everyone by surprise, ranging over subjects far beyond cricket. He was rewarded, in addition to receiving a tremendous ovation, by the genuine astonishment of the next speaker.

The General arose and, in beautifully turned phrases, said that he would always have expected decent sentiments from bone-headed athletes. 'But,' said he, 'I was not prepared for oratory on the plane to which we have just listened.' It was a most happy start to our trip.

Our first match against Cape Province was drawn due to rain, and we passed on to Kimberley where Griqualand West were beaten by an innings. For my own part I was having trouble with that elusive leg-break so, at the nets, I started to bowl quick off-spinners with an occasional cutter the other way. When Herbert Sutcliffe had finished his knock he said to those standing by: 'This boy's off-spinner comes quicker from the mat than anyone else's.' I was much flattered, and took the observation to heart.

Our next match was against Orange Free State at Bloemfontein, and for once the leg-break operated very well – to a point. I got a couple of wickets, and remember Ewart Astill saying, 'If you keep bowling like that you'll have them all out.' Then, sure enough, it came unstuck again and, remembering Herbert Sutcliffe's remark, I switched to fast-medium off-spinners. The result was ten wickets in the match, and great jubilation on my part. Thereafter I made this my basic style for the tour. Herbert was rewarded by the gods with 279 not out, and that on his birthday, so we won by an innings.

The first Test was played at Johannesburg, and was not only a most interesting cricket match but also a comprehensive demonstration of the virtues and limitations of cricket on matting wickets. As matting has long since disappeared from first-class South African cricket, and in Britain is little known except for practice pitches, it may be timely to describe briefly its nature and effect on the game. The old Wanderers ground at Johannesburg, now a railway marshalling yard, was the best ground of its type in South Africa, and its pitch ideal of its kind. The whole area was like a vast, red tennis court, with a fine, sandy top-dressing which made a surprisingly agreeable surface on which to field. The matting was stretched out on a harder strip on a foundation of gravel, and gave a fast, true pitch. The ball would do exactly as dictated by the bowler: if spun it would always turn, and the bounce was high but constant. To cope with the sharply turning ball a batsman had to be technically sound but, because of the absence of anything unexpected in the nature of shooters or lifters, he could play his strokes with complete confidence. It was in fact a more precise science than cricket on turf, and held an absolutely fair balance between batsman and bowler. Those who could bat, and anticipate the bowler's intentions, made runs; but the unsound were quickly eliminated, as the South African bowlers were adept at concealing their intentions whilst cutting and spinning the ball. This they did at a medium-fast pace, slow bowlers being at a disadvantage with the constant bounce and turn which laid them open to attack with the flat bat.

For the first Test the South Africans had Cyril Vincent, a left-hander, whose leg-breaks turned a foot at medium pace; Buster Nupen, who spun a ferocious off-break at fast-medium; and Henry Promnitz, around medium pace, who bowled top-spinners and occasionally a googly – a well-balanced and penetrative combination. To counter them we had four experts – Holmes, Sutcliffe, Tyldesley and Hammond, and a young, rapidly developing Wyatt.

Of these Ernest Tyldesley was probably the best of the lot on the mat. For a great player he had two faults which occasionally undid him on treacherous turf. He picked the bat up to third man and, more importantly, brought it down from that point, which meant he might be trapped on grass by the ball keeping low. The other slight flaw was that, when he hooked, he did not always get outside the line of the ball. The consistency of the matting pitches completely discounted these weaknesses, and upon it he was a superb player of all bowling.

We won the toss and put South Africa in to bat and, George Geary taking 7 for 70, got them out for 196. Percy Holmes was given LBW for 0, a bad decision, but Herbert Sutcliffe and Ernest Tyldesley both made hundreds and the second wicket fell at 230. The third fell at 252 and, although Wally Hammond was still there, one end was now open. Wally made 51, the rest of us made 13, and the innings got to 313. George Geary took 5 for 60 in the second innings and Wally Hammond 5 for 36, so South Africa only got 170, to lose by ten wickets. It had been a very instructive encounter.

The battle between the South Africans and our top players, and between their batsmen and George Geary, was some of the finest play I have ever seen. The bowlers attacked incessantly and every ball had the quality of life and death. Herbie Taylor said that, on the form of the first Test Match, George was the nearest thing he had seen to Sydney Barnes.

Unfortunately this great spell was the last that George was to bowl on the trip for, in the course of it, he injured his elbow so badly that he was out for the rest of the season. Even so we won the second Test comfortably. The Newlands matting was laid on turf, and a gentle proposition compared to hard Johannesburg gravel, but our batting was largely a replica of the previous match with Bob Wyatt getting 91. I stayed with him whilst we added 55 for the ninth wicket, and was then caught at short-leg off Henry Promnitz. There was some doubt, as a number of people, including Bob, thought it had been a bump ball. Just last year the bowler, a charming man, wrote to me recalling the incident and saying that he had his doubts, but that the umpire had been quite satisfied when the fielder had appealed. He reminded me that, by way of compensation, I had knocked his castle down and so taken my first Test Match wicket.

The second Test was notable for the first appearance of George Bissett who had come to England in 1924 but, handicapped by injury, had met with little success. He was now a magnificent fast bowler whom our experienced players put in the first line for sheer pace. Like Frank Tyson, he was to have but one glorious series but, even so, it is strange that one seldom hears his name quoted when people discuss the great fast bowlers.

The third Test at Durban was played in a temperature of 107 in the shade and 100% humidity. This was without doubt the most trying spell of weather I ever experienced, and we spent our days and, in the times before air-conditioning, our nights, in a cloud of steam. The match was a high-scoring draw, the most remarkable feature of which was that Bob Wyatt opened the bowling, and finished with the astonishing analysis of 10 overs, 4 runs and three wickets in a total of 246. The satisfaction this feat afforded him was off-set by his being LBW to Cyril Vincent for nought. His indignation at what he considered a criminal decision exploded when we went down to the sea for a swim in the evening. Suddenly he came scuttling back to the beach. 'I'm not going to bathe in the same sea as that chap,' he said with some heat. At this we discerned the ample figure of umpire Laver, the responsible official, floating gently on the waves. The depth of Bob's feelings may be gauged from the fact that the sea in question was the Indian Ocean.

Going back to Jo'burg for the fourth Test we were beaten by four wickets. The South Africans brought back Alfie Hall, who bowled quickish left hand with a low arm so that, unlike so many who bounced over the top on matting, he usually hit the stumps. He and Bissett took 17 wickets between them, and decided the match.

I had my moment of glory, going in sixth wicket down and being last out when 91 runs were added. I only made 26, but it took about two and a half hours, and must have been infinitely tedious to the opposition. However, they took it all in good part and I can remember, as I battled away, Nummy Deane, their captain, passing at the end of an over. 'Well played, Stonewall Jackson,' he said with a smile, 'you're a bloody nuisance.'

So we went to Durban dormey one. I did not play in this one, which we lost by eight wickets, not that there was any connection between these two events. The deciding factor was again the bowling

"YOU'LL NEVER GET HIM OUT"

BUT FOR THE STAND MADE BY PEEBLES, IT IS PROBABLE THAT THE M.C.C.
WOULD HAVE BEEN DISMISSED LONG BEFORE CLOSE OF PLAY ON SATURDAY.

of George Bissett who, in our second innings, bowled with a gale behind him. Such was the force of the wind that when Greville Stevens held his bat pendulum-wise by the top of the handle, it blew out horizontally. The result was that Bissett bowled, so locals said, as fast as Jack Gregory, which was the fastest they had ever seen, to finish with 7 for 29.

Percy Holmes had been caught at the wicket off Bissett for nought in the first innings and, as he buckled on his pads again, there was a certain amount of raillery about Bissett being a bit too quick for an old man. As he left the dressing-room Percy turned to the company. 'I could play yon Bissett with bludy broom 'andle,' he said, and strode forward.

A couple of minutes later there was a deafening appeal for LBW, and our champion returned – beaming. As he unbuckled his pads he suddenly sat up, still smiling broadly. 'You know,' said he, 'it's first time as I've bagged 'em.'

From Durban we returned to the Cape, our last official fixture being against the Western Province of Newlands. We also played a delightful one-day match against Constancia, in the midst of the fruit- and wine-growing country. As our batsmen were soon well entrenched I went with a couple of local lads to bathe in a nearby river. The time passed more quickly than we calculated and, when I got back, we were in the field and I was soundly and properly berated by Ronny. However, no one was more amused than he when next day the *Cape Times* in their score of the match had a line: 'Peebles, absent, bathing o', an entry surely unique in the score books of the world.

Our last operation before boarding the *Saxon* for home was to have our money changed into gold, as we were told that we would get 27/6 for each sovereign when we got home. Out of the one hundred pounds with which I had set out I had fifty-seven left, which made a nice litle jingling bagful, and I could savour the miser's delight in letting these beautiful shining new coins run through my fingers.

It had altogether been a wonderful experience for a nineteen-

My top score in a Test Match – 26 *v* South Africa at Jo'burg in 1928. The cartoon is from the *Rand Daily Mail*.

year-old. Being so young and naïve I was received wherever we went with a warm and friendly indulgence. The South African side were not only a fine cricket team but a group who always made me feel welcome, and with whom I kept up over the years. Buster Nupen showed me how he bowled his leg-cutter, and Bob Catterale taught me to play the ukelele. This is not to say that on the field we didn't play hard and keen, but it was a series which was without lapse or ugly incident.

In my youthful enthusiasm I was too young and green to take any serious interest in the historic, social or political aspects of this beautiful and fascinating country. Apart from Ronny, who was naturally fascinated by the military history, Greville Stevens was the only one of our number who gave intelligent thought to these matters, reading widely and taking a lively interest in every place we visited. He would occasionally pass on the fruits of learning, but these were rather lost in the activities of a touring side's daily life.

We were little affected by the political divisions of the time. The lowly status of the natives was taken for granted as God's will. We were mildly aware that the Boers still resented our presence, and that *Verdomfer roinek* meant 'a bloody red-neck', and was synonymous with 'Britisher'. Even so, at Bloemfontein the First Lady of an extreme Afrikaaner group gave a party for us, and a good evening it was.

Of all the States and Provinces we visited Natal was the general favourite, as being the most British in population and tradition. Personally I loved the Cape, with its beautiful and varied country-side, and the gracious city, with its splendid and unique background of Table Mountain. Our hotels were usually in the surrounding suburbs which nestled amongst the deliciously smelling pines. This no doubt contributed to the impression that there was a distinct re-semblance to the Scottish Highlands, with the advantage of the climate rather on the South African side.

They had been four glorious months, and I had learned a little about life in a very pleasant school.

# FOUR

# The Age of Progress

To the player with love for the game and reasonable ambition there can be no more agreeable form of cricket than the first-class English system, involving the counties and the two senior universities. The standard of play is high enough to make county cricket a pleasant end in itself and, for the more aspiring, it remains the only route to international cricket in England. The system has been basically unchanged since the 1890s, but has naturally been affected by the vast upheavals and social and financial changes of this century.

Historians incline to regard the period between the '90s and the first war as the 'Golden Age' of English cricket, but those who played in other times would naturally believe theirs to be the pleasantest span. I certainly think myself lucky to have played in the late '20s and early '30s, a time which was a half-way house between the turn of the century and the present age in cricket shapes and forms. Between the eras there was much change, both subtle and obvious, in techniques, manners and philosophy, yet there is a great deal of common ground upon which both the cricketer of the '20s and his grandson would be perfectly at home.

Manners were more formal in cricket, as in all walks of life. The professional was addressed by his first name, and replied to the amateur as 'Mr So-and-So'. It was a convention both sides observed unself-consciously, for social divisions were part of the period. It could in theory lead to such unlikely situations as a new, unfledged amateur addressing Jack Hobbs by his first name upon introduction; but human nature doesn't change, and the senior professionals were regarded with some awe by the young, amateur and professional. In passing I may add that, many years ago, I advocated the abolition of any distinction between pro and amateur by the simple and sensible means of changing both titles to that of 'cricketer'.

There were still a considerable number of genuine amateurs in those easier days. Some were men of means, some had jobs which allowed or encouraged them to play, whilst undergraduates and schoolmasters came along in numbers during the holidays. They would wear heavier boots, and their caps would have smaller peaks, but their flannels and regalia would be quite familiar to a modern eye. The only difference in the equipment would be in the new 'boxing glove' now making its appearance, and the bats adorned with large and conspicuous trade marks to catch the eye of the television cameras.

It used to be said that in England love of county was greater than love of country, and this may well have been true before regional differences had been flattened out by modern communications. At any rate, there was a great sense of comradeship in the county cricket teams. Middlesex, as befitted the centre of the Commonwealth, had a cosmopolitan air, with players from all over the United Kingdom, and a strong tradition of overseas visitors. Affection for Lord's was so strong that there were several cases of professionals, offered better terms and prospects elsewhere, preferring to stay on the MCC staff.

By the start of the 1928 season I was qualified for Middlesex, but an unforeseen situation arose on my return from South Africa. Faulkner and I fell out. The *casus belli* was something trivial, but what with his impatience and my resentment all the friction of years flared up, and this time I felt sufficiently well-established to resign. He was obviously much taken aback, but it seemed that business-wise we were never likely to agree. He asked me to see him through the Easter holidays on the terms of an assistant instructor, and this I did, after which we parted. This left me with the problem of finding other employment, but whether it would be such that I could play county cricket was still to be seen. The answer turned out to be a compromise. Julien Cahn was a multi-millionaire who lived in Nottingham and had a passion for cricket. Much of the vast income he derived from the furniture trade he devoted to his own private team, and he was keen to recruit likely players into his business. Not long after leaving Faulkner's I was approached by a henchman of Julien Cahn's, one 'Lofty' Newman, whose wicket I had taken twice when playing for Plum the previous season. He offered me the prospect of a commercial career in the furniture business, a good future, and plenty of cricket. The salary was £350 a year, a princely sum by my standards of the '20s. At the same time two good friends whom I knew through the School, Peter Judd and George Kemp-Welch, were bound for the same destination, so I would be in agreeable company. Acceptance meant moving to Nottingham, but it was agreed that I could play a few matches for Middlesex if wanted, provided there were no prior claims of business or cricket. The result was that I played a few matches at Lord's early on but, finding it difficult to serve two masters, soon dropped out. I did, however, take part in one remarkable game which became famous as 'Constantine's Match'.

This took place at Lord's in June and started quite unremarkably when Middlesex batted first and declared at 352 for six wickets. Doing my 'Stonewall Jackson' act I made nought, not out, whilst Pat Hendren went from the mid-fifties to a hundred. This was useful, if tedious, and at least I was afforded a close-up view of Constantine's astonishing acrobatic fielding when I snicked a catch off Joe Small to third slip who dropped it quite low to his right. Constantine at second slip shot behind him, flipped the ball up just before it touched the ground, and had five snatches at it before it just escaped him, by which time he had covered about ten yards.

The West Indies made a pedestrian start and were 79 for five when 'Learie' came in to bat. We were immediately caught in the eye of the hurricane. One of his many spectacular strokes was a square cut off Gubby Allen which went for six into the balcony of the grand-stand, but he attacked every bowler with a fine impartiality. In less than an hour he had got to 87 and I was bowling to him with some trepidation. I still bowled basically medium pace but, in desperation, I let go a slow googly. He went to give it such a clip that I could hear the swish of the bat at our end of the pitch, but it dipped in and he hit outside it. To his manifest disgust it hit the middle stump.

By the end of the day we were nearly 250 ahead with seven wickets in hand, so seemingly well on top. But the third morning Learie, who had bowled a pretty sharp pace throughout the match, suddenly took off as one possessed and, from the pavilion end, he bowled at an awe-inspiring pace. No one looked like coping with this tempest, and the morning's haul brought him six wickets for eleven runs. There stays in my mind the picture of little Jim Powell, our last man, looking in imminent danger of sudden death as five whistling deliveries flashed past without his seeing one of them, a perilous state of affairs which caused Frank Mann to cry out from the dressing-room balcony, begging him to knock his own stumps down.

The West Indies finally needed 259 to win and five went for 121. Learie started again exactly where he had left off. J. W. Hearne, a most courageous man, sought to catch him off his own bowling and suffered such damage to his hand that he played no more that season. The ball in this case went smack into the bottom pavilion step whence it rebounded almost to the bowler's feet. Runs came at a roaring pace and in under the hour Learie had reached his hundred and his side were all but home. This was the greatest all-round performance I was to see in my career – and possibly my life.

The season with Julien Cahn was a qualified success, but what I saw of the furniture trade was not inspiring, and I still yearned to play first-class cricket. Furthermore, both Peter and George had decided to try something else, so I had little to keep me at Nottingham.

At the end of the season I went down to Folkestone to play in the Festival, and had the considerable pleasure of travelling with George Gunn. Of all the great players I have known he was in many ways, as player and man, the most quaint and attractively original. The tales about him are legion. He had set out to be a professional pianist, hoping to succeed as an accompanist, but when he had failed to attain the high standards he had set himself he turned to cricket instead. His play always had the air of virtuoso, with all the moods and shades of music, and he always played as *he* felt, regardless of the bowling or other circumstances. Figures meant little to him so his record, although very good, gives little idea of his mastery as a batsman. One of the strangest features of his career was that, when still the finest player of fast bowling in the country, he was not picked in 1921, the year of Gregory and McDonald, although thirty others were.

As we journeyed I said I very much hoped I would get a wicket in the forthcoming match, Gentlemen *v* Players, in which we were on opposing sides. 'Well,' said he, 'I need forty-six runs for my two thousand, and if I get them you might get a wicket.' I didn't attach any great significance to this remark at the time but, when he came in to open the second innings for the Players, he still wanted 12 more runs for his goal. I went on to bowl when he had made six. He walked casually to meet my first ball and struck it for two. The next he hit for four. The third he walked out to meet again, but somehow missed it completely and just kept on walking. It is in *Wisden* to this day: 'Gunn st. Benson b. Peebles 12.'

In September I went home on holiday to Uddingston and my parents broached the idea of my going to Oxford. My brother was already up at University College, and they felt that, with the prospect of my getting a Blue, Oxford would be a great help in my career. It would certainly be a strain on their limited resources, but they were very keen that I should take the chance, which accordingly I did. As things turned out I think they got much pleasure from such success as I had, and I hope I was duly grateful.

As I had been negligent in my last years at school I had to do a winter's studying in order the following spring to tackle Responsions, the entrance examination to Oxford, but, with the aid of a local Uddingston *dominie* I made the grade and was accepted as a commoner of Brasenose College, to go into residence in the following autumn. With this glorious prospect before me I returned to London and had my first full season with Middlesex. It was one of the happiest times of my life.

Frank Mann was officially captain of Middlesex in 1929 but, since he was unable to play more than a few matches, Nigel Haig took over. Six feet tall and well built, Nigel was so spare that he weighed little over ten stone, yet he was strong and wiry, and was a first-class all-round athlete. He was temperamental, but a wit and raconteur on the grand scale.

We had a bunch of young amateurs, and about the whole side was a light-hearted air. The only professionals were J. W. Hearne, Pat Hendren, Jack Durston and Harry Lee – a most stalwart veteran phalanx. Joe Hulme, 'the Arsenal Flyer', was a regular member and a number of youngsters making their way also came into the side from time to time.

We were a very fair team and out of 30 matches we won 13 and lost 9. At first our chief snag was that Pat Hendren was out of luck, and nothing went right for him. After a month of frustration he had just got started against Notts when a ball from Sam Staples pitched very wide of the off stump. Pat 'shouldered arms' but the ball pitched in a rut from the previous match, rose almost vertically and hit the end of his bat handle, whence it shot as from a billiard cue into the stumps. Pat might have been forgiven for giving way to despair, but he battled on, to end the season in a blaze of glory.

Walter Robins at this time was the best English leg-tweaker I ever saw. He bowled at around medium pace with a fine, long, swinging action, and spun the ball more than anyone else in the game outside Australia. His googly was hard to read and came off the pitch with the same venom as the leg-break. He made no great pretensions to flight and was occasionally erratic, but his pace and spin discounted this. He was then unfortunately prevailed upon by some pundits to flight the ball and, though always a rare good tweaker, never fulfilled his glorious potential.

Gubby Allen occasionally came into the side and was by this time a truly splendid fast bowler. Arriving late for the Lancashire match at Lord's he went on first change, and took all ten wickets for 40. He was a great personality, and unaffectedly nice to me when I was very small fry. Indeed, and not surprisingly, I took to him right away. They were happy days whenever Gubby, Walter and I played together.

My career for the first part of the season was rather in and out. Persevering with my quickish method I never reproduced my form of the Faulkner School days. Against Yorkshire at Lords I got a chance with the new ball and was quite successful. Bowling seamers I got six wickets in the match, including those of Wilfred Rhodes and Emmott Robinson with successive balls, a noteworthy brace. Wilfred was caught at the wicket and, departing, put me in my place. 'Can't see 'em like I used to,' he said. But, apart from a few overs to warm me up, I wasn't interested in seam bowling and persisted in the hopes I would, as the Australians say, 'come good'.

By the second half of July I had played 17 matches for Middlesex and taken 52 wickets for 25 apiece. At Leicester we lost the
toss and I got nought for 59 when Leicester made 377. It was not
good enough. When they batted again I cut my run by half, and
my pace by roughly the same margin, and wound up with 6 for
56. In the next match, against Derby, I took 5 for 70, then 8 for
95 against Worcestershire. It seemed I had got the answer, and was
supported in this by the whole-hearted approval of captain and
team.

At the beginning of August we went to Old Trafford for Ted
McDonald's Benefit. Walter Robins and I shared the wickets between us but I felt I was robbed of one further wicket in observing
the proprieties by getting Ted off the mark. Having bowled a
series of half volleys and full tosses, I accidently bowled a straight
one which struck him on the pad and, by pure reflex, I appealed,
to be answered by Nigel Haig from mid-off, who shouted 'Not out,
you bloody fool,' before the umpire could speak. When Ted eventually got his first run he was not in the least grateful, saying
he didn't need any help. This I found disillusioning from one I
regarded as a hero.

Neville Cardus took a great fancy to the bowling of Walter and
myself and wrote me a letter which I have to this day. It reads:

'Dear Mr Peebles,

Congratulations on your fine bowling against Surrey today!
I admired your attack at Manchester last week; did you see
what I wrote about you? Here's a future to you if you'll keep a
cool head.

Yours sincerely,
Neville Cardus'

Although we were to know each other well in after years we
had not met at that time, so it was a kindly gesture on his part
to encourage a young unknown. As time went by he looked back
on this period with such nostalgia that I felt that, with Walter,
I had become a minor figure in the grand Cardus tapestry. The
change to the slow-medium style which he was kind enough to
admire brought me a good bag of wickets at a much smaller cost,
so that I finished the season with 107 wickets at 19 apiece. By each

taking 100 wickets Nigel Haig, Walter and I set up a record for Middlesex, and possibly for any county, as it was the first time that three amateurs had done so in the same season.

My first two terms at Oxford were extremely enjoyable, but uneventful. Each undergraduate had his own set of rooms in college, or comfortable digs nearby, and life was pleasant and relaxed. There was no compulsion to work and, although ostensibly reading law, I never opened a book. At the end of the Easter term I sat the first examination, known as 'Law Prelim', and, knowing that I had made little impression, I asked my tutor how I had done. He was Dr Stallybrass, a great authority on international law and an immensely keen cricketer, known to all as 'Sonners'. He eyed me with doleful countenance. 'You got one per cent in one subject,' he said, 'but you were not quite so successful in the others.' This was a performance for which a modern undergraduate would be sent down forthwith but, in those easier days, no action was taken. I was soon off on a successful trip to Egypt with Hubert Martineau's Water Martins, and got in good training for the serious business of the season to come.

When I returned to Oxford I played in the Freshers match and took five wickets, but was firmly dealt with by a young South African, Alan Melville, who made a hundred. With my record for Middlesex I felt fairly confident of an extended trial for the Varsity and Melville, hitherto unknown in England, could now well think the same of his own case. We were both included in the side for the first match, against Kent, and both got off to a good start. I got six wickets and he got 78 before rain came to prevent either team from batting a second time. The next match was against Yorkshire and was again confined to little more than a single innings apiece. I again got six wickets, while he made 118. This was a very fine performance on his part, for he was a newcomer to turf wickets and Yorkshire, on a soft pitch, were the best bowling side in the country.

The bad weather had its compensations for, as the rain poured down, I sat with Emmott Robinson, one of cricket's major characters. It was his benefit year and, with the aid of a map of the Headingley ground, we set about knocking a bit more money out

of what we hoped would be a capacity crowd. This we did by
various devices such as turning some of the bob seats into two bob.
We also schemed to prevent members giving their passes to friends
and, although I thought this a base suspicion to be aimed at our
patrons, Emmott was unsentimental in matters of business. When
all was said and done we had increased the maximum possible return
by a hundred or two pounds, always given that capacity crowd.
He was a great financier, and we both thoroughly enjoyed the
exercise.

When it was over he looked at me with those keen blue eyes.
'Tha'll play for England this year,' he said. I was much flattered,
but said there were surely stronger claimants, naming Walter
Robins for one. 'Nay, nay,' said Emmott, 'he hasn't got that *control*
of the ball that you have.' Hearing his heavy emphasis on the word
'control' I was reminded that accuracy was one of the canons
of the Yorkshire creed, to which Emmott was an ardent subscriber.
One of my favourites of the thousand-and-one tales told of this
stalwart and devoted man underlines this very point. When Hedley
Verity took all ten wickets for ten runs against Notts in 1932 there
was as usual much discussion in the evening amongst his team mates
about the day's play, and this extraordinary feat was naturally the
main topic. Emmott for once was inclined to be silent as the conversation, for the most part congratulatory, rolled on. But when
there was a pause he burst forth. 'Eeh,' he said, 'if only you hadn't
given them yon fower.'

Fairly early in the season I was asked to play for MCC *v* the
Australians at Lord's. This was an encouraging sign, for MCC
against the touring side was usually regarded as a dress rehearsal
for the first Test Match. A somewhat unexpected situation had
arisen in the Australians' progress. When, six weeks previously,
they had set out for England three young men had been publicized
as coming champions. The first and greatest prospect was Archie
Jackson, born near Glasgow, and regarded as a second Victor
Trumper. There was a young man named Bradman from Bowral,
in New South Wales, also of great if less spectacular promise. The
third and youngest was Stan McCabe, another New South Welsh-
man, said to be a fine stroke player. When they arrived at Lords,
their side having played five matches, Bradman had made 556

runs for thrice out. Jackson had made 138 in 7 innings, and McCabe had batted 5 times for the modest total of 44. The gates at Lord's closed early on the first morning, and it was clear that the chief attraction for this large crowd was Bradman.

When Jackson came in first and was out for nought few people realized that he was a sick man suffering from advanced TB. McCabe was not in the side, but Bradman shone with sufficient brilliance to dispel any doubts as to his supremacy. He got 66 and 4, but the first innings was a revelation. What caught the eye was his extraordinary speed of foot in playing the slow bowlers, when he would wait till the ball was well on its way, then dart out to kill the spin. Gubby Allen had the mortification of having him missed by Greville Stevens in the slips and, by way of explanation and apology from that cheerful wit, had to be content with a curt enquiry as to why he didn't 'bowl at the bloody wicket'.

Otherwise the match was an unspectacular draw. My own share in the proceedings was to get three wickets at fair expense but, what with a good press, I was not discouraged. One interesting comment in this match came from Alan Fairfax, a very good all-round new-comer from Australia, who was playing at Lord's for the first time. In after years he told me that the crowd seemed so restrained and well-behaved after the Hill at Sydney that his first impression was that he was playing on an empty ground.

In being picked for this match I escaped something at Oxford. Gloucester had scored 627 for two wickets to defeat the Varsity by an innings. Denis Moore, a Freshman from Shrewsbury, made 206 for Gloucester, so forcing his way into the Oxford side, and Wally Hammond made 211 not out. Wally always did have a liking for the Parks and University bowling and, not long ago, David Macindoe told me an intriguing tale concerning their encounters.

In 1939 David was attacking Wally at his best fastish-medium when, by way of variation, he let go his slow ball, a delivery good enough to baffle many a first-class player. Wally played a beauti-ful swinging forward stroke, and the ball shot back over David's head whining like a shell. It was still going up when it cleared the pavilion and disappeared from sight and, as it happened, from human ken, for it landed in the rough behind and was lost for good.

THE AGE OF PROGRESS

The war was just over when Gloucester next came to the Parks, and David was again bowling to Wally. By way of variation he tried his slow one and this time, he says, an evil leer passed momentarily over Wally's features. He played forward, majestic and unhurried, the ball whizzed back over David's head and was still rising when it cleared the pavilion. It was never found. Perhaps some day two lovers, sporting in the long grass, will expose two decomposed cricket balls nestling together in the undergrowth – who knows?

Apart from Gloucester's great onslaught the one other occasion upon which we were collared was when the Australians won the toss on a beautiful wicket on the Christ Church ground, where we were playing as we could not take gate money in the Parks. Bill Ponsford, dropped at the wicket early on, made 220 not out, and they declared at 406 for a couple of wickets. By evening my part in the proceedings had ended with the first real complaint from a 'googly shoulder', which the Australian masseur kindly worked on, and advised me to rest. Relieved of responsibility I went to the Pembroke Ball that evening, not meaning to have a very late night. However, on leaving with a friend in his car, we offered a lady a lift home. This she accepted with alacrity which was not surprising when it turned out that she lived, not in Oxford, but in London. Gallantry prevailed, with the result that I arrived back at BNC early in the morning, still resplendent in white tie and tails. Absence without leave was a serious offence and so I was somewhat shaken when I ran straight into the arms of a don, a good Scot named McKie. He took one look at my outfit. 'Been to see the Pope?' he asked, and passed on his way.

Our batting failed miserably and, sleepless night or not, I had the glory of making top score of 22 not out, and had the unusual experience of receiving a full toss from Clarrie Grimmett which I hit for four.

During the match I attended a memorable dinner party. The hosts were Pat Kingsley, the Noob and myself, and the guests were Charlie Macartney, Clarrie Grimmett and Bert Oldfield. They were wonderful company, and we undergraduates were enthralled by their talk. But the dominating personality was Charlie Macartney, 'the Governor General'. He was, without being con-

ceited, a very confident man, a characteristic reflected in his
aggressive and original batting. It was also evident when I asked
him how great Syd Barnes had been. He pondered the question for a few moments then pronounced. 'I'll tell you how
great,' he said. 'In 1912 at the Oval I said to the boys, "I'm
going to hit the blooming Barnes for six today."' He paused
to give full weight to his words. 'I had to wait until I had made
sixty-eight,' he said. This unusual measure of Barnes's supremacy
was quoted without affectation or conceit. It was one which kept
Neville Cardus happy all his days.

The Oxford side of 1930 was potentially a very good one but,
in practice, it turned out to be a great disappointment to its supporters. The University Match was a fiasco, the memory of which
still makes Oxonians shudder. We had a splendid batting order
with Kingsley, Moore, Melville, Pataudi, Ford and Garland-Wells.
It was completed at the end of term with the arrival of Aidan
Crawley, who had been working hard for his Finals during the
early part of the season. He was a splendid opening batsman, and
a good counter to Killick on the other side.

Our bowling, on the other hand, was always suspect. Charlie Hill-
Wood, a quick left-hander with a strange off-the-wrong-foot action,
had lost the fine form of the previous season and so we lacked an
effective spearhead. E. M. Wellings, the best stock bowler in residence, and possibly the best all-rounder, was *persona non grata*
in certain quarters and was dropped at the first opportunity. He
had been a 'Blue' the previous year and was reinstated in 1931.
He later achieved fame as a most knowledgeable cricket writer on
the London *Evening News* where his opinions were sometimes con-
troversial, but always courageous, qualities which may have aroused
the opposition which cost him his place in the 1930 side. John
Mayhew was a very good wicket-keeper who had occasional off days
but these always seemed to occur at crucial times. He was a particular friend of mine, so that I suffered with him as well as from
him when he had a lapse. This variable element was an added
imponderable.

It was not our material state which led us to disaster so much as
dissension and uncertainty within our ranks. Our captain, Pat
Kingsley, was a fine cricketer and a charming man who would have

led a normal and happy university side with success. But we had a large proportion of relatively experienced and certainly opinionated cricketers, often at sixes and sevens, for whom the ideal leader would have been someone in the Douglas Jardine mould. As things were it seemed beyond normal human ability to weld us into a team. In making these strictures it is well that I should add that, with the conceit of youth and a certain substance of fact, I considered that I was the mainstay of our bowling, and so entitled to make my views heard – which probably did nothing to help. Despite these internal stresses we had a very good season until we arrived at Lord's. There all our latent flaws came to light, mostly on the last day as we staggered from one disaster to another.

The first serious accident occurred in the last over of the second day. John Mayhew dropped Killick whilst standing back to Charlie Hill-Wood. Had he taken this chance it would have meant the first five Cambridge batsmen would have gone with a lead of only 40 runs. Even so, we had six of their wickets down for 110 next morning, and should have been home and dry. But Tom Killick, who knew my every trick from Faulkner School days, got up to my end and batted splendidly, sheltering the weaker, to my rage and frustration. Our fielding then steadily deteriorated, and catches fell like autumn leaves. I volunteered to bowl with the second new ball, an offer which was inadvisedly accepted and, what with one thing and another, four very average batsmen helped Tom to add 210 runs. Cambridge eventually declared at 332 for nine.

We then embarked on the crowning folly. Left 307 to win in about two-and-a-half hours, we yielded to the clamour of one faction who felt we had a good chance if we went for the runs. That this was never on became clear when, instead of keeping pace with the clock, we found ourselves desperately defending on a dusting wicket which gave the spinners quite a bit of turn. We lost with time to spare by 205 runs, and it remains in my memory as the saddest and most futile major cricket match in which I have played.

My next visit to Lord's was a much happier occasion. Playing for the Gentlemen against the Players I got seven wickets, including those of the opening pair, Hobbs and Sutcliffe. This was the only time I ever took wicket of 'the Master', in fact one of the very few times I ever beat his bat. He was LBW and very out, for umpires had to be well satisfied before giving a decision against the top players, whilst the small were occasionally less fortunate; it is probably still so. Hobbs was now in his forty-ninth year. When young he had been a most dashing player, fleet of foot and always on the attack. Now he was a beautifully orthodox batsman, his judgment of length impeccable, and his reading of the bowler's intentions seemingly infallible. By now, however, he did not chase bowlers to destruction, but played the spinners from the crease, showing the full face of an impeccably straight bat. Thus, although I got the impression that he spotted the wrong 'un as soon as I started to run up, it was not alarming, but rather an intensely interesting experience to bowl at him, and always something of an occasion.

As we came off the field after the first innings in which I got six wickets (the second innings being limited to a few overs), someone said, 'You'll soon be on your way to Manchester,' to which my old friend and compatriot Gubby Allen replied, 'He can start packing his bag now.' The realization dawned on me that I must be well in the running for the fourth Test Match starting at Manchester in less than a fortnight.

During this time in London I was staying with the Warners, who had a delightful house in Tedworth Square, Chelsea. They made me very much one of the family which consisted of their daughter Betty, and two sons, Esmond and Johnny. This, and their kindness generally, went to make one of the most wonderful summers any young man could ever have enjoyed. Now we all waited breathlessly for the hoped-for news that would crown it all. In due course the selectors, 'Shrimp' Leveson-Gower, Frank Mann and Jack White met and announced their teams. I was one of the twelve and, as Walter Robins was also named, I was to be in happy and familiar company.

There was great jubilation in the Warner family at this even if the tidings were not unexpected. Sir Pelham and his wife Agnes — a great expert — were so delighted that I might have been their son. I was myself aglow but awed and rather chastened. To play cricket for England against Australia is the ambition of every cricketer in this country. To a boy in Scotland it was a faraway dream that had become a hope, then a probability, only to fade again as my true form continued to elude me. My mind went back to the afternoon just over a year before when on the impulse of a moment, doubtless prompted by a cricketing guardian angel, I had abandoned the pursuit of the quick leg-break and turned to slow-medium. It had worked out.

I would be the first Scot born and brought up in my own country to play cricket for England.

# FIVE

# Encounter with the Don

The 22 players taking part in a Test Match will almost all have played against each other before, the veterans perhaps a large number of times. The newcomers are largely picked on the strength of a good performance against the visiting side for their counties, or some representative side. The majority will know the ground on which the match is to be played, and have grown accustomed to the accommodation and officials over the years. But despite the familiar ingredients the match will be quite different from any other game of cricket. On arrival the player will be aware of a special sense of competition and of an anxiety to succeed which pervades the whole atmosphere. That the crowd is much larger and manifestly more expectant than on lesser occasions adds a sharp tang to this awareness, and is a reminder that maybe millions eagerly await the performance of teams and individuals. The play, physically and psychologically, will be more intense and of higher standard than any other form of cricket competition. All this is popularly known as 'Test Match atmosphere', and is a strong trial of temperament even to the most phlegmatic. Even those of long experience and success continue to be affected, and Jack Hobbs himself once said that he occasionally felt physically sick on the eve of a Test Match. Withal, for those with stomach for the fight, it is the grandest of all cricket's thousand fascinating forms.

Each cricketing nation adds its own particular flavour to the scene. To English eyes the South Africans have a certain friendliness, the West Indies an underlying gaiety, New Zealand arouses a family affection, and all wish the relative newcomers, India and Pakistan, well in what until recent years has been an uphill battle in this country. All are most welcome but, with all their talents and attractions, none quite arouses the tremendous interest and feelings of rivalry that an England *v* Australia Test Match generates in both camps. This is the oldest of the international fixtures but still the freshest and, at best, productive of the greatest skills most shrewdly applied. Sir Gerald du Maurier, who knew something of such matters, once said that, for him, the most dramatic moment in life was the moment when, in an England *v* Australia match, the umpires were out, and the fielding side was about to appear.

It was therefore in a do-or-die but slightly nervous frame of mind that I set out for Manchester on the eve of the fourth Test Match. Apart from normal anxieties of a newcomer making a first appearance against Australia there was the uneasy reflection that at that stage Bradman had batted five times against England and made just 728 runs.

The first news that came to hand on arrival was that the selectors, considering the weather to be uncertain, had sent for Tom Goddard, the Gloucestershire off-spinner. This meant that, with Walter Robins and myself, there were now three slow bowlers of whom two would play. Walter's selection had been a surprise in the first place, as he had had a sharp altercation with the chairman of the selectors, 'Shrimp' Leveson-Gower, during the Lord's match. At a crucial moment in the game Walter, who was like a greyhound between the wickets, had run out Jack White. Walter was much upset by this and when he got back to the dressing-room he had high words with the Chairman, who had attacked him in somewhat intemperate terms. The result had been a heated scene and, in the opinion of those present, the end of Walter's prospects for the current series. In the event he was the one to be omitted at Manchester, but whether this was in any way due to the scene at Lord's no one could say.

We lost the toss and Stan Nichols and Maurice Tate started off against Woodfull and Ponsford on a softish wicket under a dull, grey sky. Having fielded at long-leg and mid-off for the first hour I was presently called up to bowl from the practice ground end. When I had measured off my run and was waiting whilst Percy Chapman directed the field, Jack Hobbs made a detour in his journey from cover to cover to give me a word of encouragement. What he said was, in essence, that this was just the same as any other cricket match, and to bowl as I would in the ordinary way. It was a characteristically thoughtful gesture and started me off on just the right note.

My first spell achieved nothing material, but I caused Bill Woodfull quite a lot of trouble and he might twice have been caught at second slip, had there been one, and once he failed to pick the googly and was nearly bowled. But Ponsford was the best of all the Australians on soft wickets and was unperturbed.

After lunch I went on again with Maurice Tate, who soon had Woodfull caught at the wicket. Don then came in, his habit of walking very slowly to the wicket to accustom himself to the light lending a dramatic air to his entry. He took a single off Maurice and then he and I joined battle.

We must both have been aware that this encounter had very much the air of a personal duel, for it was hoped on our side that, as he had only had a brief glimpse of me at Lord's and Oxford, I might deceive him. The press had fostered this idea to the point that my inclusion was solely aimed at Bradman, but this was only true to the extent that he was obviously the largest target for any English bowler. One could feel the tremendous tension as I ran up to deliver my first ball to him. The only plan of attack which I had was to drop a googly at him right away before he was settled, and this I did. It pitched outside the off stump, and he moved across his wicket and 'shouldered arms'. But he had gone so far that he had left all three stumps visible. The ball nipped back behind him, and went so close over the middle stump that George Duckworth let it go for four byes. Had we been playing with the larger stumps already in use in county cricket, it must have hit.

Although Bradman was already much too shrewd a tactician to show it, this hazardous start may well have disconcerted him, for he then made several mistakes, and was clearly ill at ease. When he had made ten he came down the wicket to drive a leg-break past extra cover, but failed to get to the pitch of it, and snicked an easy catch to Wally Hammond at first slip. To the dismay and astonishment of the English camp Wally dropped it.

It now seemed inevitable that he would run through this period of uncertainty and, having found his touch, build up another enormous innings. His confidence must have been increased when I bowled a full toss which he hit effortlessly for four. But in my next over, when he had made 14, he again came down the wicket and played the same off drive to snick the ball to second slip, where Duleep made no mistake. A roar went up from the crowd which must have lasted a full minute and, for the moment, I had fulfilled my purpose. A well-known artist named Nevinson wrote later, in a book entitled *These Savage Islands,* that he had returned to these shores in the midst of a bank crisis, and various other disasters, to find, much to his disgust, that all the evening newspaper hoardings said was PEEBLES DOES IT.'

Much has been written about this duel and many commentators have been very generous to me. Over the years I have given the matter a good deal of thought and imagine that I see it in proper perspective. I believe I bowled my best, especially the leg-break, and I am sure Don could not pick my googly. That being said, there is one more important factor. It is that, for the first time in his life, Don was seeing a slow, soft English wicket. Any good Yorkshireman would have met with little difficulty on it but, to the batsman brought up on fast Australian wickets, it had always been a problem at first sight. Curiously enough it was the one type of pitch upon which Don never looked at ease, presumably because he didn't really apply himself to what, for him, was a rare and not very important matter. Bill Ponsford, with a good strong top hand, was always a great player on soft wickets – as Don must have been had he tackled them seriously.

When Don was gone in came Alan Kippax. He played forward at the first three balls and received them all on his front pad. 'Ducky' and I shouted our heads off, and were always agreed in after years that the first two were plumb out, and the third a 'good ask'. But Joe Hardstaff, a very conservative umpire, said 'not out' to all three. On the third one he started violently and shouted his answer, at which I realized the awful strain of umpiring a Test Match.

It was just not my day nor, for that matter, my match, for next morning nothing went right, and when the innings closed at 345 I had taken 3 for 150. I make no bones about saying that with any luck or, indeed, had we played with the larger stumps, I should have taken twice as many wickets for less than half as many runs. I took cold comfort from recalling Cecil Parkin once saying that,

after he had had an unfruitful and expensive day on a plumb Australian pitch, Warwick Armstrong had gone out of his way to say
'well bowled'. At first Parkin suspected sarcasm but, on reflection,
realized that he had bowled very well, and here was a good enough
judge to appreciate it.

Hobbs and Sutcliffe gave us a fine start with 108 for the first
wicket and by the end of the second day we were 221 for five. Next
day we had only 45 minutes' play in the semi-darkness during
which we lost three wickets and, on the fourth, it rained incessantly.
The general feelings of the players in these depressing circumstances were summed up by Maurice Tate who, jerking his pipe
at the sky, said to Percy Chapman, 'See that cloud, Skipper?' and
on Percy's saying he did added, 'It but flatters to deceive.' With
which enigmatical observation Maurice put his pipe back in his
mouth, and waggled his head in an oracular manner.

There was much reflection in press and in cricket quarters
on this match. Some were led into a hasty and erroneous reassess-
ment of Don Bradman as the wonder of the era. They had to
make a further revision when, almost immediately, he resumed his
triumphant march to finish the season with phenomenal figures
in both Test Matches and county matches.

Percy Chapman came in for a lot of adverse criticism, chiefly
on account of his field placing for me. He loved to field at silly
mid-off right on the bat, which he did with the utmost brilliance,
but I sorely needed an extra cover against batting of this calibre.
Thus I was largely the unwitting cause of Percy's downfall.

In the course of the match Ranji gave a dinner party at the
Midland Hotel where we were all staying. The guests were Archie
MacLaren, Plum Warner, Sir Arthur Priestley, Duleep and myself.
I sat opposite Sir Arthur who had played for MCC in days gone
by, and whose alarmingly apoplectic complexion was due to his
falling asleep in his bath just before the dinner. After a few
pleasantries with the company in general he bent a disapproving
eye upon me and asked abruptly, 'What were you doing at long
leg today, young man?' to which I replied that I had been directed
there by the captain. 'Hmm,' he said, 'you might have thrown your
arm out.' This I parried by saying that when possible I had lobbed
the ball back to save my arm. At this he rapped the table. 'Lobbed

the ball back, sir,' he exclaimed, 'you have outraged every canon of the game!'

From Manchester I travelled south to Hove for the August Bank Holiday match with Sussex. This was always the most festive fixture of all the glad New Year. It coincided with the Brighton Races so the town was usually full of enterprising and amusing citizens.

The amateurs stayed in grandeur at the Metropole Hotel and entertained the opposition with an open-handed generosity which contrasted sharply with the treasurer's annual and vocal misgivings. There was adventure, incident, and romance to say nothing of the attractions of Brighton pier. There was a financier whose joy in life it was to conduct the band in Palm Court. Unfortunately for him the ozone seemed to stimulate Frank Mann's own humbler musical ambitions and, taking advantage of the conductor's short sight, he would conceal himself amongst the musicians. So, much to his annoyance, the maestro's finest moments were liable to be blown asunder by the discordant blare of a trumpet, or a thunder of drums, according to the novice's fancy of the moment.

There was a 'bombe surprise' which lived up to its name by exploding in the chafing dish and sending the flesh-pots diving for cover in all directions. There was a dog which somehow fell six stories down the lift shaft, to emerge like cannon shot and complete three dizzy laps of the lounge, before disappearing into the night. It turned up next day a mile away, thoughtful but unscathed. Such simple pleasures, allied to a plentiful intake of champagne at the club's expense, kept everyone happy on and off the field.

Nor was the spiritual side neglected. One year Walter Robins, returning after a trying day in the field, referred to the bedside *Texts for All Occasions* thoughtfully provided by the management. Appropriately he turned to the section devoted to difficult times and days of trial. Apparently some previous tenant had done likewise for, scrawled underneath the official words of comfort, was the footnote: 'Go to 78 Marine Parade, knock three times, and ask for Maisie.'

The match on this occasion was Maurice Tate's Benefit, and a deserving occasion for the greatest seam bowler of modern times. No country has since produced his equal in this particular line, and

it is difficult to think of even a near resemblance. With the perfect
rolling momentum of his body and the enormous whip of the arm,
no one who played an over from Maurice would subscribe to the
scientist's view that a ball cannot increase in pace off the pitch.
To this ability was added the sharp and late switch of the ball,
chiefly from leg to off, but now and then suddenly dipping in
from the reverse direction. No one ever seemed to know whether
this was by design or just nature's bonus to an unusually great
natural talent. As it turned out this Benefit was scarcely just reward
for the amount he had given to the game of cricket in general, and
his county and country in particular.

The Saturday was relatively uneventful. Sussex batted first and
made 243 and Middlesex were out for 214. But over the weekend
a great storm of wind and rain blew in from the sea. The force
of the wind blew a lot of water under the cover at the sea end and,
when the pitch was uncovered on Monday morning, there was a
neat line dividing the sea end, which was soft and wet, from the
north end, which was bone dry, hard and fast. Just to perfect the
situation from the bowler's point of view there was still a stiff wind
blowing in from the sea. When Sussex batted again Gubby
bowled down the breeze into the hard end and quickly took the
first four wickets, at which point I came on to bowl into the soft
end. The unfortunate batsmen on running a single must have felt
as though some malevolent magic carpet had swept them off to
some entirely different cricket ground. The result was that I took
the next five wickets in a row but Gubby, by way of a bit of justice,
got the last. Maurice, the beneficiary, was caught off the back of the
bat at short leg and the game ended on the second day.

The following week there was a great sensation when the
selectors announced that they had dropped Percy Chapman from the
team for the last Test Match. This decision stirred up strong feelings, for it was a sad ending to what had been a spectacular and,
indeed, romantic career.

If cricket ran to such extravagances Percy Chapman would doubtless have been the 'Golden Boy'. A large and handsome young man,
he had been a great favourite with the public ever since his university days, when his dashing left-handed batting and magnificent
fielding had promised a great future. This promise was fulfilled

when he succeeded Arthur Carr and defeated Australia in 1926 for the first time in fifteen years. It was enhanced and confirmed when he won the 1928/29 series by the wide margin of 4–1. His personal and private fortunes seemed to be blessed with the same happy touch (he had a most attractive wife, and a very good job with the Distillers Co.) and he became a national figure, epitomizing all the public wanted in a sporting hero. No one regarded him as a particularly subtle tactician, and it would have seemed out of character for him to have been so, but he was a sound captain, and one whom his team would follow with a cheerful smile.

With the arrival of the Australians in 1930 Chapman's admirers had confidently looked forward to the continuance of his triumphant career, and a further victorious series. But no one in England had foreseen the strength of the Australian resurgence, led by the phenomenon of Don Bradman. Since their defeat in the first Test Match at Trent Bridge the Australians, largely due to Bradman, the perfection of English pitches and the added fourth day, had transformed the nature of international cricket in England. Now, with the last and deciding Test at hand, England's early position as favourites had declined until a fair share of odds lay against them.

The captain had, of course, to accept the responsibility for his side's reverses, but how far he had personally contributed to them in fact was the cause of much controversy. He had averaged 43 with the bat – although this was largely dependent on his spirited century at Lords – and he had fielded with his customary brilliance. His leadership was less certain. His tactics had been criticized and, at Manchester, specific field placings had been questioned. If he was to be superseded the obvious choice was Bob Wyatt, and this added further weight to the arguments of those who wanted a change. The match was to be played to a finish, and many considered that Wyatt's sounder batting and possibly more cautious approach was more suitable than Chapman's flamboyant presence. The selectors apparently leant to this view and so Chapman, ironically, found himself in the same position as his predecessor – deposed, undefeated after four Tests.

The last Test Match of 1930 played at the Oval was notable as being Jack Hobb's last appearance for England, and deciding in their favour a series which the Australians had unexpectedly dominated ever since their first defeat. The pitch was the most perfect the Oval could produce, which is about as good as anything on this imperfect earth. Here the Aussies were better qualified than we were, with Bradman leading a tremendous batting order, and Grimmett spear-heading a bowling side accustomed to dig out batsmen on perfect wickets.

They did well to get us out for 405, and would have done much better but for Sutcliffe and Wyatt, the latter surviving the emotional shock of a tremendous welcoming ovation. Together they carried the score from a disappointing 197 for 5 to 367 for 6, but after that there was little to come. Australia started with a beautiful hundred from Bill Ponsford. I had been told how tough and sharp the Aussies were generally and that Ponsford was the toughest and least approachable of all. However, as he got to a hundred by hitting me for three I felt I must say, 'Well played, Bill,' which I did. He turned to me with a most friendly smile. 'Ah,' he said, 'thanks, Ian.' This I thought a strange gesture from such a hostile and taciturn nature. It was then I reflected my informants had been one-eyed men, who had never been out, and always hard done by in life by umpires, gods and tax collectors. Thenceforward I had the sense to make my own judgments.

We got two wickets on the first day of the Australian innings and only one in the second. There was an element of luck about the last one in that, half way through an over, I said to Bob Wyatt I would rather have him at extra cover than forward short leg. He wisely told me to wait till the end of the over, and next ball made a splendid catch when Alan Kippax miscued and hit the ball in his direction.

By lunchtime on the third day we had got three Australians out for 371 and Duleep and I were sitting disconsolately in the dressing-room when Mr Leveson-Gower came in to announce the arrival of the Prince of Wales. As he shook me by the hand the Prince said, 'You've just come down from Cambridge, haven't you?' To this I artlessly replied that I was still up at Oxford. The Chairman got over the ensuing hiatus by introducing Duleep, to whom the Prince said, 'Of course, you're still up at Oxford, aren't you?' Duleep replied that he had come down from Cambridge two years before. Dismayed at our ineptitude the Chairman then fetched in some of the Aussies who, untrammelled by academic complications, were unabashed in the royal presence.

Don Bradman and Archie Jackson batted out the rest of the day but next morning, when a shower had livened the wicket, they had a roughish time from Harold Larwood. Thinking how easily they had cruised along the previous day, one marvelled at how little it took to affect the balance between batsman and bowler. Don's consummate skill saved him from injury but Archie Jackson took some nasty knocks, despite his ill-health, unflinchingly. Eventually we got them out, Don going to a decision so dubious that some said the umpire was making amends for a previous mistake. Thereafter we made some progress and eventually we finished the innings at 695. 'Bosser' Martin, the Oval groundsman, was disappointed by this, saying, 'If they could make 728 for six at Lord's they ought to have made a thousand here.'

We had now 45 minutes to bat, and Bob Wyatt was concerned as to whether Jack Hobbs would want to go in that evening. The 'Master' was adamant. This was his last appearance for England and he was determined to open the innings, a desire which Bob granted without further argument, and so it was. On his arrival at the wicket the Australians gathered round and gave three lusty cheers. There was no doubt as to the heartfelt warmth and sincerity of this gesture, but it greatly increased the tension of an already highly emotional scene, and one wondered whether it would not have been better to accord him this salute on his departure.

As it was, not being an excitable or demonstrative man, he batted quietly and soundly for a few overs. Then, in trying to cut Alan Fairfax, he got a bottom edge and nicked the ball on to his wicket. He paused sadly for a moment, then walked quietly back to the pavilion and out of Test Match cricket. He took with him much of England's hope of recovery in the current match, and a quarter of a century of glorious memories. A great sense of anti-climax descended upon the scene, and the large crowd seemed quiet and subdued in the realization that a unique era in English batsmanship had just ended.

Perhaps the gods also mourned this event for next day the rain poured down. By lunchtime there was no prospect of any play and my hostess, Mrs Warner, started to look up the cinemas. Suddenly she had a much better idea. 'Sydney Barnes is playing at Lord's,' she said, 'I'll take you there and introduce you to him.' Barnes was in fact playing against the MCC for Wales, where he had been living for some years. It was a splendid thought, and we set forth without delay.

We found the great man sitting by himself, puffing his pipe, and possibly conjuring up visions of Victor Trumper and days gone by from the damp Lord's turf. He was delighted to see Mrs Warner, and obviously a Warner introduction was my guarantee. Having made the introduction Mrs Warner packed us off to the Long Bar where I spent one of the great hours of my life. Barnes was most expansive and, given a cricket ball, demonstrated the whole technique which was of his own invention, and which has never been wholly or successfully imitated. I was much elated and, having said my thanks, parted on warm terms to return to the Oval. Here I naturally told the rest of the team where I had been and all I had learnt.

There was a most unfortunate sequel. Early next morning Barnes rang Plum in considerable wrath to draw his attention to an article in the *Daily Mail*. Its headline was to the effect that Barnes told me how he would get Bradman out, and the entire article was imaginary and wholly inaccurate, giving the impression that he had been boasting freely. He was understandably infuriated, and suspected that I had given the story to the press. Plum assured him that this was not so, and suggested that it had been the fabrication of an enterprising newspaperman on hearing that we had met. This was indeed the true explanation and, because of his faith in Plum, Barnes eventually acknowledged my innocence.

The next day proved to be the last of the Test Match. Percy Hornibrook, a left-handed dentist from Queensland, bowled us all out on a wicket exactly made for him, and we lost by an innings and 39 runs. Bob had proved a very fine captain but not, at that point, a very lucky one.

# SIX

# Last Fling

By the close of the season of 1930 I was half-way through my twenty-third year. The last two had been periods of almost uninterrupted joy, and it seemed that this happy state of affairs could continue for some time to come. There remained, however, the awkward fact that I was still an undergraduate living on an allowance, and that jobs were hard to find in the slow recovery from the financial disasters of 1929. My academic progress at Oxford had been nil and, having failed to get down to hard study, it seemed that I was not cut out for the more scholarly professions.

The time had come to make a decision, and I was helped in this by the fact that an MCC side was due to set sail for South Africa in the autumn. This seemed a good opportunity to have one grand last fling before settling down to making a career in earnest and, accordingly, I dropped a hint in the appropriate quarter that I would very much like to make the trip again. Plum Warner, on hearing this, said he thought I would be very welcome, but raised the question of my return to Oxford. I replied that I was sure that the authorities would be sympathetic and let me come up again in the summer term. The authorities were understanding, but pointed out that I had been failed in the only examination that I had sat, and had not since tried again. The upshot was that I had to choose between going to South Africa or going up to Oxford.

There seemed little prospect of my doing anything of much consequence during the next two years at the university so, with some misgivings, I chose the South African tour. It was a decision which, despite my love for Oxford, I never really regretted. At least the *Daily Express* did me proud. Under the headline CRICKETER'S SACRIFICE their correspondent inferred that I had made a noble gesture in abandoning a promising academic career in the interests of cricket and country. I fear he cannot have been very well briefed on the details of the academic career.

Again, as in 1927, in the absence of Sutcliffe, Larwood and Jardine we could hardly be considered to be the full strength of England, but were still a very fair side. Besides Percy Chapman, who captained the side, there were five amateurs, Jack White, Bob Wyatt, Maurice Turnbull and myself. The professionals were Andrew Sandham, Pat Hendren, Wally Hammond, Maurice Leyland, Tom Goddard, Maurice Tate, Bill Voce, George Duckworth and Bill Farrimond.

We sailed on the *Edinburgh Castle* and the itinerary was as before, with a stop at Madeira, and then a pleasant fortnight's sail to Cape Town. Again we danced, played deck games, fed like fighting cocks, and enjoyed brief shipboard romances.

Our first match against the Western Province was played on turf, and a very good wicket it turned out to be. J. J. Kotze, the great South African fast bowler, who had worked so hard to produce turf pitches in his native country, was delighted with it. By the time he died the following July he had seen one of his fondest ambitions borne out. It was also an occasion for his erstwhile teammate, 'Old' Dave Nourse, who was playing his last match against a touring side. He was an international character in cricket and, apart from his ability as a player, boasted the biggest hands of any cricketer. My recollection is that, when he got hold of the bat, the handle disappeared entirely leaving a bit of overlap at the top.

The home batsmen were less at home on their own pitch than we were and, with Wally Hammond and Bob Wyatt both making hundreds, we won easily by an innings. 'Old' Dave had the satisfaction of making top score of 36 in his team's second innings, before stepping down in favour of his son 'Young' Dave, who was to have a long and highly successful career in the years ahead.

The tour posed some tricky problems for a touring side, as the South Africans were in the midst of changing from matting to turf pitches and our fixtures were divided almost equally between the two. This meant constant readjustment for our players as there was a considerable difference between the required techniques. It was remarkable how quickly most of the side sorted out these differences, the only really sad man being Tom Goddard whose off-

1. A studio portrait taken in Inverness in 1931.

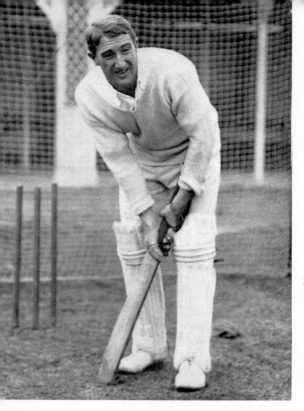

2. Aubrey Faulkner. The stance is slightly 'two-eyed' and the grip very low on the handle.

3. My first Test appearance against Australia, at Manchester, 1930. From my left: Tom Goddard, Wally Hammond, M.S. Nichols, Maurice Tate, Herbert Sutcliffe (with Duleep behind), George Duckworth, Jack Hobbs and Percy Chapman.

spinners did not seem to be suited to either medium. At least he had the consolation of returning some years later and doing well enough on the turf to perform a hat-trick in a Test Match.

From the Cape we moved up to Kimberley where the directors of the diamond mines said they would present a stone to the top scorer. This caused such a commotion amongst the later batsmen, like myself, that they tactfully changed this generous offer to a stone for every member of the team, set exactly as the recipient wanted it. I had mine set in a platinum ring and my wife wore it for some years until it was unfortunately lost or stolen.

Having played Natal and the Transvaal we went on up to Bulowayo to play Rhodesia, which gave us a chance of seeing the Victoria Falls. This meant a further trip to Livingstone where we played a match against Northern Rhodesia. There we spent a pleasant week seeing the full majesty of the Falls from every vantage point and playing a nice friendly game of cricket. For all of this we were indebted to the local chief of police, a keen cricketer who had made a tremendous effort to get MCC to visit his parish. Little reward did he reap for his efforts.

The week before our arrival his chief prisoner, due to come up on a charge of murder, had taken advantage of his preoccupation to skip across the border and disappear. By way of consolation for this set-back and in gratitude for his efforts, I was instructed to get him off the mark when he came into bat, and duly bowled him a half-volley. Unfortunately I bowled it straight and, in his eagerness, he missed it and was bowled first ball. He then missed a couple of catches and, at the end of a miserable day, decided to drown his sorrows at the ball held that evening.

It was evident that he had at least succeeded in this when he started to drive some of us, including Percy and Beet Chapman and Maurice Tate, back to our hotel some miles away. As he swerved giddily from side to side of the road I couldn't help thinking of the narrow unrailed bridges over various streams on the way, streams I imagined to be stiff with crocodiles. He was deaf to all suggestions that someone else might drive and no one could get to the ignition switch, so eventually I asked him if he would stop for a moment whilst I went behind a bush. He did so immediately and out I got and said, 'I don't know about the rest of you, but I am going to walk.' The rest of the company, with the exception of the police chief's girl friend, said they felt the same way so he gracefully surrendered the wheel. To our alarm and astonishment he turned round at the hotel and set out again for Livingstone, accompanied by his lady who must have had blind faith in him, or in the Lord, or in both. Anyway, having just scraped through a spacious hotel gate on the way out he turned up next day in good heart. It would have been much better in every way if I had not bowled that ruddy first ball straight. Incidentally, it turned out to be the middle one of a hat-trick.

The first Test Match was a very good game of cricket on the mat at Johannesburg. Bill Voce and I had nine of the South Africans out for 81 when Quintin McMillan hit me very gently into the hands of Percy Chapman at mid-off. As I reached for my sweater the ball popped out again and the last wicket put on 45 runs. We lost the match by 28 runs but, undiscouraged, said, 'Wait till we get them on turf.' This we did the following week at Cape Town where they made 260 for the first wicket, which stands as a record to this day, and went on to declare at 513 for 8 wickets. We batted unevenly on a still perfect pitch to make 350 and 252 for nine, so had much the worst of the draw. Thereafter Percy Chapman won all three tosses and twice put South Africa in to bat but, despite this enterprise, we never caught up as all three matches were draws.

The start of the last Test Match at Durban was delayed by one of the strangest causes ever to have interfered with a serious cricket match. The larger stumps had recently been introduced, and were due to be used on this occasion. On winning the toss, Percy Chapman, being one down in the series and there being a bit of rain on the wicket, put South Africa in to bat. But, just as we were about to take the field, it was discovered that the only bails on the ground were the smaller wicket and would not fit the new larger one, there being less space between the fatter stumps. There ensued a frantic but fruitless search, after which an emmissary was dispatched to the nearest sports shop. *Wisden* says that the umpires themselves whittled down the bails to the required size, but my recollection is that they were fetched from the shop, by which time the best part of half an hour had been lost. As things turned out no great harm was done as the wicket proved to be a lot less helpful than we had hoped and, after a fairly short spell, we were rained off for the day. Had circumstances been different there might have been a very ticklish situation indeed.

The South Africans were at this time a very good side and quickly adapted to the turf wickets now becoming widespread in their country. Many cricketers might regret the passing of matting wickets in South Africa as losing something unique in the game, apart from the fascination they brought to the play. That the decision to go over to grass was the right one was underlined by the fact that the next South African to visit England, in 1935, won a series abroad for the first time ever in their cricket history. It had been an interesting experience for our side to have taken part in the actual transition, and most had surmounted the difficulties of changing overnight from one type of wicket to the other. Hammond, Hendren and Leyland led our batting and Tate, Voce and myself were the most successful bowlers. But the best bowling on our side was undoubtedly Bill Voce on the mat, cutting the ball from the leg stump to the off.

During one of our stays at the Cape we played a match against the Navy at Simonstown. They were led by a splendid cricketing sailor known as 'Bonham the Bad' whose active career was to extend from Zebrugge to the Arctic Convoy and who later, as Admiral Sir Stuart Bonham-Carter, was to be President of Hampshire. It was an enjoyable, not to say hilarious day, starting with a fine, bibulous luncheon aboard *HMS Calcutta*. In those days the Navy's preprandial drink was pink gin, and they shot a few good broadsides of this into us before lunch. Some days before in the House of Commons Lady Astor had said if the MCC drank less they would win more matches, but we found a champion in Lord Hawke. He said that her ladyship was wholly mistaken and that most of the team in South Africa were extremely temperate and some indeed total abstainers. Neither was completely accurate but while right was on his lordship's side it was unfortunate that his timely reply was published on the morning of this particular fixture. It was read out by the ship's chaplain amidst scenes of great enthusiasm.

The match, as might be expected, was not a very serious affair. Pat Hendren and Jack White played for the Navy, arrayed in

*HMS Calcutta* caps, and Percy Chapman and I opened the innings. He made nought and I was run out by Pat Hendren calling me for a run when I wasn't looking. Maurice Allom batted twice, once as himself and once, with beard, as 'W.G.' He was perhaps a little out of character in the second role for, being given out LBW first ball, he walked without demur. A good sailorman being c Chapman b Peebles was kind enough to say that it was his finest cricketing moment.

There was a cheerful young sub-lieutenant named McMullen who was very friendly with all the team. Our paths did not cross again for many years but, returning recently from Teneriffe, my wife and I had the honour to sit at the captain's table. The warmest greeting of all came from Admiral McMullen, almost indistinguishable from Sub-Lieutenant McMullen. He was a great hit at the ship's concert as a nautical man in a yachting cap called 'a Chap named Morrice'. Our Navy may be smaller than it was but the material still seems to be the best in the world.

It was not long after my return from South Africa that I was approached by the *Evening Standard* in the person of their representative Jim Swanton. We had seen each other before at the Faulkners School but not actually met. He explained that his paper was going to recruit some of the younger generation to write a series of articles about their particular game or sport throughout the coming summer. Henry Cotton would write about golf and Fred Perry about tennis, and they wanted me to write about cricket. The terms were 15 guineas an article, and the series would run to about a dozen of these. This sounded to me like a fortune, and I accepted with alacrity. Under Jim's tuition I put pen to paper, and the *Standard* seemed content with the results.

After a few weeks a complication arose when I found myself the proud possessor of a bunch of cheques, but with no bank account in which to lodge them. Accordingly one morning I walked round the corner from Lower Grosvenor Place, where I was living, and went into the first bank I came to, which happened to be Barclay's, Belgravia. On hearing that I wanted to open an account the clerk summoned the manager, a splendidly portly Pickwickian figure named Dickinson, with a florid complexion and G. K. Chesterton *pince-nez* askew on his nose. He enquired my name and on

hearing it he looked at me thoughtfully. 'Do you play for Middlesex?' he asked. I said I did. 'Well,' he said, 'Tich Freeman's a
bloody sight better bowler than you'll ever be – hand over.'

We never looked back from this happy introduction. All through
the '30s 'Dickie' looked after my fluctuating fortunes, and many
a happy half hour we had in the 'Feathers' where he met his friends
and clients and conducted much of his business. This he did with
a genial efficiency until the war years and, when our business restarted in 1946, I was able to take our firm's account to his branch
where it remains to this day with my own. It is difficult to realize
it is 45 years since our historic first meeting, and that we are now
bidding adieu to a good friend who is about his seventh successor
as manager.

Having made this major financial advance I then addressed myself
to the approaching season. The New Zealanders were due to play
their first Test series in this country, which was to consist of three
matches of three days apiece at Lord's, the Oval and Old Trafford.
They were not expected to extend England's full strength but were
an enterprising and attractive side under the able captaincy of Tom
Lowry, Percy Chapman's brother-in-law. The England captaincy
was in abeyance and, with a tour of Australia coming up in eighteen
months' time, the appointment was going to be one of considerable
consequence. Douglas Jardine was known to be available and, in
accordance with general expectation, was duly appointed to captain
England for the New Zealand series, a selection made with an
obvious eye to the future. The choice was a popular one with the
public but amongst those in closer touch with cricket affairs there
were some misgivings.

Jardine, even to his closest acquaintances, was an enigmatical
character, and plainly the very opposite of his predecessor Percy
Chapman, who had made such a success of the previous tour. He
had been a member of that team, and was known to have an almost
irrational dislike of all things Australian. Where 'Chappie' was
cheerful and genial Jardine was reserved and sardonic of manner,
lacking entirely in the common touch. What was never in doubt was
his iron determination and unshakeable courage, moral and physical.
Whilst he was not a bully he despised weakness and, in one's deal-
ings with him, one had to stand firm at all points within reason,

an attitude which he appreciated and which made for good relations.

He embarked on his command with the first Test at Lord's at the end of June, leading a side which ranged in years from Frank Woolley down to an experimental and youthful opening pair, Arnold and Bakewell. Les Ames made his first home appearance for England behind the wicket, and Gubby Allen and Bill Voce opened the bowling, to be supported by Walter Robins and myself.

We lost the toss and had not been long in the field before the first signs of friction arose. Instead of putting Frank Woolley at slip — his accustomed position — Jardine sent him down to fine leg. Habitués of Lord's will know that each stand or section of it is distinguished by a letter, starting with A on the left of the pavilion and going clockwise round the ground. The letters are large and displayed on the railings at convenient intervals. Douglas, wishing to station Frank accurately, called out 'B. Woolley,' but it was clear that Frank was unaware of the lettering so the message had no meaning for him, who, using his own judgment, stationed himself by chance under the letter C. As the bowler, Wally Hammond, was running up Douglas stopped the game and called out in stentorian voice from mid-off, 'I said "B", Woolley – not "C".' Frank's confusion was not lessened by Wally Hammond pointing in both directions at once, all of which led to a certain hilarity amongst us young. But Frank was very much affronted, and felt that he had been humiliated in front of the large crowd.

Relations between the two worsened when, having disposed of the New Zealanders for 224, Douglas went to the Professionals' room to discuss the batting order. 'Woolley,' he said, 'you will bat number five and I shall bat number six but, if there is a crisis, I shall bat number five and you will go number six.' As we lost three wickets for 31, and four for 62, there was a crisis, and Douglas preceded a now thoroughly disgruntled Frank.

By twenty past six we had lost our sixth wicket for 188 and I went in as night watchman to be promptly stumped off Bill Merritt for nought, at which we retired for the day. As things turned out my nought stayed up on the board for Saturday, Sunday and most of Monday as Gubby and Les Ames both made hundreds. This afforded the two Walters, Hammond and Robins, the most exquisite boyish pleasure. All through Monday they kept enquiring of each other what the last chap had made – who was he? – Hobbs, Sutcliffe, Tyldesley? – No, Peebles. My batting ambitions had long been a cosy family jest so everyone was happy, or mostly everyone. On arriving on Tuesday Douglas drew me aside and said it might all be very funny but it was what one would describe as rather 'fourth form'. So accustomed was I to these innocent irreverences that it was only on enquiring I realized he was talking about my nought, and the simple pleasure it had afforded my friends and associates.

When Walter Robins arrived Douglas spoke to him on the matter but unfortunately did so with his back to the glass doors leading to the balcony. The effect of his rebuke was rather lessened by an admiring group standing behind him waving encouragement to the accused interspersed with some less courteous gestures!

The New Zealanders batted pretty well in their second innings to declare at 469 for 8 so, if we never looked like losing the match, we soon lost all prospect of a win. Douglas could derive some satisfaction from the fact that his first Test as captain had thrown up a few unexpected problems and provided him with some useful experience. A month later at the Oval we overwhelmed the opposition by an innings in a match that produced no difficulties of captaincy or personalities. But the third and last Test at Old Trafford produced a strange and unprecedented situation.

On 15 August when the match was due to start the rain fell heavily in Manchester and continued to do so for two and a half days. On 17 August the skies suddenly cleared and the sun shone down, but by this time everyone had given up any hope of play. However, the ground being in surprisingly good condition, the gates were opened and quite a number of people came in. There then arose the problem of reassembling the opposing terms. The English team were pretty well all present having, as they thought, a farewell lunch before departing for home. But the New Zealanders had sought to relieve the tedium in various different quarters. When, not without some difficulty, all were corralled it was apparent that a few, on the general assumption that no play would be possible, had spent a convivial morning and were in no shape to bat in a **Test Match**.

The official record says that New Zealand won the toss, but whatever the outcome, there being nothing in the match, the captains agreed that England would bat for the few remaining hours. This was safely accomplished but not without an anxious moment when, half way through the English innings, some generous, if misguided, sportsmen started to call for a declaration. The immediate result of this was an urgent message from Tom Lowry asking Douglas *not* to declare.

Presently a large and hostile group arrived under the dressing-room window calling upon Douglas personally in loud and aggressive terms. At this Douglas threw the window open and, leaning out, fixed the chief protesters with a basilisk eye. It was as though the headmaster had suddenly appeared in all his awful majesty. The more raucous voices faltered and, as presently the group started to break up and slink away, Douglas closed the windows without speaking, and the game proceeded in peace. It had been a very minor and gently amusing incident, but it foreshadowed an uncompromising attitude towards protestors in very much uglier situations to come.

The Middlesex season was, as always, very pleasant but we still bumped about in the lower half of the table. The truth was that our mainstays were getting to the age where lessening elasticity called for increased effort, but produced less result. Neither Nigel Haig nor Jack Durston now bowled to much effect with the new ball and, as Gubby Allen only played seven matches, we lacked a spearhead. Walter Robins played but two, and this was a great loss.

When the season was over I was faced with the fact that a major slump still prevailed and that, having had my last fling, I would still have to earn a living. A friend ran a printing agency and I joined him for a spell, but the business was itself in a precarious state and the trade extremely competitive. The first winter months were extremely bleak, and no prospect was apparent when my fortunes suddenly took a turn for the better.

Staying with Percy and Beet Chapman for Christmas, my fellow guest was Tim Molony, a director of Ladbrokes, the famous firm of bookies. During our stay he suggested that I should join them but, whilst delighted at such an opportunity, I said I was not a racing man and wholly ignorant of horses and betting. However, he assured me I would soon learn, and duly introduced me to Arthur Bendir, the founder and almost sole proprietor of the business. The meeting was a success and I was recruited there and then. My connection with the firm lasted most happily until it was finally sold in the 1960s, by which time I had been a director for some years.

Ladbrokes considered themselves rather 'Bank of England' amongst bookies, and the office in Old Burlington Street was a most cheerful place. The other directors and staff were most welcoming, doing all they could to initiate me into the mysteries of the turf, and I was extremely happy keeping them informed on cricket in which most were keenly if not, at that date, professionally interested. We always seemed to have a number of interesting visitors looking in either on business or for a lunchtime drink, over which Arthur Bendir would preside. There were Rothschilds, and golfers, and cricketers, usually led by Lionel Tennyson or Percy Chapman, and a good cross-section of London's sporting world. Amongst them was a most distinguished elderly gentleman named Wilfred Edgerton, who wore rather Edwardian clothes and very high collars, and who used to sit in the office for long periods. Once when asked why he replied that no cloistered calm could afford him such peace of mind as the gentle melancholy of a bookmaker's office where, he said, it seemed no one had seen a profitable day for the past fifty years, but all were able to smile and soldier on.

In days long before Women's Lib was heard of we boasted the only lady bookie, Mrs Helen Verney, who was always on the rails at any meeting of consequence. She was a chic, comely woman of mature years who did a great business amongst the gallant gentlemen of the turf. Her other particular interest in life was ballroom dancing, and it was said that her clerks were selected as much for their poise and skill on the floor as for their command of figures.

In the autumn Jim Swanton and I set up house together in the Temple. Ever since our meeting in the spring we had got along splendidly. We had common cause in our love of cricket and, importantly, we seemed to laugh at the same jokes. We now, as a couple of needy young bachelors, wanted somewhere to live.

Jim, whose close friends address him as 'James' or 'Swanton', was at the beginning of what was to become a very successful career, and already had the application and ambition which went to make it. He was always a personality of much presence with his great size and his resonant bass voice and, throughout his life, has occasionally overawed the uninitiated. But the same close friends used to bait him unceasingly and affectionately, to find that he was extremely adroit in the counter-attack, giving at least as good as he got. This may cast a leavening light on occasional accusations of pomposity, although it might be said that he does not deliberately seek the company of fools in order to suffer them gladly.

His cricket writings and commentaries have the virtues of profound knowledge, readably and lucidly expressed with force and decision. I do not necessarily agree with all his views but admire the sincerity of his judgments and the courage with which they are presented, even when unpopular. These attributes, in their very nature, have created critics and sometimes enmities, but they have also made a host of friends and an enormous and loyal following which has carried him to the top of his profession.

Our friendship, punctuated by occasional rows when we were young and spirited, has lasted uninterruptedly over the years. He was prevented from being my best man as the calls of duty precluded the long journey to the Highlands, but I was able to perform the same office for him some years later. He was, by that time, godfather to my son.

The Temple days were a time of much incident and entertainment. Our landlord was a worthy Irish barrister whose practice, I suspect, had dried up for lack of customers, a calamity which necessitated his return to his homeland. The flat was ideal for a couple of bachelors, and we were further lucky in having the services of a paragon amongst dailies. Mrs Smallbone cleaned, cooked and performed all manner of domestic services without complaint. She was a lady of great character and, when an officious porter made trouble about Jim parking his car, Mrs Smallbone routed him whilst we lay pusillanimously concealed behind the door. Her methods were oblique but firm and moralists might have detected a hint of blackmail, but she won and the porter departed with his tail between his legs, never to reappear.

The car in question had claims to being a historic vehicle and

"JIM' ALIAS ERNEST.

was the centre of one of the many tales about its owner which so delighted his friends and admirers. Jim had bought it from an acquaintance who had been compelled to leave the country, the purchase price being a fiver, cash down, and the car a bull-nosed Morris Cowley of long service and uncertain age. It resembled its new owner in that it was clearly a machine of considerable personality with certain characteristics all its own. One was a wheel wobble which developed at low speeds and imparted a shimmying motion to the whole contraption. As the fastenings had long since perished the sides of the bonnet would start a violent flapping, so completing a general effect of a huge agitated bird striving to take off.

When, one wet day, a young policeman sought to halt the London traffic the Morris, in the van, responded with a beautiful slalom which landed it right under his nose. Unabashed, Jim berated the officer for having all but caused a serious accident, and unnerved him with dark speculations as to the effect on his future career should he find it necessary to refer the matter to the Commissioner. However, he conceded that, if a passage was cleared for him, he might overlook this particular offence, at which sundry Rolls-Royces and Daimlers were halted and diverted to that end. With a conciliatory wave of the hand Jim started on his way. There was a gentle wobble, followed by a violent shimmy as the wings burst free from their moorings and frantically beat the air, so terminating the triumphal exit in a sadly undignified emergency stop. A great shout of laughter went up from those who had gathered to enjoy the encounter but none, said Jim reflecting on the incident, laughed as heartily as the policeman.

# SEVEN

# Cricketer's Midsummer

In the spring of 1932 there came an invitation from Hubert Martineau to make another trip abroad, this time to Egypt.

The tour turned out to be a splendid series of cricket matches, combined with delightful travel and unending social engagements. We travelled overland to Genoa where we boarded the *Ausonia*, the flag-ship of the Sitmar line, and had three or four days on the blue and gentle Mediterranean.

Our first week was spent at Alexandria and, from the cricket point of view, was the best fun. The ground was small and the surface was of baked mud, which may not sound attractive but made for lively and exciting play. The pitch was matting and lightning fast, which as at Johannesburg in the old days gave the bowler opportunity for attack and the adequate batsman fine scope for stroke play. If the ball beat the fielder it kept on rolling, without loss of pace, all the way to the boundary. The combination of these factors would lead to high scores rapidly compiled, while wickets fell with corresponding frequency. Thus over four hundred runs in a day would be a good combined tally for one innings completed, and another well under way.

On moving south to Cairo the visitor found a rather different scene. The pitch was part of the Gezireh Sporting Club, a very famous institution, and was matting on grass – an easy-paced wicket, much less to the taste of bowlers like myself. This objection was to some extent compensated for by the splendid surrounding amenities and, if roughly handled by the opposing batsmen, one could seek solace in the swimming-pool with the bathing belles, of whom Cairo boasted an abundance.

We played against the Alexandria Club, the Gezireh, the Army and Egypt. At that time there were numerous British soldiers in Egypt, and the cricket was good and keen. We had an adequate side, with Geoffrey Lowndes, Ronny Stanyforth, Eddy Dawson and Alan Hilder to lead the batting.

Off the field our social progress was spectacular. The rumour ran that alone of the team I had got a night's sleep, the explanation being that I had fallen asleep on a tram and gone to the depot. Though not strictly true this was indicative of the unceasing series of balls, parties and functions which made for great enjoyment if not for the strictest training. We were mostly billeted in military messes and, when no official meeting was scheduled, our hosts were determined to show us the town in style. Geoffrey Lowndes was billeted with a Guards Battalion and, by way of repaying hospitality, took the CO's beautiful daughter out to dine. Arriving back at the barracks' gate in the early hours he clasped the lady to him, and bestowed upon her a warm goodnight kiss. This idyllic scene was interrupted by a stamp of ammunition boots and a crash of arms and, over the lady's shoulder, Geoffrey saw that the Guard – possibly expecting her father – had turned out smartly, and was now standing at the car window. It would have been interesting to hear what comments were made once the soldiery were ensconced again in the safety of the Guard Room.

Nemesis fell upon us when we got back to Alexandria. We batted first and made 336 and, having got half All Egypt out, as ever danced the night away. Next morning the effects of so much cricket and revelry were plain to see and we bowlers, having disposed of the other half of All Egypt for a total of 140, gratefully threw ourselves into deck-chairs and looked forward to a lazy day. But, much to our alarm, one faction took the view that we must put them in again and, despite our strenuous protests that this would lead to disaster, our captain yielded to them. Things went as forecast by the pessimists. We got three quick wickets then blew up, and a very good player named O'Brien made 177. To this day I remember standing in the slips making bitter complaint to my neighbour, Geoffrey Lowndes, at which moment the ball went through my hands to hit me on the chest and fall to the ground. He was just making sympathetic reply as the next ball eluded his grasp and, taking him in the navel, was also lost to our cause. The upshot was that, set about 250 to win, our batting failed miserably and we lost by 130 runs. There may be several morals to this tale, stern or commonsensical, but one certainly is: Beware of follow-ons when the pitch is unchanging and there is bags of time in hand.

On the ship bound for home I embarked on the first real affair of my life. It was not long before I felt myself to be much in love and, as she was the daughter of a peer and very social, my life in London became something akin to the one I had just left in Egypt. This again did not make for good training, and my right shoulder was now starting to complain more ominously. Whether I was 'sick of love' or whether I had bowled too many googlies, or both, my start to the season was much less impressive than the previous two. The results in figures were fairly good, but I knew that a lot of the life had gone out of my action, with a consequent loss of spin and bite.

In the first match which I played for Middlesex there occurred an unusual train of events which at one moment I believed had brought me lasting fame. Tommy Jameson, who had only come to Lord's to support Hampshire and see old friends, was pressed into playing despite the fact that he had no practice whatsoever. He came in with Hampshire six wickets down, and the first ball I bowled just touched his leg stump and knocked the bail out of the groove, although it did not actually fall to the ground. This was out under the existing law but, as Umpire Dolphin galloped to the scene in answer to the wicket-keeper's appeal, a puff of wind blew it back again, at which Tommy laughed and said, 'That's good enough for me – you get on with it.' My next ball hit his middle stump, and this time the bails flew in all directions. Years afterwards when I had almost forgotten the incident Tommy said to me that we jointly held a world's record for, he said, he was LBW to me first ball in the second innings. To have received three good balls and true from the same bowler in one match and been out to all three must be rare if not unique. The pedant may argue that the second was not eventually out, but most concede that the batsman, like Lazarus or a man given the kiss of life, had arisen from the (nearly) departed to play again. In any case, a reference to *Wisden* rendered the whole question academic, for it revealed that he had indeed been out first ball again, but to Jack Durston in the second instance.

A friend of mine hearing this went some way to matching my

story. He had played in a club match in which their opening batsman had been bowled first ball of the innings. After a few overs it
was discovered that the pitch was a few yards too long so a fresh
start was made, with exactly the same result as far as the unfortunate batsman was concerned. He then took a first ball in the
second innings, all of which adds up to a pretty tidy day's work.

In June I played for the South against the North at Old Trafford, but failed to strike any sort of form. I was mildly surprised
to find Douglas Jardine an understanding and sympathetic captain
in my difficult time. He took much trouble to get me on at advan-
tageous moments and got me off again when things were unpromising. But this consideration had its disadvantage as well, for in short
bursts I failed to settle down and was inclined to lose confidence.
By way of encouragement he got me on at the tail so that I picked
up a few mediocre wickets but, although grateful, I knew they
meant very little.

The match was played on a perfect Old Trafford wicket, and a
lot of people made runs. Frank Woolley went in first, drove Larwood and Voce all over the ground then hit Tommy Mitchell's
first ball, a full toss, down long-on's throat. Wally Hammond
and Duleep made hundreds for us, and Herbert Sutcliffe 96 and
110 not out for the opposition. Two strokes still live in the imagination as though they had been played yesterday. Larwood bowled
a good-length ball to Wally who, up on the toss off his back foot,
hit it like a cannon shot past cover's left hand. Lol moved his
cover two yards squarer and, to the next delivery of similar length
and line, Wally played the same majestic stroke and the ball flashed
over the spot he had just vacated. I used to think that, if cricket
was played only on the offside, Wally would have been the greatest
of the lot.

This match was a turning point in my cricket career. On the
evidence of my indifferent showing I was omitted from the team
to play against All-India, who were playing their first Test Match
ever in England that season. England were well placed for leg-
spinners at that time, with Walter Robins and Tommy Mitchell of
Derby both well established, and Freddy Brown now arrived as
a high-class wrist spinner of lively pace. Plum Warner was, as ever,

4. Jodrell Hall, during the 4th Test. The Don tries his hand at tennis – but shows no ambition to get to Wimbledon.

5. In another part of the grounds Ranji and Duleep watch whilst Arthur Mailey advises me on the leg break. Accused by Australian manager Kelly of betraying State secrets, Arthur replied: 'Bowling is an art, and as such international.'

6. Send-off party, 1938. Percy Chapman and I say 'goodbye' to Wally Hammond, bound for South Africa. We three had been members of the 1930/31 MCC team to S.A.

7. The Master: Jack Hobbs in full cry during a Middlesex/Surrey encounter in 1931. From the left: myself, Jack Hobbs, Greville Stevens, Pat Hendren and Fred Price.

kind and considerate, telling me not to despair as I was still in the running and would soon return; but I had a feeling that this was a much more serious situation. At the end of the previous season I had had acute trouble with my shoulder and, despite much attention to it, no one had been able to diagnose the cause nor alleviate the pain. Nine months later it had recurred, and at that stage of medical advance there did not seem to be any cure. Although I had many years of happy cricket of all sorts before me I never did regain my true form.

There were those who attributed my decline to the good life and the bright lights, but this was not so. I did enjoy life tremendously but I always trained hard and kept in first-class physical shape. The Press had always been good to me in the good times and never tried to make any capital of my troubles although, as I shall later describe, they did quite rightly rise in wrath when I was preferred to Bill Voce in 1934.

It was during the 1932 season that I met a very unusual cricketer. Dining one night with Max Aitken we returned to Stornoway House to be told that his father had gone to his office on some urgent mission and had left instructions that Max was 'to entertain Winston', who had been dining with him. Presently I was also summoned to the presence, and found the guest still seated at the dining-table, armed with a glass of brandy and a cigar. He still had a certain amount of vivid red hair, and was naturally much slimmer than the famous wartime figure. He arose courteously and shook my hand, saying, 'You play cricket, young man?' to which I replied, 'Yes, sir.' After a few random remarks he launched forth on his own cricket career which ended with a broken finger when he was ten. He could not remember the rules or the names of the implements very clearly, but the delivery was tremendous, enhanced by the squishy sibilants which the Boers had remarked on thirty years before when describing him as an escaped prisoner. Prompted occasionally by myself he warmed to his tale. 'The ball came pascht,' he said, 'and hit the little things behind – what – schtumps? yesh.' In all we had a glorious twenty minutes, but I do not recall that we progressed to matters of high strategy.

The remainder of the season with Middlesex was spasmodic,

but I had good days enough to come out second to Walter Robins in the bowling averages. He was only able to play five matches and Gubby but four, whilst it was plain that Nigel Haig's span as captain was nearing its end. Other amateurs like George Newman, Greville Stevens and Tom Killick found that the calls of business and profession were always growing more insistent. It seemed that our splendid and happy brotherhood was starting to disintegrate, and it was with feelings of sadness that I departed north for a holiday at home.

When there I met another great man. For many years I had been a great lover of Paul Robeson's bass singing, which still seems to me to be one of the most beautiful of all sounds known to man's ear. Having collected his records over the years I saw with some excitement that he was giving a series of concerts in Glasgow, and I made sure of attending one of the first. There was an introduction to each performance in the form of a one-act play, the star of which was an old cricketing friend, Mike Shepley, and at the end of the show I looked him up. After some talk he said, 'You must meet Paul,' which I was delighted to do. The introduction was made the easier, for Robeson's secretary and manager was 'Andy', an abbreviation of Andrews, who had opened the innings for his school in the West Indies with Leslie Hutcheson ('Hutch' of cabaret fame). He was a very keen cricketer and most welcoming when Mike introduced us, saying that I was something of a player too.

Robeson was the most charming of men, with a magnificent and gracious presence. Hearing us talk of cricket he told me that he used to sit at Lord's, but usually reading a book, until one day he saw Percy Chapman flaying the bowlers and, thereafter, took a lively interest in the game. Being something of a baseball player – as well as all-American footballer – he was induced to turn out for the Thespids, the actors' side, and was said to be a first-class cover point. We met again on several occasions and I was greatly flattered that, on arriving at Aberdeen in later years, he quoted me as saying that they would love to hear him sing in the Highlands. This was a true if not very startling prophecy and, when he sang the 'Eriskay Love Lilt', that tremendous Highland man and holder of a record number of Scottish Rugger caps, Johnnie Bannerman, told me that Robeson might have been a Highlander himself so beautiful was his interpretation.

Middlesex affairs went through a rough patch in the years from 1930 to 1932. The many good players who came and went were seldom available in any number at any given time so, apart from the solid but veteran nucleus of Hearne and Hendren, the sides had an *ad hoc* air. It was decided that for the season of 1933 there would be a joint captaincy, shared between Nigel Haig and Tom Enthoven.

A divided rule is seldom satisfactory in the best of circumstances, which was not exactly the condition of Middlesex cricket at that moment. Neither were the partners ideally suited to the task before them: Nigel, a very good captain in his heyday, was at the end of his career while Tom, a fine cricketer and popular man, was a surprisingly inept captain. Up at Cambridge Tom's chief liability as a captain had been a wild lack of judgment in running between the wickets which, it was said, resulted in him running his entire side out once, and getting half way down the list a second time. His failure to complete the remaining half was attributed to the fact that, every time he awarded a Blue, the recipient was emboldened to refuse his wilder invitations.

Tom was well aware of this frailty and, in later years, loved to tell of his appearance in a Fathers *v* Prep School match during which he shared a lengthy partnership with a stranger. In this partner he at once found a perfect understanding; his calls were immediately answered, and never a moment of hesitation arose. It was towards the end of their association that they met in mid-wicket at the end of an over. 'By the way,' said his new-found friend, 'don't bother to call – I'm stone deaf.'

A tendency to absent-mindedness also led to some oversights. When Wally Hammond thrashed us all over Lord's throughout a May day we were at our wits' end as we came off the field at tea-time. Knowing it to be long overdue Walter Robins said to Tom, 'I suppose you're keeping the new ball till after tea?' His harrassed captain halted in his tracks. 'Oh, dammit,' he sighed, 'I'd forgotten all about it.'

The happiest part of the season for me came in the latter half

when Julien Cahn took a team to Canada. He supplemented his own
side by the inclusion of Jim Swanton and myself, so that, with
Walter Robins already a member and Roger Blunt, an old New
Zealand opponent, Denis Morkel, whom I had played against in
South Africa, and George Heane of Notts all making the trip it was
a splendid company. The supporting cast were all of county standard. By way of a send-off we had a lunch at Claridges where the
guest of honour was J. H. Thomas, then Secretary for the
Dominions. Possibly under the impression that he would not be
quoted he made a somewhat indiscreet speech, saying, 'You can
do what you like, but for God's sake don't take Larwood to
Canada.' The scars of the bodyline row still being raw, this caused
a certain amount of adverse comment but the Minister, with his
reputation as a wit to be upheld, may have felt the laugh it raised
at the moment outweighed this. An echo of the incident arose
again later when Larwood, writing in a Sunday newspaper, quoted
this sally and Jimmy Thomas blandly denied having said it.

We sailed in August in splendid style, setting out from Southamp-
ton on the *Empress of Britain*, the pride of the Canadian Pacific
line. As a fellow traveller, in the best sense of the term, we had
David Niven whom I had last known as an officer in a Highland
regiment. This particular episode in his career had just come to
an end largely, it was said, owing to his electrically disturbing effect
on the regimental ladies, and he was now seeking a new life and
fortune in Canada. He was very good company and, to judge from
his success with the girls aboard the *Empress*, we were inclined
to accord full credence to his reputation for gallantry whilst a
soldier. In passing, Middlesex could perhaps lay a tenuous claim
to having aided his subsequently successful career, as it was his
friend Nigel Bruce, a great Middlesex man, who helped launch
him as a film star.

We landed at Quebec and had a day seeing the city which was
fascinating and in parts beautiful, but one had an impression,
possibly imaginary, that as visitors from the UK we were not particularly welcome. Montreal, on the other hand, gave us a warm
reception, and we played a couple of matches there on a matting
pitch against opposition of mostly English and West Indian im-
migrants. One of the latter was rumoured to have been bailed out

of gaol for the occasion. It was said that his wife kept a brothel but
he, being a gallant man, always pleaded guilty and served the resulting gaol sentences. This rumour was embellished by the unlikely
addition that, having had an indifferent match, he was stuffed back
in again on our departure.

At Ottawa we played within the grounds of Government House,
and the match was memorable for me in that I made an enormous
on-drive. One of the change bowlers practised a slight off-break
at a gentle medium pace, the main effect of which was to tee the
ball up perfectly for the real old-fashioned clumping pull-drive.
Jim Swanton and I were batting together at this juncture, and
there was fierce competition to get opposite this philanthropist
and stay there. Jim was so crafty in keeping the strike that it was
only after some time that I got there by calling for two, and reso-
lutely refusing to stir when I had arrived at the desired end.

I let fly at the first ball and it sailed out of the ground – which
was all right. But the second one was the hit of a lifetime. I middled
the ball with all I had got, and felt that beautiful whip of the
handle which means that everything has gone just right. The
ball soared away out of the ground over a small wood and struck
a church behind it. The opposition were delighted and the bowler,
a good-natured man, seemed as pleased as any. Now, I thought, I
really will show them. The next ball was a slow full toss, and I went
to hit it over the church. I connected with the splice of the bat, and
was caught and bowled off the tamest of returns. Afterwards I was
told that the only other batsman to get a hit on the church was
W.G.; but, as so often, this warming statement was not supported
by the records, from which it was fairly certain that W.G. had
never played there.

Toronto was the premier club of Eastern Canada and the
amenities were first-class. We played on a good turf pitch and,
although we won our matches fairly easily, the standard of the
cricket was good, the chief problem to the home batsmen being
that they had no experience of the googly, and were severely handicapped in playing Walter and myself. Thereafter our travels took
us by pleasant but easy cricketing stages to the Niagara Falls, which
were magnificent, but hardly as awe-inspiring nor as majestically
placed as the Victoria Falls. There was, however, no reason to dis-

agree with the verdict of George Ulyett, the Yorkshire cricketer, who when asked his opinion of the scene long ago replied, 'I see nowt to stop it.'

Our first call in the United States was Chicago, which we approached with some trepidation as it was then the scene of a series of gangster films, and the actual home of Al Capone and his notorious brethren. We were surprised to find a fine city, to all appearances peaceful and well-ordered. We also found that the citizens were inclined to be sensitive on the subject of gangsterism, feeling that their city had been exploited whereas many worse towns went unnoticed. So far as we were concerned we saw no trouble, and spent our first day peacefully and pleasantly at the World Fair which was then in progress.

The closest resemblance to a film gangster we encountered in Chicago was one of the main supporters of the cricket club, a very tough citizen indeed, of rugged physique and character who spoke out of the side of his mouth about 'dem and dose' and 'toity-toird' in the best gangster film manner. To our surprise he turned out to be an Englishman who, down on his luck after the first war, had tried his fortune in Illinois, apparently with success. He had married a charming American wife who, after being introduced to the mysteries of cricket, helped him look after us, which they both did wholeheartedly.

At one point he approached the reigning Mayor, 'Big Bill' Thompson, with a view to getting a site for a cricket ground. His Worship, whom my friend unequivocally described as 'a big slob' (his opinion was endorsed by the *New York Times,* which described the appointment as a 'national disgrace'), was very welcoming. He assured his visitor that he was indeed fond of Limeys, and there had been nothing 'poisonal' in his statement that if the King of England came to Chicago he would 'boff him in the snoot'. However, he said that in his city were great Irish and German communities, and that to grant the English a cricket ground would be ruinous to his hard-won, and doubtless very expensive political career. So he said good luck, but no dice.

Our first match was therefore played in a public park, on a rough surface, with baseball games going on all around. Characteristically Walter Robins was soon in the midst of one of these where he was made very welcome, and astonished the players with his bare-handed fielding. Of the game in which he was officially engaged his baseball chums could make little or nothing.

We played a second match at Winetka, about twenty miles outside Chicago, and then set forth for New York. This was a notable journey for me, a confirmed railway lover, as we travelled on 'The Twentieth Century Limited', one of the world's famous trains, which did the near thousand miles to New York in about twenty hours. In the '30s it was, of course, steam-hauled by one of those enormous American 4-8-2s, complete with bell and enchanting chime whistle which moaned sweetly and musically from time to time as we swept along. The sleepers were commodious almost to the extent of a liner's cabin with a most comfortable bed in which, having had a wonderful farewell party in Chicago, I slept the sleep of the just and, heavily hung-over, good.

New York like many cities is a matter of taste. For me it was splendid and stimulating and the natives, contrary to general reputation, extremely helpful and friendly. All seemed to be imbued with a great civic pride, and one had the feeling that they were especially glad to demonstrate its beauties to a 'Limey' for which, until I had proclaimed that I was a good Scot, I was always mistaken. Prohibition was soon to be on its way out, and we found it much easier to get a drink in the States than it had been in Canada.

We stayed at the Waldorf Astoria Hotel on the nineteenth floor. The floor is impressed on my mind because Phyllis Cahn's father, mother and aunt were all travelling with us, and occupied a suite thereon. The two old ladies, a sweet couple much loved by the entire party, used to do their daily dozen together every morning in their undies at their bedroom window. Unbeknown to them they were clearly visible from the landing and, such a popular spectacle did they become, that all lifts paused at the nineteenth so that the passengers might enjoy this innocent diversion before plunging into the hurly-burly of the day.

We played on Long Island and Staten Island and, if the cricket was undistinguished, the ferry trip to and from Staten Island was exhilarating, and the hospitality unstinting. The teams were again mostly immigrant English, Australian and West Indian but one of the hosts, the president of one club or league, was a German. He

was a portly, middle-aged man with an imperial beard which gave
him a very Teutonic aspect, and it was most curious to find him
in this situation. We had a coach to take us to and from the ferry
on which I happened to sit next to him and I found him a most
engaging companion. He talked freely and frankly and said that in
the First World War he had been bitterly opposed to everything
British but had gradually come to know a number of his old
enemies who had also settled in New York. He had been introduced
to cricket and, too old to participate actively, had become a patron
and supporter. He was a good and patriotic man, and I have often
wondered how he reconciled his loyalties and emotions when the
Second World War threatened to burst forth. One would hope that
a taste for cricket would ever be incompatible with sympathy for
Herr Hitler.

A further rare cricket experience befell me on Staten Island.
Fourth ball of the last over before lunch I took a wicket to make
my analysis three for nought. By lunchtime this was three for
twelve, the incoming batsman have struck the two remaining balls
out of the ground. Surely, in terms of time and situation, a right
royal defiance?

On a beautiful September day we boarded the *Queen of Bermuda*
and set sail for the islands of that name. The voyage itself was
rather less romantically known as the 'Booze Cruise', for in days of
prohibition, this was an ideal way in which the aridity-stricken
American citizens could combine a modicum of ozone with a few
days' unlimited consumption of legal and palatable liquor. Some,
it was said, paid very little attention to the ozone.

Bermuda in the '30s was as agreeable a collection of islands as
could be found in the civilized world. Its charm was enhanced by
the prohibition of all mechanical transport beyond the fire engine
and the ambulance. The gently tranquillizing influence of horse and
bicycle were happily apparent, distances were short, and time was
unimportant, so that the difference of twenty minutes instead of
five to the cricket ground was soon unnoticed.

Apart from the beauties of the scene the first things which struck
us on arrival there were the tremendous enthusiasm for cricket
amongst the inhabitants, and the general confidence that their team
would beat us. The superior smile with which we greeted the latter

attitude faded slightly when we ran into real opposition. This we did when, having won three comfortable victories against lesser forces, we took the field against Somerset, the strongest side in the islands.

What determined the balance of power was the pitch, a good stout coconut mat laid on concrete. This gave the ball a steep and lively bounce and called for a good deal of acclimatization, a situation we only realized on meeting more hostile bowling. But, until that time, we enjoyed the pleasure of the island and being the centre of the most intense 'Test Match' atmosphere.

The whole of Bermuda was in a state of happy excitement, the blandly partisan factions being the Bermudians on the one side and the troops of the Northumberland Fusiliers on the other, whilst American and other tourists were fascinated by the general air of intensity the rivals exuded. The enthusiasm of the home party could be gauged by the tale of an owner of a fruit store who had employed two coloured assistants for many years. When they asked for the day off to see the match he gravely replied that they would have to mind the shop in order that *he* might go to the match. They retired for consultation and shortly returned to say that, with much regret, they jointly tendered their resignations, at which he rounded off his little joke by saying that, on the contrary, they were sacked – until the day after the match.

On the morning over 8000 people crowded into the ground, which was roughly oval-shaped, and dished like a saucer. This sizable gate represented about a third of the population at that particular moment and, on one side of the ground, a solid block of soldiery gave us moral and vociferous support.

We won the toss and batted first, to see the game get off to a dramatic start. A large Bermudian named Benavados ran up and delivered a fast shortish ball which kicked up to hit our opening batsman, Paul Gibb, high on the forehead. Paul, tough citizen, ran a somewhat zig-zag single as the ball soared, first bounce, to third man. By dint of hard travail we had made 66 for two by lunch-time of which Paul had made six not out, but had no recollection whatsoever of having batted. However, he resumed quite cheerfully after lunch, under instruction to push things along in order to build on our promising position.

Those optimistic directions led to immediate and total disaster. A left-hander named Simon started off after lunch, and bowled almost exactly as Bill Voce had bowled three years previously on the South African mat – at fast-medium pace, pitching on the leg-stump and hitting the off. Our batsmen had not the experience and practice of the South Africans and, in a short time, we were all out for 85, Simon having taken 7 for 19.

Sir Julien did *not* like being beaten, and there was some degree of consternation as we discussed the situation in the dressing-room. It was decided to dispense with any seam bowling and start with Walter and myself. This was immediately successful in that we got two out for six, but then saw a stand led by Alma Hunt, the left-handed 'star' of the opposition, which got the score to 45 before he was caught in the slips. Thereafter things went with a rush, and nine wickets were down for 66. It was about this time that drinks were somewhat unaccountably brought on, one of the bearers being a sergeant of the Northumberland Fusiliers. He was a state of nerves to which no hostile salvo or barrage would have reduced him, and there was a desperate light in his eye as he said to me, 'For gawd's sake get this over, sir – the troops have got every button they could raise on you.' I said things were now going to be all right.

It was a rash assurance. Almost immediately I was hit for six into the very midst of the soldiery, and this made the score 76 and the end of the over. Walter's first ball was a good length leg-break, but the tail enders were no respecters of persons or reputations, and the striker caught it a slicing off-drive that sent it first bounce for four. The next he struck for two, and defeat seemed very near at hand. The third ball of the over he again drove forcefully with the spin, and it skimmed over mid-off's head. Right on the rim of the saucer George Heane started from deep extra cover, measuring the flight of the ball as he bounced along, flat out, inside the line. Ball and fielder met almost at the sight screen and George caught it, a foot above his head, like picking an apple off a tree. As he slung the ball up heavenwards everything else on the ground seemed to rise vertically in sympathy, including the spectators. In the excitement of the moment all rivalries were forgotten in the appreciation of one of the best cricket matches that anyone present could remember.

The troops celebrated in style, the home supporters consoled themselves in the splendid and sporting performance of their side. As for the Americans and other disinterested parties, it was, 'fools who came to scoff remained behind to pray.' Our American friends, of whom we had made many, reproached us for concealing the true nature of our national game. They had, they said, always understood that cricket was a slow, tedious game but, what with the infectious delirium of the partisans, they proclaimed that it was the most exciting feature of the whole sporting calendar. We had in honesty to confess that every cricket match was not quite like the one they had just seen.

A hard-earned draw against All Bermuda the next day was a complete anti-climax, but we again encountered the leading all-rounder in the islands, Alma Hunt. He was a right-handed, fastish bowler and left-handed batsman, and good enough in both departments to have played in a West Indian trial match, a great distinction for one outside the regular circuit. Soon afterwards he became professional with Aberdeenshire, and proved such a success that he remained there until the outbreak of war. He is now a leading figure in the administration of cricket in Bermuda.

If the names of our ships were any guide, our progress was royal indeed. Having sailed in an empress and a queen, we now embarked on the *Monarch of Bermuda* for the return trip to New York. It turned out to be a very different journey from the outward passage for, about mid-way up, we struck a hurricane. It was a most awe-inspiring spectacle, and we were glad to have 23,000 well-found tons to combat it. So violent was the storm that we were told the *Bremen*, outside New York, and the *Queen of Bermuda*, on the southward run, were hove to. This we could well believe as we stood behind the heavy glass windows of the promenade deck and saw the enormous seas break over the bows, the spray rising like thick mist, mast high. The little tube in my ear again stood me in good stead and, although much impressed, I did not miss a meal. There were in all four other diners, including Roger Blunt and a convivial American who, exempt from the laws of his country, was in such a permanent and delicious state of intoxication that nature's upheavals were to him a matter of complete indifference.

We had a few very enjoyable days in New York then sailed for home in the *Aquitania*. On the ship I met an American actress, as sweet as she was beautiful and, if not ever afterwards, we lived happily together for a year or two to come. Here I should add that I do not propose to go into the details of my youthful romances. A raconteur must exercise some discretion, a point made by another American. Wilson Misner, asked to write his memoirs, replied, 'Why blow a police whistle?'

# EIGHT

# Not by Bread Alone

In the 1930s a young bachelor without private means but with a good job could expect to make between £500 and £1000 a year. This was my situation and I got along well enough, living cosily in the Temple with occasional cricket tours abroad. I had enough money from steady employment and part-time writing to exist comfortably, a vast company of friends and acquaintances, and, since my meeting on the *Aquitania*, my love-life had been sweet and full and happy. My parents had moved back to the Highlands so I had a base in the midst of my favourite country where I was always welcomed with open arms. It was a happy and eventful period of my life despite occasional personal setbacks and the increasingly black international outlook.

In 1932 I joined the International Sportsmen's Club. It was a proprietary club belonging to the management of Grosvenor House, wherein it was housed. When originally founded it had been intended as a resplendent counterpart to such transatlantic institutions as the New York Rackets Club, and its sponsors had hoped for a large influx of American millionaires in a generally wealthy membership. The crash of 1929 had put an abrupt end to such hopes, and the proprietors had to set their sights on a more work-a-day scheme, and welcome the less affluent such as myself. Their earlier aspirations did mean, however, that the amenities were first class, and included squash courts, Turkish bath, gymnasium, and swimming-pool all built on a comfortable scale.

It was a mixed club with a large membership, but boasting few international sportsmen within the strict meaning of the term. Above all it was an immensely happy institution, with great harmony amongst the members, and between members and staff. There were strictly male preserves in the shape of a bar and a smoking-room, and the regular supporters of these tended to become a club within

themselves. Its subscribers were sure that it was quite the best
and friendliest bar in London.

Despite all these advantages I returned from Bermuda in a state
of indecision for, although very happy at Ladbrokes, I suffered
from occasional doubts. My liking for horses, racing and betting had
remained tepid and, as these were the principle ingredients of the
business, this was not a good portent for the future. There was
obviously need for a change to something better suited to such
talents as I had, and which offered better prospects.

Apart from an ill-formed idea in my early teens that I would like
to be a surgeon I had never had any pronounced ambition apart
from the wish to excel at cricket. As it now seemed that I had
got as far as was likely in this line I was in a vacuum. The professions had no appeal for me, and in any case, at 26 years old
and without any capital, for me to undergo prolonged training was
out of the question. All this I discussed with Walter Robins, who
himself was happily and profitably employed as a member of Lloyds,
and who was anxious to see me settled in some similarly agreeable
situation. He said that a friend of his, Henry Horne, had just become
managing director of the gin-distilling firm of Seager, Evans and
Company which was now branching out in all directions. It looked
a possibility. He suggested he should arrange for us to meet, which
he duly did.

Henry Horne was a remarkable man. He was a handsome Scot
of well-set-up figure, which qualified him as one of Lord North-
cliffe's good-looking young men. From there he had, on North-
cliffe's death, joined Lord Rothermere but, for some reason, had
later fallen out with him. He then became 'involved in cement'
and, always a whole-hearted performer, went in big. Caught in
the slump of 1929, he went bust for around seven million pounds,
but after resting awhile he was now trying again.

Thus through Walter's introduction I joined the firm of Seager,
Evans and Co., who, as well as being gin distillers, were general
wine and spirit merchants. It was a long-established family firm
which had fallen into a decline and, according to Henry Horne,
was a dull and dreary institution when first it caught his eye. He
soon wrought a great change in its character, and before long
none could have criticized it as lacking in enterprise or gaiety. In

certain respects it was positively hilarious, if not always so in the eyes of its shareholders.

As the firm was run by two managing directors it resembled the two-headed giant of the fairy tale. Henry, as one head, was the essence of good cheer and optimism. His opposite number was gloomy and drear, viewing any new trends with grave suspicion. My appointment obviously did nothing to lessen his gloom; amongst other doubts he may have regarded me (erroneously) as a rival to his son, for whom he entertained great, if unsupported, hopes.

Henry was a firm believer in entertainment as a force in the furtherance of business, and he had soon acquired a number of original props to lend spice to his hospitality. We had a portable darts parlour (the game enjoying a boom at this time) which went round various social functions. It was specially designed and painted for us by Anna Zinkheisen, the motif being crafty old mariners trying to harpoon and net ravishing mermaids. It was, on one occasion, inspected by Queen Mary who approved in general but remarked that the mermaids' hair might, in the interests of propriety, be a little longer. This being regarded as a royal command the artist was summoned, and duly provided the additional locks.

We had a four-in-hand coach which trumpeted its way round the streets of London and provincial capitals, to the joy of the masses and mild dismay of the traffic department. But perhaps the most spectacular exhibit was acquired by chance. Henry, gliding by in his grey Rolls-Royce, espied one day the remains of an old London horse-drawn bus doing duty as a henhouse on a wayside farm. In no time at all he had bought it, had it restored, and hired Mr Barley and a team of his famous coach horses to propel it. Filled with distinguished guests it made a novel and ideal vehicle for pub crawling.

My first official mission was to hire a river steamer from which to view the Boat Race, and to see that it was adequately stocked with our products. This was the sequel to a great banquet on the previous evening, and I only made one serious miscalculation. Owing to our nocturnal hospitality there was such a demand from the guests for brandy and ginger ale that we ran out of both before we had cast off. It was a cold, unpleasant day, and very few actually ventured out of the bar to watch the race. Nor was much attention payed to the somewhat garbled accounts of the event with which they returned, but the occasion was generally voted a great success.

I was next given a roving commission and sent off to recruit the support of a great darts expert who kept a pub in Camden Town. But here my triumphant career was nigh wrecked beyond repair. On my saying that I came from Seagers, Mine Host, a large, craggy man, regarded me with darkening brow and bluntly stated that he had been insulted by our sales manager. Neither honeyed words nor expressions of regret had any effect, so I ordered a pint over which to review the situation.

The pub was starting to fill up and I realized that the clientele was mostly railwaymen from Camden Town depot. As a locomotive-lover I got into conversation with the group next door and soon, my troubles forgotten, I was listening to expert chat on cut-offs and valve gears, to say nothing of pacifics and blast pipes. After a round or two the proprietor joined us and all was forgiven and forgotten. I got all the information I wanted, invited the expert to our next darts function, and was driven home by his son, my reputation saved by a last-minute fluke.

Some months later I was introduced to Mr Foxwell, a director of the firm who daily toured the pubs, wine shops and certain favoured merchants to minister to their needs. This he did in a manner which could be described as the best of Charles Dickens, yet all his own. The barmaid, be her charms a trifle faded, was never less than the 'Lily of the Valley' or the 'Flower of the Forest' and once, a less fortunate address to a lady of ample bosom, 'The Maid of the Mountains'. Never was the lady asked to take a drop of something. Rather was she invited to brush her dainty lips with our incomparable distillation, which, being Seager's gin, was guaranteed to 'bring the flush of beauty to her cheeks', and so enhance her already established reputation for wit and allurement throughout the district. All of this was delivered with such courtesy and grandeur as to elicit squeals of delight from those addressed, and broad grins from all around. Sometimes we would laugh aloud at his more extravagant fancies, at which Mr Foxwell would survey the company with majestic serenity, then his eyes would twinkle and all the goodness of his heart would smile forth. For in my travels with him I was to learn that he was simple, patriotic, loyal and generous to the point of nobility.

Right away I realized that introduction to Mr Foxwell was quite something in itself. He did not quietly clasp the outstretched hand but, in moments of bonhomie, would take a great round-arm swing at it, so that the palms met with a resounding smack. However, if he mistimed his grasp the unsuspecting subject was liable to be spun like a top. When, so to speak, order had been restored, Mr Foxwell almost invariably congratulated his new acquaintance, sometimes upon such points as his inspiring appearance, but more often than not just on general principle.

We progressed from pub to pub in an old and dignified Rolls-Royce driven by Irving, a splendid Irish chauffeur. The dialogue, usually conducted in a vast traffic jam, ran to a well-established pattern.

Mr F.:  Irving! What's the time?
Irving: 'Alf past twelve, Mr Foxwell.
Mr F.:  *Good gracious!* To the Bull, like a flash of lightning.

This latter might be varied by, 'Non-stop to the Grapes!' or other instruction impossible of implementation in the London traffic but, as Irving always had the day's programme in hand, all was well.

I used Foxwell shamelessly. Any particularly deserving friend to whom I owed, or whom I deemed worthy of the honour, I would invite to have a day with us. Because Mr Foxwell's performances were absolutely natural and he never strove for effect, it was a never-failing and heart-warming excursion. A gigantic American friend attempted to apologize for being a little late, but Mr Foxwell waved this down. 'For,' said he, 'your appearance fills us with the utmost enthusiasm.' One day, when I prevailed upon Lord Claud Hamilton to leave his desk in Queen Anne's Gate and join us, he was rewarded with a splendid scene. Mr Foxwell was on this occasion selling port, for which purpose he naturally employed his own wholly original methods. Calling at Stone's Chop House he asked to be given a sample of their standard port. On the manager supplying this Mr Foxwell took a sip and staggered backwards with, I fear, a highly theatrical bout of coughing and spluttering. Having, on recovery, described the wine as poison and the manager as a bandit, he waved an arm in the direction of a much-embarrassed Claud.

'Had you offered such stuff to his lordship's ancestors,' he declared, 'they would have washed their feet in it.' The manager was delighted and Mr Foxwell left triumphantly with an order for six dozen of his superior brand.

In 1933 my father retired from the parish of Uddingston, moving to Birnie, in Moray. The parishioners lived about a mile away in the village of Tomshill, and were mostly employed in Glen Lossie distillery, which belongs to the Distillers Company. The manse was by the river Lossie, and was a delightful house. There was no gas or electricity, so one was dependent on coal fires and oil lamps, both of which were a delight to the guest who did not have to attend to them. My mother and her unmarried sister, Auntie Mary, who had always lived with us, ran the house with the aid of a wonderfully competent cook named Bella, while other help was readily available from the nearby cottages if required. This was just as well, for in addition to its lack of mod cons the house was large and rambling. At Christmas and in holiday time it could comfortably accommodate the entire family, as at this time my eldest sister was the only one of our generation to be married, and had but one daughter. These were happy times.

Whenever – despite Dr Johnson's dicta – I got tired of London I boarded the night sleeper. At Aberdeen I got on the dining-car of the Elgin train and, having breakfasted on fresh herrings done in oatmeal and warm, fluffy baps, would head for the manse. Its natives claim that Moray is the best climate in these islands, bar Devon and Cornwall, and I for one believe them. Frequently I left King's Cross in murk and damp to arrive in sparkling sunshine and glorious clean fresh air. Perhaps I was lucky because, at one time, I so regularly brought good weather that neighbouring farmers remarked on it. Later, being inclined to boast about this, I seemed to lose something of my magical touch; but whatever the weather the scenery is always beautiful and the air fragrant.

It is said that Scots talk and dream of Scotland but never go back there. In my case this is not entirely true for, although I have lived over fifty years in the south, I have taken every opportunity of returning, originally for holidays, and latterly on business. In addition to my parents at Birnie there were, in pre-war days, my uncle and aunt in Inverness who, with their two daughters, were a wonderfully happy family. The girls were young and very sweet, and made such a fuss of me that I used to think I was something of a hero to them. My cousin Hilda caused me to think again, just the other day, by saying they looked forward to seeing me because I always used to bring the biggest boxes of chocolates they had ever seen.

Cricket in Scotland is of much higher standard than is generally realized in the south and to tour in Scotland was a delightful, and for me, a nostalgic journey. In the mid-'30s Julien Cahn took his side to the north on a particularly agreeable short tour. We stayed at Gleneagles, and played at Broughty Ferry, Perth and Glasgow, each ground bringing a happy memory. Broughty Ferry I knew from the Kinnaird week, and Perth is beautiful – the North Inch, on the banks of the Tay. In Glasgow we played at Hamilton Crescent, the West of Scotland's ground at Partick. It is very much an urban ground, but of great character and attraction. There I had seen the great Australian side of 1921, and played against the Australian schoolboys some years later. On this occasion the pitch took spin, and Walter Robins and I had a field day.

A little farther north in Aberdeenshire I used to stay with Mo and Sass de Mier, whose father had been the Mexican ambassador, and whose mother had remarried into the Arbuthnot-Leslie family after his death. They were a spirited couple, and soon became the most ardent highlanders north of the Border. It was an enthusiasm which carried them into the services right at the start of the war. Mo joined a Highland regiment and spent four years as a prisoner of war, and Sass was killed early on as a rear-gunner in the RAF.

This made a happy half-way house on my road to the manse, and we usually raised a cricket side, playing a hearty match against a nearby village. After one such convivial game the three of us came back on a real 'braw, bright, moonlicht, nicht' in Mo's Ford convertible with the top down, enjoying the crystal evening air. We wound through a sizeable park then turned sharp left over a narrow bridge, spanning a burn running in a deep, wide cleft. Once over that we ran up a slope for about thirty yards, which brought us to the front door. Mo knocked on it, then, after a short pause, he said he would put the car away while we were waiting. He turned round and stopped in amazement. The car had entirely disappeared.

I had never seen a ghost, but at that moment I knew exactly how it must feel. In the bright moonlight and flat countryside we could see a mile in every direction, but there was no visible trace of the car. We stared at each other in amazement, and presently one of a very sober trio said, 'There *was* a motor car there a minute ago.' There certainly was no sign of it in the cleft where it must have gone had it run backwards, and a wider search lead to nothing.

There I fear my story as a ghost story ends. We found the car next day. The hand brake was ineffective, and the car had taken off gently and noiselessly. Gathering speed, it had miraculously shot the bridge with inches to spare on either side. It had then run on a considerable distance over a sweep of hard turf, leaving no trace, at the end of which it had gone through a high hedge. The hedge had sprung up again, completely shielding it from view, and, in the bright moonshine, the deep shadow had made it quite invisible from the other side.

It was left, therefore, to my grandfather to be the only one of the family who was supposed to have seen a ghost in a land full of ghosts. This he did when driving a horse and trap along a lonely highland road as night was falling. A sturdy, matter-of-fact citizen, he maintained that what he saw was an ordinary, rather large dog, which circled the trap a few times in the dusk, and accompanied him for some way along the road. At his destination, however, the locals insisted that this was in fact a spectral hound as good as anything the Baskervilles could do.

It was well that he was not impressionable for, in middle age, he was cursed by a witch. As agent to a highland chief it was his unpleasant duty to evict her from her cottage, at which she made a wax dummy of him, stuck pins in it, and threw it into the canal, pronouncing a terrible incantation to the effect that, as it withered away, so would he. That he was pottering around his garden the day before he died at 91 is testimony to her British workmanship rather than to her powers of darkness.

Once I had savoured the beauties of Scotland to the full, and the

autumn started to draw in, I would yearn for the excitements of
the big city, and travel back to the south bursting with health
and enthusiasm. London was a wonderful place to which to return.
One of its grandest entertainments in those times was a play,
*Young England*, which both Jim Swanton and Henry Longhurst
have described so well elsewhere. Contrary to general belief I was
not one of the most frequent attenders, but think I could claim to
have 'discovered' it. A female member of the ISC said to me one
day, 'There's a most wonderful play on at the Victoria Palace. It's
unbelievable – like an old melodrama – but it can't last for a week.'
It sounded so good that the friend with whom I was lunching
agreed we might see one act of the matinée that afternoon. It *was*
unbelievable. From the moment the hero was born (illegitimately)
in a tube station during an air raid in the first war there was never
a false note. The impossibly noble Dr Col. Frank Inglehurst, VC,
etc. comforted the pregnant lady by crying out in clarion tones,
'I shall telephone your mother, and she'll come here by underground
right away.' Having given vent to this plug for London Transport
he then set about throttling the cringing, sneering villain (Jabez
Hawk – who else?) with one hand, whilst raising the index finger of
the other in denunciation. The villain responsible for the lady's
condition turned out to be the hero's father, a complication revealed in the dénouement of the whole compelling drama.

I went into the club in the evening and said that, although the
rest could not possibly live up to the first act, it had to be seen
before its removal at any moment. We went in a body that very
evening to find that the rest was not only as good as the first act:
it excelled it. As the word went around more people joined the
gang and the play ran for six months; some people saw it almost
every night of its existence. It was about saintly boy scouts, a diabolical mayor (Jabez Hawk), dissolute young bloods and a heroic
young architect. The audience helped, making its own interjections
and suggestions as the play went along. Thus the ringing announcement, 'Your son was born in lawful wedlock' somehow got dis-
torted into 'Your son was born in awful Matlock.'

Better qualified critics than I gave it their spontaneous approval.
A friend of mine, Dick Shanks of literary fame, found himself
sitting next to a beautiful stranger, film star Laura la Plante, a

position many might well have envied him. They had further grounds for envy when the scoutmaster hero declaimed in all innocence, 'Rubber can be stretched, this we know.' Miss La Plante let go a piercing whoop of joy, cast her arms around Dick's neck, and hugged him.

It was about this time that I was playing in a match for Julien Cahn. Remarking that I was in the wine and spirit trade he said he had a distant kinsman, a Mr Siegel, who was a wine-grower in Germany. Things were becoming very difficult for him as a Jew in Germany and, with Julien's aid, he hoped to set up in Britain. He had been here on occasional visits so had a small connection, but Julien tactfully suggested that I might be able to give him some further introductions. To this I replied that I would be delighted to do all I could, but that my influence with my firm or in the trade in general was strictly limited.

Not long afterwards word was brought me in the office that Mr Siegel was in the sample room. We had an agreeable chat and went out to lunch, and in due course I reported back to Sir Julien that our meeting had been a success, and I would muster what forces I had on his kinsman's behalf. He pondered this for a moment, then said: 'If you and he liked to set up together, I would finance you.' This was a tremendous thought. Sir Julien's income was said to be £1000 a day in good pre-war currency and his wealth, derived from the furniture trade, beyond computation. A mirage of a large marble-fronted block of offices emblazoned with the sign 'Peebles & Siegel' flashed before my excited vision, but I managed to reply that I would certainly like to discuss the possibilities.

Hans – for we were soon on first-name terms – was equally ready to pursue the idea, and we discussed the situation, which was slightly complicated by the fact that I was employed by Seagers. This difficulty was solved by Henry taking a third share on behalf of Seagers, with the understanding that we should get the bulk of their German wine trade.

Things are never as easy as they seem, and seldom as rosy. Sir Julien was a generous man but, as millionaires occasionally are, he was surrounded by some very hard-headed financial advisers with whom we had to deal. Aware that Hans was a kinsman, they may have reckoned that blood was thicker than water, but they also believed that it was readily dilutable by stern business considerations. The outcome was that, after over a year of negotiations and prevarications, we were given a small loan, admittedly on easy terms, and set up the firm as Rhine Wines (Walter S. Siegel) Ltd on a very modest scale. Our offices consisted of two small rooms off Baker Street, and bore little resemblance to any marble palace.

Support from our allies was also uncertain. The Sales Manager of Seagers said he would do what he could but, over the years, he had many commitments and, indeed, he had a German House of their own which he was expected to promote. Despite this there came a great day when our German wines were put on at a large luncheon at Queen Anne's Gate. Henry Horne, the host, perhaps forgetting that they were also his wines, inspected the glass submitted for his approval, blew a great cloud of cigar smoke into it and, with a majestic wave of the hand, said, 'Corked.' An embarrassed butler later showed Hans and me the bottle in question. It was clear, cool and quite perfect.

Mr Foxwell, of course, remained loyal. He took our list with him and, what with such terms as Auslese, Liebfraumilch and Schlossberg, he hissed and blew like the contemporary Flying Scotsman, but they were not for his clientele. Hans was not one to be discouraged and, if we did not make great profits, he was busily laying foundations which were to stand us in good stead in the years ahead.

There was another trade connection which was to have a profound influence on our future progress, although this was not for the moment obvious. The Glasgow firm of Ross and Coulter, whisky merchants, was composed of two large burly Scots, Herbert Ross and Sam Coulter, connected with Seagers through Strathclyde Distillery, which Seagers owned and for which they were agents. The two men had been friends at school together, but had not seen each other for some time when they met in a military hospital in the first war. Each had lost a leg, and Sam the sight of an eye as well. On being discharged from the Army they set up in business together, first as photographers, at which they were not very successful, then in their old trade as whisky brokers, in which they were astoundingly so.

Stumping around together on their wooden legs, usually in argument about something, they became a great and popular part of the scotch whisky scene, and Herbert especially was a first-class man of business. Sometimes in moments of jollity they would throw off their wooden legs and dance together on the pair God had left them. Sometimes in the pub hard by their office they would stage a mock scene, and one would up with a club-like stick and fetch the other a resounding whack on the leg, which would immediately be returned with interest. Strangers not in the know had to be restrained from rushing into the street and hollering for the police.

Some years before I had met them when playing cricket at the Poloc Club in Glasgow of which they were members and supporters. We met again when I was in Glasgow with Henry Horne, who was going to do a large whisky deal with them. They arrived together at our hotel, arguing about bodyline bowling, and after we had exchanged our greetings the company sat down round a large table and prepared to do some hard bargaining. Herbert opened the proceedings. 'Now, Sam,' said he, indicating me with a wave of the hand, 'we've got an expert here so we'll just hear what he's got to say.' The company, avid to do business, then found themselves involved in, or spectators of, an argument on bodyline, which raged and blew between the two partners, the 'expert' not being called upon to say very much. When the subject had been exhausted (without any sign of settlement) they turned to the business in hand and, in a very short time, had settled the whisky question with a sure and dexterous touch.

Out of this meeting grew a warm friendship between us, for they were great lovers of sport. If not expert on the subject of cricket, they were much interested, and the fact that I was, at that time, the only Scot born and bred to play for England seemed to please them, for they were the stoutest of patriots.

With the firm of Rhine Wines set up it was agreed that I should fly to Germany to meet Hans's father, and possibly acquire a little first-hand knowledge of wine production. The first leg of the journey was to fly to Cologne, whence I was to take train to Wiesbaden, where Walter S. Siegel had his home and his business. The flight lasted some hours, the plane being *Heracles,* one of Imperial Airways' large, four-engined bi-planes, which cruised along at a

steady and comfortable 96 mph, according to the speedometer
thoughtfully placed in the passenger compartment. At Wiesbaden
I stepped off the train into the arms of my host, which I took to
be a good omen. He was short of stature, very bald with a pleasant
face, given an expression of great animation by an exceptionally
bright blue eye. He welcomed me warmly and took me to the Nas-
serohoff Hotel. He lived with his wife and daughter in a large house
in the Beethovenstrasse where I was made equally welcome, and it
was, for me, a very enjoyable stay. It was also an interesting first-
hand experience of a totalitarian State.

By 1937 the Nazi régime was causing acute alarm by its military
expansion and increasing persecution of the Jews. It struck me
then that the Rhinelanders were mostly reluctant Nazis, but had
little choice to be otherwise in the circumstances. My admiration for
the Siegel family steadily increased as I saw how bravely they coped
with this mounting threat. When Mr Siegel and I walked together
in the streets certain citizens would give him a half-hearted 'Heil',
at which he would raise his hat and occasionally say to me, 'I used
to know that man very well.' There was little doubt as to which
party emerged with the greater dignity from these encounters.
Wherever we called it was evident that he was a much respected
citizen and, if there was any uneasiness, it was never on his side.

We hired a car, and Mr Siegel, his daughter Greta and I went
off to visit his vineyards at Osthofen. On arrival we walked up the
hill to his land, where a small army of workers gave him a most
affectionate welcome, after which there was a slight but obvious
pause. Mr Siegel drew me aside and said, 'Will you take the chauffeur away and pick a few grapes? They know who you are, but
they won't speak freely to me in front of a stranger.' Accordingly,
the chauffeur, a decent enough chap, and I went grape-picking,
conversing to the extent of 'twelf-cylinder' and 'Rolls-Royce'. This
incident I found revealing, and I was reminded of a friend in
Germany at this time who was a victim of the rather lighter side of
these pressures and fears. He essayed to halt a bus between official
stops by holding up his hand. He was obviously mistaken for an
enthusiastic party member, for the driver and the entire bus load
gave him the 'heil' salute, but the bus went straight on.

On our tour we stopped for tea at the Kroner at Assmanshausen.

It was a delightful inn, and the sun blazed down as we sat under a canopy formed by a huge spreading vine beside the River Rhine, just where some rocks caused the water to break and foam like a Highland burn. 'When I get married,' I said, 'I am coming here for my honeymoon.' This I failed to do, but ten years later, not long after our wedding, Ursula and I visited the Kroner with some friends. It was a dull, misty autumn day, the vine was bare, the tables and chairs had been stowed away, and the river was muddy and black. I was compensated to some extent by the railway running very close by, but the rest of the party objected that the magnificent belching steam locomotives merely added to the gloom.

The year after our meeting Mr Siegel came to London, where he was a popular visitor. His English was fluent and original for, knowing that his vocabulary was limited, he divided all things into two categories. If you won a football pool or were knighted it was 'agreeable'. If your house was burnt down or you went bust it was 'not agreeable'. One morning, seeing that he was not entirely at ease, I asked him if all was well with the accommodation we had found for him. After a moment's hesitation he said, 'Dere is de vindow. Now I am putting mine head out. Dere is de iron bar. It is not agreeable.' At that he raised his hat to reveal an enormous bump in the middle of his bald head.

It is altogether agreeable to record that, having stuck it out to the end in Wiesbaden, he and his wife got to Sweden, and later to this country. Both died in the '50s, but had the joy of seeing their son and daughter firmly established. Father Siegel also seemed to be very happy with the branch of his firm which we had set up, and always had an encouraging word when he called to see us.

## NINE

# *Decline and Oriental Fall*

My playing career had almost come to an end as far as first-class cricket was concerned, but I played a lot of highly enjoyable club and country house games. Twice I had come within measurable distance of playing again for England.

In August 1934 I had been a guest of Charles Carnegie (now Southesk) who yearly had a particularly pleasant cricket week centred on Kinnaird Castle, in Angus. We played the neighbouring clubs by day and attended the various highland balls and parties by night. It was after a ball at Kirriemuir that I came down late to breakfast to find a telegram awaiting me. To my astonishment it came from Pete Perrin, the chairman of the selectors, and asked me to come to the Oval prepared to play in the fifth Test against Australia. I had not played any county cricket for some time but, as I had taken a few wickets the day before, my surprise gave way to suspicion. No one round the table showed the slightest interest so I put the wire in my pocket, and waited for the hoaxer to show his hand.

The morning papers resolved all doubt. The *Mail* carried a front-page headline – WHY PEEBLES? WHY NOT VOCE? – while others expressed surprise, some politely, some less so. I could not but agree with their sentiments, but was not going to miss the outing. I took the prepaid form, addressed it to Pete Perrin, and wrote, 'Many thanks. Will be there if not lynched *en route*.'

My first over of that day's match also resolved all doubts about my final inclusion. The first ball was a full toss which was hit for four, and thrown back by one of the small crowd. Casually I put out my right hand, and the ball knocked back the top joint of the third finger at a sharp angle. Arthur Hazlerigg, an old friend and an opponent of Cambridge and Leicester days, was at mid-off. He came over and, taking my finger in a firm and competent grip, had it in its place again in a few seconds. However, by lunchtime it was very swollen, and by the time I got back to London it was like a banana. An X-ray showed a bit of bone had been chipped off as well, and soon my finger was in a splint and any prospect of playing had evaporated. The selectors were sympathetic, and told me to come along anyway, which I did. I had escaped something. We lost the toss, the first Australian wicket fell at noon for 21 runs and the second at 6.15 with the score at 472. Ponsford and Bradman each making over 200. England was overwhelmed by 542 runs.

At the start of the next season I had a good match for MCC against the South Africans, getting four cheap wickets in their only innings, and was one of the twelve to be invited to Nottingham for the first Test, only to be omitted on the morning. This was my last summons and, if disappointed, I was also relieved for now I knew I was a crock and below form. Playing a couple of days in a week I enjoyed myself very much, but any heavy work I found very soon led to severe shoulder trouble.

It was in the summer of 1937 that Lionel Tennyson told me he had been invited to take a side to India later in the year, and asked if I would be available. I said I would talk to Henry Horne, and also said I was always something of a risk with my uncertain shoulder. Henry was most helpful, saying they were anxious to increase their trade with India and it would be a good opportunity to visit our various agents. I therefore returned to Lionel and said I had the firm's blessing, and he disposed of my remaining worries by saying that the best possible cure for my shoulder would be the Indian sun.

Lionel was one of the richest characters of his age. He is lovingly remembered by a vast number of people as a great personality, whose whole-hearted enjoyment of life gave equal joy to all who ever met him. He belonged ideally to another age, for even the now spacious-seeming days of the '30s hardly offered sufficient scope for his gusto and vitality. His heart was as great as his massive, sturdy frame, and stuffed full of courage and kindliness. His conceits were enormous, unaffected and endearing, a sitting target for the shafts of his friends, whose badinage was the truest gauge of their affection. Wherever he went, whatever he did, he was sure to start something, if sometimes untoward, for he had a flair for attracting disaster in his more portentous moments.

He was the subject of countless anecdotes, and his name seemed to arise whenever the conversation turned to cricket. There was a certain artlessness about him which was wholly disarming. It was said that in the dressing-room, during a Gents *v* Players match, he laid all comers ten to one that his grandfather had written *Hiawatha*. If several present had never heard of either they could all recognize a nice price, so it proved an expensive assertion.

When he dropped a brick, as he did from time to time, it was not just a slight misjudgment, it was a good old-fashioned hay-maker, game, set and match. One popular example of such a coup given wide currency concerned a cricket dinner at which he sat next to Joe Lyons, Prime Minister of Australia, a devout Roman Catholic and proud father of a large family. They got along splendidly and, when there was a pause in the conversation, Lionel was ready to fill it.

'You've got a lot of Roman Catholics in Australia,' he said.

'Yes, indeed,' replied Mr Lyons with pardonable pride, 'about a third of the population.'

'You want to watch 'em,' cautioned Lionel, 'you can't trust 'em – and, what's more, the buggers breed like rabbits.'

Sensing something had gone wrong, Lionel afterwards remarked that the PM was a funny chap who suddenly shut up and wouldn't talk any more.

Once started on Lionel I find it difficult to abandon the flood of memories he evokes. He had a chauffeur named Bailey whose salary, to say the least, was somewhat erratically collected. The story went that master and servant had come to an understanding. In lieu of cash, if unavailable, Bailey was allowed to hire out the car, a fine vintage Austin Twenty Landaulette, for such functions as weddings, Council do's or private assignments.

There was a memorable morning at Lord's when Lionel arrived for Hants *v* Middlesex match flush with a gigantic wad of notes, the fruits of a profitable Ascot. His first gesture was to call for the faithful Bailey. Flourishing this impressive bundle and affecting an elaborately casual air Lionel said, 'Let me see, Bailey, don't I owe you some wages?' His face fell slightly when Bailey replied, 'Yes, sir – three months.' But honour was satisfied by a full settlement.

There was only one slight snag to domestic bliss – it rained. To while away the time Lionel joined Nigel Haig, Tommy Jameson and one or two other shrewd operators in a game of poker. Alas for human hopes and aims. Before lunch Bailey had to be summoned thrice to bail out his master's honour, and by lunchtime his original financial position had changed for the worse. If anyone had said to Bailey that he had been hard done by he would probably have been asked to step outside. In fact any word of criticism of Lionel, such as that he had played a lucky innings, would always get a dusty answer from this true and loyal man.

Our first official function in Bombay was a dinner at Government House, where Lord Brabourne presided. It was a formal occasion, and the uniforms and robes of the various dignitaries made a beautiful scene in a lofty and gracious chamber. The speeches, equally formal and extremely discreet, were received with polite applause and subdued murmurs of approval. Or so they were until the guest of honour arose, well charged with good fare and brandishing a large cigar. After a few preliminaries he got into top gear. He was delighted, he said, to see his old friend Lord Brabourne doing himself so well in India, and it was his intention on his return to England, he added, to put in a word for him personally at Whitehall. The faces of the VIPs at this unexpected furtherance of their host's interests was worth the price of admission alone. What other joyous indiscretions the Lord let go I cannot recall, but his whole oration was a riot of pleasure among the irresponsible.

We set forth on our tour by going to Karachi, Baroda, and then on to Peshawar in the foothills of the Khyber Pass, a very attractive town. Here I got a fair bag of wickets on the matting, but my old shoulder trouble started up again and this was the only success I had on the trip.

At Peshawar I stayed with a cousin of Douglas Jardine's. On the first morning we parted on his doorstep, I to play cricket, he to settle a tribal war. In the evening we compared notes and, for once on this trip, I seemed to have fared relatively well. He had arrived on the scene where a truce had been arranged in order that the warring chiefs might parley, and all went well, up to a point. He joined one of the warlords in his entrenchment, and together they advanced into no-man's land to meet the opposition half way, all of which had been agreed beforehand. When they reached the appointed place exactly on time there was no sign of the other party, and they settled down to await their arrival. Suddenly there was a rattle of musketry from the enemy position, and the air became alive with humming, whistling bullets. My host said that it had been no time for heroic gestures, so they took to their heels and got safely back. When I left the war was going merrily on, and my host was considering his next move. My suggestion that he might advance into no-man's land from the other side met with little enthusiasm.

From the cricket point of view the trip was a disaster, for I was completely crippled with a bust shoulder. *Wisden* summed the matter up in one terse but accurate sentence: 'Peebles was a failure.' It was an eventful and occasionally enjoyable trip just the same, and I was lucky to have as a half-section Tommy Jameson, an imperturbable Irishman whose unfailing good humour was equal to every situation.

Midway through the tour Lionel, encouraged by his obvious and immense popularity, customarily opened his speeches with the words, 'When I come back as Viceroy . . .', a prospect which was always greeted with acclamation. What the reigning incumbent thought of it was not recorded, but as he had known Lionel at Eton it is unlikely that he viewed it as an immediate threat.

We stayed with a number of Nabobs and Maharajahs, who were still a flourishing society. At Patiala the choice of transport from the guest house to the cricket ground was by camel, elephant or Rolls-Royce, the latter upholstered with tapestry and fitted out in gold and ivory. But the most impressive show of wealth was an exhibition of some of the 'crown jewels'. Although this was said to be but a small portion of the whole treasure house it covered three billiard tables and was closely guarded by a posse of gigantic Sikhs. One piece, presumably worn round the neck to rest on the bosom, consisted of 500 perfect stones in platinum, the centrepiece being a small pink diamond of exquisite clarity. The whole necklace had recently been reset by Cartier of Paris who, apparently, had been unable to put a price on it but thought that the pink stone alone was worth around £50,000 in pre-war currency.

The Maharajah was a suitably magnificent figure who walked among his people like a mediaeval emperor. His son, the Yuvraj, was an equally impressive figure, six foot six in his puggaree, which was always of pink or Cambridge blue. The Yuvraj played against us at Patiala and also in the unofficial Test Matches, and was a fine batsman with a good, flowing style.

At Jamnagar, the home of Ranji's successor, there was a different entertainment. In a clearing in the jungle a goat was tied to a stake and, all being well (except for the goat), a leopard would come and eat it. To enjoy this spectacle we had to sit in a hide in complete silence for a considerable time, as leopards have very acute hearing. As they were also growing scarce only one shot was allowed, and this, of course, was given to the guest of honour. The Jam Sahib's party, including Lionel, sat scarcely breathing for more than two hours but were eventually rewarded by the arrival of a beautiful young leopard which came stalking cautiously but majestically into the arena. The host pressed a musket silently into Lionel's hand, and the great hunter drew a bead on the leopard – and shot the goat dead.

This slight set-back gave all concerned, including the marksman, infinitely more pleasure than the more usual result of a live goat and a dead leopard and, next day, Lionel received a cable from White's Club offering to pay its passage home if he would have the goat stuffed.

Most touring sides have found some difficulty in keeping their members fit and well in India, the diet, the heat and the water all tending to upset the unacclimatized European stomach. In the dark days before antibiotics and such medical aids we were no exception, and midway through the trip we found ourselves with only about ten usable bodies. We were due to play an up-country match at a place I have always referred to as 'Porundapore'. The immediate problem was thus to get a complete side on to the field and, in order to help in this, Alf Gover heroically rose from a bed of sickness to lead the attack. He did not lead it very far. We lost the toss, and Alf started off at a very respectable pace. About his third over a desperate expression compressed his features, and his run-up developed into a wild gallop. He shot past the umpire, the crease, the batsman, and fairly flew up the pavilion steps in a cloud of dust and gravel. We all hoped he made it, and were soon reassured by sounds of primitive plumbing.

This left us one short with no reserve, so there was a delay whilst a junior groundsman was pressed into service. To pass away the time George Pope, our only remaining bowler, and I were idly bowling the ball to and fro when something distracted him and the ball took him smack in the crotch. He went down in a heap and had to be carried off. When the game eventually restarted Lionel was standing in the gully pondering these various disasters when one, Wazir Ali, made the most tremendous square cut. The ball took Lionel a crack on the shin which must have broken a lesser leg and, with a bellow of rage and pain, he shot into the air. When he descended none of his team was able to go to his assistance, not, I regret to say, on account of their various frailities, but because of their callous laughter. The batsman alone ran up to offer his sympathies, but was driven off with blows and curses.

To round off this sombre day we then had a series of truly diabolical decisions. Lionel arrived at the wicket just in time to see Peter Smith given out LBW in making a perfect leg-glance. It was too much. We saw the Lord turn on the umpire and deliver a good old-fashioned broadside which obviously shook the offender to his foundations — so much so that he changed his decision. We were later informed that the address was, in essence, a stupendously phrased enquiry as to whether, having started the day blind, the official was now bereft of his hearing as well.

The cricket went very well on the whole. Four unofficial Test Matches ended in a draw, two-all, and it was decided to play a decider on the newly opened Brabourne Stadium in Bombay. This might have drawn a crowd of 100,000 a day, which would have gone a long way to paying for the stadium. However, as seemed so frequent in Indian affairs, there was a row between the Hindus and the Moslems. So far as we could gather the Hindus had sufficient seats for their own needs, but thought that the Moslems had been allotted too many. So the Hindus boycotted the match and staged a rival match of their own to coincide with the Test. The result was that a paltry thousand spectators came to the stadium, whilst its finances were said to be well in the red.

# TEN

# Partial Recovery - and Captaincy

My complete failure in India seemed, on my return to England, to mark the end of my cricketing days in all but the most modest circles if, indeed, in any active form at all. As things turned out it may be that the Indian sun did some good for, after a cautious start to the 1938 season, I had a partial resurgence. This led to an unexpected return to county cricket and, in time, to the captaincy of Middlesex.

For the first few months after my return I perforce rested, had a lengthy course of massage on the ailing shoulder and, apart from a few tentative nets, remained inactive. During this period my interest was as keen as ever, and I followed the fortunes of the touring Australians as closely as the calls of business would permit. For the Lord's Test of 1938 I had a box on the Father Time stand. The view from this was broadside on, roughly amidships from a vantage point well above the level of the play. The purist may insist on looking end on in order that he may follow every deviation of the ball in flight and from the pitch, but one gets a much better idea of the pace of the bowler and the beauty of the straighter drives and front-of-the-wicket strokes from the side. It is, to my mind, essential to be slightly elevated in order to see the pattern of the field settings and movements of the fielders which contribute so enormously to the spectacle as a whole.

Where that particular match was concerned our position turned out to be absolutely ideal to enjoy to the utmost two enthralling performances. The first was an opening spell of fast bowling by Ernie McCormick who, having at last got his run up in order, shot out Hutton, Barnett and Edrich with just 31 runs scored. All fast bowlers have an optimum spell when everything seems to detonate at that precise moment that the ball leaves the hand, and this was McCormick's.

The second phase was Wally Hammond's tremendous retort to this early catastrophe. Aided by Paynter he added 222 for the next wicket, and then went on to score 240. Once again our vantage point was an ideal one from which to appreciate the full beauty and power of Wally Hammond in full spate, especially through the covers, off back or front foot. As, after this opening flurry, both sides settled in to make large scores, the game soon had the appearance of the inevitable draw, which eventually it was.

In the course of the match I met Sydney Barnes walking round the ground. It may be remembered that our first meeting eight years previously had almost ended in disaster, but now all was forgiven. He came back to the box with me and, over a drink, I asked him what he was doing at the week-end. He replied that he was writing for a Welsh newspaper, and staying in a hotel in Bloomsbury, with no plans of any kind. I asked him how he would like to come to a real cricket match, explaining that Seager Evans was due to play the Bar Tenders Guild on the Sunday, and that it would be quite a day. He smiled and said, 'I'll umpire.'

It must have been a familiar situation to find himself the centre of attraction, and it was one which, on the Sunday, he handled with great charm and dignity. He made the speech of the day after lunch, signed autographs in an impeccable copper-plate, and answered innumerable questions, sensible and otherwise. He then re-affirmed his offer to umpire and, properly arrayed in white coat, proceeded to the middle, adjusted the bails and gave the Bar Tenders' opening batsmen middle and leg. From then on he performed his duties with a painstaking care which everyone appreciated as the ultimate courtesy. When a visiting bowler mildly protested that he had only been given five balls in the over there was a flash of the old spirit. 'I'm umpire,' said the official with an imperious flash of the eye, and the protester conceded the point with bowed head.

It was a glorious opportunity. Every time a wicket fell I fetched the ball, stationed the wicket-keeper, and asked Syd to swing an arm. This he was most willing to do. He was 67 in umpire's coat and trilby hat, but he skipped up five high-stepping strides and his arm sailed over in a beautiful sweep, brushing the brim of his hat as he demonstrated the technique he had explained to me

those many years before at Lord's. When one remembered that, in
his prime, he delivered at fast-medium, it was easy to imagine why
all his generation, and any competent judge who had seen him in
action, considered him supreme.

By this time I had given up any thought of playing serious or
regular cricket but greatly enjoyed the occasional one-day match.
About mid-season Gerald French, the cricketing son of the Field-
Marshal, asked me to play for his MCC team against the National
Provincial Bank which ran a very strong club side. We batted
first to make 189, and by tea they had made about 90 for no wicket.
The batsmen had taken about half their runs off my seamers, which
I loved to bowl with the new ball but which, on a perfect pitch,
were no doubt very friendly. It so happened that Jack Durston, the
old Middlesex fast-bowler, was the umpire at my end and, as we
walked out after tea, he said, 'Have a go with your proper stuff,' at
which I rather reluctantly reverted to spinners. It was one of my
days, and the result was nine wickets in a row for very few runs,
and an unexpected win. Our captain was delighted, and Jack bore
the tidings back to Lord's that I had rediscovered my touch.

Almost immediately Walter Robins asked me to come to Trent
Bridge where Middlesex, having a fair chance of the Championship, had a needle match with Notts. I had always liked Trent
Bridge which, although a beautiful wicket, had a bit of bounce and
pace in it, and I was delighted to pick up seven wickets. The match
had a most feverish end. Batting first we had made Notts follow
on 189 runs behind, and got nine of them out in their second
innings for just over two hundred on the third afternoon. This was
fine, but down the Trent Valley was rolling an enormous black
cloud obviously with the most evil intentions. To our exasperation
the last pair got stuck, and it soon got to be a very finely run thing.
The atmosphere was in a double sense electrical when as a last
resort Walter called for his fast bowler, Jim Smith, and the new
ball. As I threw it to Jim from mid-off, feeling the Championship
might well depend upon it, he looked at it and grinned. 'Look
what the silly buggers have done now,' he said, 'cost the club another thirteen-and-six.' With that he dispatched the last man, and
our batsmen roared home at 43 for 1 as the heavens opened. It
is a sobering reflection that, at modern prices, the silly so-and-so's

would have cost the club around twelve pounds.

My performance at Trent Bridge had re-established me and, with the exception of a most enjoyable visit to Holland with Ronny Stanyforth's MCC side, I played for the rest of the season. By judicious management on Walter's part as well as my own, I lasted the course and topped the bowling averages.

These were some of the happiest days of my active cricket life. I was back with old friends, and doing quite well. I was now older, and having suffered a good deal of disappointment and frustration I was grateful for modest success. There was also the less pleasant possibility that, to judge from the truculent sounds coming from the axis powers, this might be the last cricket season of its kind for many years to come.

As these sounds grew in hostility to the point where war seemed inevitable Jim Swanton and I, as the rest of our generation, felt the time had come to buckle to and join the armed forces. We were anxious to go together and be with congenial company, and as I was very keen to join the London Scottish we made our application. They were very welcoming, but could not find any Scots ancestry for Jim, whilst they were heavily oversubscribed by others who could. We were still considering the situation when Mr Chamberlain returned from his historic mission, and declared it to be 'Peace in our time'. In common with the huge majority we heaved a great sigh of relief and relaxed.

Jim, always competent and well organized, had meantime made a prudent move which was to have great effect upon our military careers at future date. He took me along to the Cavalry Club, and introduced me to Stanley Harris who commanded the 148th Field Regiment RA Bedfordshire Yeomanry. Stanley was a remarkable athlete. He had been heavyweight champion of South Africa, played rugger and Davis Cup tennis for England, and was a first-class horseman and polo player. He said if things should boil up again to contact him in good time. We thanked him, and assured him that we would do so but, with Mr Chamberlain's message ringing in our ears, thought it very unlikely that the situation would ever arise.

At the end of the season of 1938 Walter Robins retired from the Middlesex captaincy. He had taken over in 1935 when the team was in an unsettled state, largely because of the doubts about the

leadership, and he had immediately shown himself to be an out-
standing captain. He started with a thoroughly good cricket education. He was devoted to the game, and knew cricket history so well
that he had a fund of knowledge of the great players of the past,
their strengths and their foibles. This contributed to a naturally
shrewd tactical sense, and on the field he was alert and forceful,
always seeking to keep the game alive, and always ready to take a
chance in order to do so. He expected his players to be of the
same mind and though patient (to a point) with inept triers, he
was fire and brimstone to the slack, selfish or indifferent. His treat-
ment of a very young Compton was typical. In a very short time
Denis had become a wonder boy of cricket, and was subjected to
a degree of adulation that would have turned many a youthful
head. Fortunately he was blessed with a rare temperament. He was
even-tempered, modest and generous, and apparently wholly unaffected by the enormous degree of publicity of which he was the
centre. Like many of such wholly admirable nature he was also
extremely absent-minded, vague, unpunctual, and unmethodical.
This was evident when on the field, the play flagged and the young
hero would be seen to have fallen into a reverie more appropriate
to a monastery than to the midst of Lord's cricket ground. His captain's reactions to his periods of meditation – which usually resulted
in a misfield or failure to have changed at the end of the over –
were rather those of a strict but immensely proud nanny. The culprit was soundly berated in front of all, and sent about his business.
Once, having perpetrated a misfield, he was ordered off in front
of a Bank Holiday crowd to get a cap, although it was obvious
the error had not arisen from dazzle. These rebukes were invariably
received with becoming humility and a disarming apology. Not
long ago Denis said to me that Walter was the best captain he had
ever known.

When invited by the Committee to succeed Walter I was very
conscious of the fact that I was taking on from probably the best
reigning county captain in England. In three of his four seasons
he had brought his side to second place in the Championship.
Although Derbyshire had won in 1936 it was really the high quality
of Yorkshire professionalism which dominated the scene, they also
having an able leader in Brian Sellers, a courageous and thrusting

captain. Apart from giving Yorks a close run for the Championship Walter, in 1937, signified his defiance of this domination by issuing an invitation to a challenge match at the end of the season. The luck ran very much against him and Middlesex were thrashed. At the end of the match there was some community singing. The song rendered by a large, good-natured crowd was: 'Who killed Cock Robin?'

No newcomer to the craft of captaincy could have had better or more agreeable material on which to learn than the Middlesex side of 1939. Fred Price as wicket-keeper and head pro was the only player senior to me in the regular side, and the various amateurs who came in from time to time were naturally very old friends. Everyone was as keen as mustard, and we had no misfits. They all recognized that I was a new boy at the job and, to a man, did all they could to help me.

We had a very happy and fairly successful season, winning 14 and losing 6 of our matches, and once again we ran second to Yorkshire. This was a fair result, but at Lords we might have given them a better run given any sort of luck. As it was they batted throughout Saturday with the sun shining down on a beautiful wicket, and we arrived on Monday to find the sun shining again, but on a rain-soaked pitch. The result was an old-fashioned sticky dog, on which we were twice routed for small scores.

Tom Killick, by then a vicar, returned for the early part of the season. He started with a homeric battle against the Rev. Steele of Hampshire, off whom he made most of a splendid 53. But Providence restored a timely balance amongst its servants when Steele knocked his castle over. Asked what Steele bowled, his fellow priest loyally replied, 'Good old Church of England – straight up and down and no nonsense.'

Our success was founded on the fine aggressive batting of Denis Compton and Bill Edrich, usually given a good start by Jack Robertson and Syd Brown, and well supported by the middle batting, who were always ready to have a go. Jim Smith and Laurie Gray gave us a grand lead with the new ball, and Jim Sims made something of a come-back from a temporary decline. I think I could claim a little credit in the last case, for 'Simmo' was a nervous performer and found Walter strong meat. Knowing something of the tweaker's

problems I gave him plenty of opportunity, and sought to protect
him from the rough left-handed assaults of Maurice Leyland and his
like.

When the Universities came down George Mann joined the side.
His father, Frank, had been my first captain so I felt something
of a link in the Mann dynasty. George was immediately an immense
asset, getting runs when they were most needed, always batting
unselfishly entirely according to the interests of his side. He fielded
magnificently with only one profitless day, at Cheltenham, when he
unaccountably missed two steeple-high catches in the deep. At the
theatre in the evening, that fine old Co-optimist, Davy Burnaby,
rephrased a current song hit and sang, 'Little Mann, you've had a
missy day.'

We had a strange August Bank Holiday match against Sussex at
Hove. In rainy weather we only got three-and-a-quarter hours' play
on the first two days during which we batted and, thanks to Bill
Edrich and George Mann, had scored over two hundred for three
wickets. This was a very comfortable position, but there was a snag.
We were running strongly for the Championship, and the result of
this match was an important matter. A win was unlikely in the
limited time, and it looked as though the match must either be a
draw, which meant a result on the first innings or, under the rules
of the time, 'no result', which meant that the first innings was un-
decided. Under the prevailing method of scoring the county championship, founded on points and a percentage basis, our best result
next to a win would be 'no result', for this would leave our percentage unchanged. A draw, on the other hand, would bring a few
points but would reduce our average and percentage.

The situation seemed to be resolved when on the Tuesday
morning all parties agreed that the ground was unfit for play. But
'Sherlock' Holmes (Flight Lt A. J. Holmes), who was captain of
Sussex, said the crowd had been let in and, it being a festive occasion, he was loath to disappoint them. While sympathizing with
him I explained our position saying that, not only would it be a
betrayal to lessen our chances of the Championship, but there was
always the strong possibility of bowlers and fielders pulling muscles
on the treacherous turf, which might well put paid to our chances
altogether. At length, with some misgivings, I agreed that we would

go through the motions for the sake of the crowd, if he would guarantee a 'no result'. To this he readily agreed, so we batted in the mud, to be all out just before lunch.

When Sussex batted it was evident that some were not privy to our agreement, or were not going to subscribe to it, and despite our efforts to keep them there in mid-afternoon seven were out for 143. 'Sherlock' was a most honourable man and, with Cornford, he stayed for most of the remaining time. But, with half an hour to go, there were nine wickets down and the situation grew progressively more farcical. We kept the last pair there by means of at least one blatantly dropped catch, and were roundly booed off the field. As a final recognition of our accommodating behaviour we were later denounced at the Sussex Annual General Meeting.

'Never give a sucker an even break,' W. C. Fields used to say and, in something of the same spirit, I resolved in future I would offer honeyed words rather than material concessions should any like situations put us at risk again. One learnt the job by hard experience.

A Middlesex colleague hearing this tale of woe cast an interesting sidelight upon it. He said that in 1934 Sussex were well placed for the Championship, just behind Lancashire. A thoughtlessly 'sporting' declaration by Middlesex at Old Trafford gave Lancashire a very narrow win from which they went on to be champions. My friend said that, however friendly particular individuals may have been, Sussex collectively had never forgiven us, and we may well have given them an opportunity for retaliation. There was also a moral to be drawn: if you play in a league, always remember that your generosity in one direction may well be an injustice in another.

From Hove we journeyed to Canterbury where we had another eventful match. It was again a soft wicket and, after some consultation and much thought, I decided to bat. Gerry Weigall, that prince of cricket wind-bags ( a proud and hard-won title, this! ) described my decision as 'pusillanimous', 'criminal' and 'lunatic'. There came to my mind Gerry's friend who had once described him as the most reliable cricket commentator he knew. The glow of satisfaction on Gerry's comely features had faded slightly when his friend added: 'I have only to reverse your opinion diametrically and I can't be very far wrong.' By this token I said that, whatever my doubts, they were now at rest having heard his views. This he took in good part, telling me to 'Wait and see, Sah!'

Everything turned out for the best, and I had the satisfaction of playing a captain's innings. Some may think this a somewhat grandiose term for propping an end up at number eleven but, at the *other* end, Jim Smith made a hundred.

Having a taste for slapstick I have always considered that, for sheer entertainment value, as a batsman Jim was the equal of Woolley, Bradman or Compton, although the pleasure was admittedly fleeting. True, he had but one stroke to add to the galaxy of shots produced by that illustrious trio, but what a stroke it was. The left leg was thrown to mid-on and the striker put all his eighteen stone into a glorious supple, swinging 'Sa-woosh'. Nobody, least of all the batsman, could be certain what direction the ball would take but, if struck, it usually went so high that the prevailing wind would waft it out of the ground, leaving an osteopath's benefit of cricked necks within.

Jim's century, the only hundred he ever made, was, perforce, achieved by this one majestic cleave. That is not to say there was any lack of variety in the results therefrom. If the striker was a bit early it was a pull, if late an off-drive, or occasionally a square-cut, the result being dependent more on the bowler's variations of length and line than the batsman's placing of his stroke.

The first five balls I saw as the non-striker went over the stumps by a narrow margin, and the sixth went far over the trees at square-leg. The bowler, Alan Watt, no mean striker himself, laughed and said he must have got out of bed on the wrong side that morning. Soon we were going splendidly and the game had reached a state of complete chaos. To the spectator the scene must have had a concertina-like air with the field at one moment rushing in to surround me, then flooding back to the farthest confines of the playing area, in the vain hope of a catch, but, in fact, to help the spectators in the search for the ball far beyond. We were thrice interrupted by rain, some thought precipitated by the ball's frequent excursions into the cloud belt, but eventually Jim got to 96. Douglas Wright bowled his quick one short to the off, and Jim delivered a massive blow at it, aiming, I would think, somewhere about long-off. Since, however, this time he was late, the result was a tremendous square-cut, and there stood the hero, grinning hugely and trying to look as he'd meant it, 100 not out. What must have been one of the most improbable of all last wicket stands was described by a delighted Weigall as 'a prostitution of the art of batting'.

We won this match, but went down to Surrey and Gloucester the same month, so finished second for the fourth time running, but well behind Yorkshire. In material terms this was certainly as well as I had expected we should do. I missed the last match against Warwickshire, for the international situation had now become so menacing that Jim Swanton and I had gone to the nearest recruiting office and signed up. We were enrolled for a searchlight unit of the RA, which was something of a come-down from the London Scottish but, with the great surge of volunteers, was one of the few formations still in need of immediate recruits. We had expected to be pressed into service right away, but were sent home and told to report immediately to the Uxbridge headquarters should there be any emergency.

Everyone was extremely kind about the season, the side and my first venture as a county captain, but I knew that there was an awful lot to be learnt. Even had I mastered the mechanics of my craft I was obviously not of the stuff of Warner and Robins, but the side seemed happy and quite willing to continue under existing arrangements. With Edrich, Compton, Robertson, Mann and Brown all young, and much good service still to be had from Smith and Sims, we had fine prospects ahead, and my greatest regret is that we never had the chance to develop our promise to the full.

# ELEVEN

# The (Not So) Good Soldier

On the morning of 1 September 1939 James Swanton woke me with the news that the Germans had invaded Poland, and added, 'We're off.' We duly reported at Uxbridge and, after a few quiet days, this stage of our soldierly venture was ended by a telegram from Stanley Harris, saying that he had arranged for us to be commissioned into the Bedford Yeomanry. They were stationed at Dunstable, and there we journeyed to throw ourselves into the science of field gunnery. Shortly afterwards we moved to Great Yarmouth.

After an inadequately short spell, during which I sought to add some military knowledge to an undistinguished career in the school OTC, I was entrusted with the 'intake' – 300 recruits from a wide variety of places and backgrounds. They were a grand lot, and my conscience smote me when I reflected that my military qualifications were not much greater than theirs. However, I was very fit and so, whilst experienced NCOs taught them the arts of square-bashing, I could train with them. We boxed, heaved a medicine ball around, swam, and paddled in the ocean to harden our feet.

The winter of 1939 was one of the hardest for years, but we weathered it comfortably in our cosy billets in the best hotel in the town. Spring came and together with the rest of the population we were rudely jolted into realization that the Germans were ensconced in the Channel Ports and Britain was now fighting on her own.

Not all were immediately aware of this. I broke the news to a very popular naval officer who, apart from being extremely deaf, had been absent on leave and not heard of the disaster. Over a pink gin I said, 'It's a pity about the French.'

'Eh – what's the matter with them?' he boomed.

'They've packed in,' I bellowed in reply, somewhat surprised. For a moment he seemed slightly crestfallen, but soon brightened. 'No damn good, these allies,' he said, 'far better get out on the sea – shoot first then ask "who were you?"'

I refrained from suggesting that this might lead to certain diplomatic complications in order to save wear and tear on my vocal chords.

Meanwhile all about us was feverish preparation. Tales of parachuting nuns and other diabolical fifth column activities were rife. Conferences were called between the services and the civilian authorities. One senior Home Guard officer was considerably deafer than my old naval friend, so on arrival at an important meeting he failed to hear the clarion tones of our well-trained sentry's challenge and drove past him. The sentry promptly put a bullet into the back panel of his Austin 7. It emerged through the windscreen, right in front of the startled driver's eyes. His indignation delayed the conference some minutes whilst he berated our CO. 'Can't pull these little prams up in two yards,' he said, then sternly voiced the burden of his complaint. 'Had me old bitch lyin' in the back,' he said, 'she's *usually* sittin' up.'

In truth our troop was in no position to sneer at any shortcomings in these military preparations. For some days we were laboriously engaged in constructing a tank-trap across the main road, on the lines laid down in the manual. When finished it looked splendid, but no hostile tank came our way and it was left to a local publican to put it to the test. Deep in wine, he rammed us with his Austin 7 (a frequent and seemingly fateful model in those parts) in the dusk of the evening. The damage to him was the removal of his hat and spectacles and a slightly stoved-in radiator. The damage to our tank-trap was total; and it was with heavy and sceptical heart we turned again to the manual.

Meanwhile I learnt little about gunnery, and soon this became a decisive factor in my unpromising career. At a shooting camp my misjudgment of range, combined with the battery's unfortunate choice of the wrong charge, resulted in our nearly blowing up the CRA. This was a not unpopular gesture in some quarters, but from then on I was a marked man. When the chance of a job in the London district came up I jumped at it. This was at the height of the Blitz, so one could serve in London with an easy conscience knowing it was then the front line. Mr Chamberlain had said at one time that it was 'better to be bored than bombed'. This bromide was of doubtful truth when the contrast was one of deadly boredom in the wilds and participation, however modest, in the wonderful spirit of London. Moreover, the International Sportsmen's Club struggled on, so there was squash and companionship, for all the members turned up on leave at one time or another.

Although delighted to escape to a more active sphere I had many regrets on leaving Norfolk. I was sorry to leave Jim, but had seen little of him lately, as we were stationed in different districts. He was a good soldier, and seemed likely to have a successful wartime career. Over the course of that year I had also become fond of Stanley Harris. We played squash together, trained and ran together and I occasionally acted as his sparring partner. He was splendid company and had the type of bantering humour I had always enjoyed. Off parade we were quite informal, and Jim and I would gently attack his conceits and vanities – which were many, and wholly innocuous. He would give as good as he got any time. When he left he said that I was deserting him, but we always remained the best of friends.

My own new career was uneventful until I went to bed in my office in Queensgate on 10 May 1941. I had scarcely put the light out when an ugly report from the other side of the wall announced that the adjoining house had received a direct hit from an oil bomb. Comforted by the thought that lightning never strikes twice in the same place I pulled on some clothes and went downstairs. There was little we could do except shut what windows were left until the arrival of the fire brigade, and I joined a knot of helpers, including a policeman, on the pavement. Suddenly there was an enormous crash and (I think) a bright blue flash, and the next moment I was lying flat on my back – just where I didn't know. My first concern was that I was blind, the affliction I had always most feared. I called out, saying that I could not see and asking if anyone was about; but the only response was a hollow groaning, which presently ceased altogether. Instinctively I rubbed my eyes and, to my immense relief, I had the partial view of the moon, coloured red, and I realized that my 'blindness' was the result of my own blood running down my face.

The night was extremely noisy, with the thump and crack of the ack-ack batteries and the periodical detonation of heavy bombs, but in my vicinity there was a profound silence. The acrid smell of high explosive was intense and, as the dust still hung heavily over everything and but one of my eyes functioned, and then only in a blurred way, I had great difficulty in seeing. I wondered if I had been knocked out, and left behind by the others in the dust and dark. It seemed that I must look to myself, and I remembered that across the road from us was a section of military police. As I could at least totter, I made for this sanctuary, rapped on the door, and presently someone opened it and let go a startled 'Christ Almighty!' before ushering me in. I was in no great pain, so I said I probably looked worse than I was, but would like some place safe for a while. The MP called his corporal, whom I later learned was named Hubbard, a first-class man who bound me up and called an ambulance.

Everyone had read about the courage and efficiency of London's services, and maybe thought that a certain amount of propaganda was understandably introduced into the press accounts to encourage morale. I was about to see for myself a demonstration that fills me with pride to this day.

An ambulance arrived, driven by a WAC and crewed by several rather small women. They already had a few 'cases' aboard, but I was lifted in with care and efficiency and off we went. It was a dirty, noisy night with bombs and shrapnel all around, and these women had answered a fair number of calls already. They tended the wounded, took messages for relatives, and unloaded us on arrival at a hospital, all as though it was a peace-time exercise. This done, off they set again.

I was soon lying on a bed, with a pretty red-headed nurse trying to get my shoes off. Suddenly there came an ugly whistling sound, and a stick of bombs fell across the hospital. The last of the stick made a tremendous concussion, and all the ward windows were blown in. When the din had subsided my nurse popped out from under the bed, where she had taken cover, and joined the others in cleaning up and putting brown paper over the shattered windows. In the midst of this the matron, looking much like her counterpart

in 'Emergency Ward 10', or similar TV drama, came in, bustling
but calm. 'Come along, girls,' she said, 'hurry up with those black-
outs,' her tone that of the form mistress happening on a beano
in the dorm. In a trice they had the black-outs up and were back
at work.

As the boiler had been burst by the same bomb I was the last
case to which the surgeons were able to attend. The anaesthetist I
was able to greet as an old Oxford friend, Reggie Nissam, but our
civilities were interrupted by the surgeon who berated him for being
late – and then forgave him on learning Reggie had been knocked
flat by a door which had blown in on him just as he was about to
open it. Reggie's assistant was his fiancée, a secretary who was
pressed into service owing to the shortage of staff.

I woke up in the Royal Masonic Hospital, one half of which
was then commandeered by the services, and there spent a happy
two months. Each day my wounds were immaculately and painlessly
dressed by Sister King and, should this ever catch her eye, I would
like to underline my gratitude for her patience and skill. It was a
beautiful summer, and I used to lie out in the sun on a balcony,
there to receive a great number of visitors. By way of entertaining
them I had a tame sparrow. He was big and decidedly fat, and,
when first we met, eyed me thoughtfully from the railing whenever
I had anything to eat. Thence he advanced to the end of the bed
and soon, at the rattle of a tray, he would arrive and sit on my
thumb, however many visitors happened to be present. His girl-
friend would sit shyly on the railing, doubtless fretting at his
reckless behaviour; when he had eaten his fill he would take her a
few crumbs. On my departure I bequeathed him to a naval officer
in the next bed.

As soon as I could travel I went on a month's sick leave to the
Manse of Birnie, an ideal place to convalesce. It was a delightful
house, and the surrounding countryside had an unchanging tranquillity. Being in the midst of the finest distilling country in the
world I did not lack for medical comforts. From then on I made
a fast recovery, and finally found myself in perfect bodily health,
but blind in one eye, bar a peep, deaf in one ear, slightly damaged
in the left leg and foot, and slightly scarred about the head. A
medical board decided that these imperfections had reduced me to

8 and 9. The hopeful age. Bowling quick-medium in South Africa, 1927.

10. With two old Middlesex friends, Greville Stevens and Nigel Haig, about to take the field at Old Trafford.

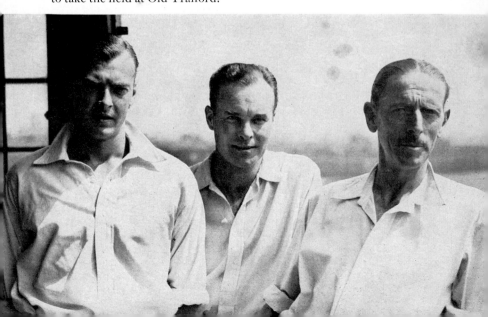

11. In the presence of the prophet. My fingers twitch as I listen to Sydney Barnes. Ronny Aird, then Secretary of MCC, is in the background.

12. Alastair's christening in 1948. Jim Swanton and Gubby Allen flank proud parents. Colonel and Mrs H.P. Hopkinson are the other godparents.

C3 on the medical scale. I was told quite frankly that there was no prospect of improvement in any of these injuries, and that I was lucky in that I had only kept my eye because of the devoted skill of the specialist, one Henry Cardell. This meant that my war would now be chairborne to the end. I had to admit that my military career had deserved little better.

On emerging into the world again I made a round of calls to all concerned without whom, I was told, I would not have survived for long. My immediate saviour was Corporal Hubbard who, it turned out, was a motor-cycle patrolman for the RAC in peacetime, and who had fortunately made a habit of keeping his first-aid kit handy. With Reggie Nissam and his fiancée I adjourned to their local, and the lady told me that she had never been in an operating theatre in her life until that night. She had been too busy, she said, to have time to feel squeamish.

From our ARP people I learnt that it had been a 2000-lb bomb which landed in the same hole as the oil bomb. There had been forty of us and, so far as they knew, I was the only survivor. I was slightly chilled to hear that all they found of my policeman friend was his head, and that was thirty yards from where we had been standing. No wonder there had been no response when I had called out for help. They consoled me by telling me that I probably held a European record for, in their experience, no one had ever got so near to a 2000-pounder and survived. The experts were chiefly interested to know whether or not I had heard the whistle as it dropped, and I was able to assure them that we had had no such warning.

By the next summer I was fit enough to play a game of cricket at Lord's. The match was the Army against Oxford University, and the wartime bowling being friendly I made fifty-odd not out. This modest success greatly excited a senior MCC member, who accosted 'Beau' Vincent, *The Times* cricket correspondent, saying, 'For many years, sir, I have said that this game should be played with one eye.' He waved a hand in the direction of the match. 'Now look at this chap,' he said. 'He was no good, he's not much good now – but he's *better*.'

The other match I remember that year at Lord's was the Army *v* the Royal Navy. I remember it because it gave rise to another

story concerning Maurice Leyland – always a happy thought. In
the role of Sergeant Leyland he had just played himself in when
the Navy made a bowling change. Their choice was a gallant
mariner, straight off the Arctic convoy, who bowled leg-tweakers.
As the nearest thing he had seen to a cricket ball for the previous
six months had been a wide variety of missiles a great deal more
lethal, it was not surprising that he was a bit out for range and line.
The first ball sailed high over the heads of Sgt Leyland and the
wicket-keeper for four byes. The second took cover point on the
knee-cap. The square-leg umpire collected the third, but the fourth
was relatively straight. It arrived third bounce at Sgt Leyland's
block hole and he, being the kindest of men, made a gesture of
playing it. In fact he scooped it very gently into mid-off's hands.
As he went on his way, tugging off his gloves, a thought crossed his
mind and he addressed the catcher. 'You know,' he said, 'ah doan't
get mooch practice against that stoof.' He was a wonderful chap.
RIP.

Cricket had become a difficult game for me as, although I could
see the ball, it was difficult to judge its pace or position. I thought
of my old friend and opponent, Buster Nupen, a magnificent bowler
on the mat and a very fair batsman despite a glass eye. It was explained to me that the eyes work as a range finder, converging as
an object gets close. In the case of a person who loses an eye,
as Buster did, at a very early age, he develops a different process
whereby he judges speed and distance by the expansion and con-
traction of his optical muscles. Whether this is true or not I do not
know, but it was clear that I was too old a dog to learn new tricks.

Squash I found was much easier as, apart from the shorter
ranges, I could measure the position of the ball against the side
walls and, on a flat, firm surface, I could move pretty well. Squash
generally was a great boon, and kept all us desk-workers very fit.
Although a very moderate player I had two great moments in my
squash career, the first being in wartime. An old friend and frequent opponent, Colonel Frank ('Froggy') Reed of the American
Army, rang me up one day and said, 'I'm playing a husband this
evening, would you mind playing the wife?' I grumbled rather at
that, saying I wanted a hard work-out to counter a couple of days'
inertia. The old rascal made no comment on that and, feeling rather

gallant, I accepted. It was not until Mrs Gordon had turned up early and we were about to take the court that he revealed she was *née* Margot Lumb, a name I recognized as a Wimbledon tennis player, and a world champion squash player. I tottered back utterly routed and exhausted to find Froggy still awaiting his opponent, but sniggering happily at my 'hard work-out'. However, to fill in the time, Margot then took him on and presently he returned in a cloud of steam, to announce defeat and confusion. At that moment her husband Bill, an army squash champion in his own right, arrived and confidently met our complaints by saying that he could 'always put her in her place', a claim which, in this instance, was smartly disproved.

An early arrival with the American forces was Dick Vidmer who, in civil life, had been a famous sports journalist on a New York newspaper. We saw a lot of each other as his headquarters were in London not far from ours. We would often dine, and I would sit up listening enthralled to his tales of Jack Dempsey and Joe Louis, Babe Ruth, Tilden, and all the other American sporting celebrities. A bit later he was joined in his billet by Bobbie Jones, who had abandoned all golfing activity to devote himself to his duties as a major in the American Air Force.

The first time he introduced me to Bobbie Jones we all went out to dine. Presently Bobbie turned to me and said, 'What's a yorker?' I did my best to explain an almost inexplicable phenomenon to a non-cricketer. However, he listened attentively, then said, 'What's a maiden over?' This was somewhat simpler, and when I had done I asked him how he came to know these terms. He told me that when he did his grand slam in 1930 he always had breakfast in bed at the Savoy, during which he read *The Times*. He had happened on the Test series, and was immediately fascinated by the terms and figures. Thereafter he followed the play daily with much interest, although of what actually took place he had no idea. He could also recall many of the names but not, as I remember, mine. Soon after he was posted abroad, but he left an impression of one of the most truly unaffected of any celebrities or champions I ever met.

Some time afterwards Joe Louis came over to entertain the American troops, and Dick introduced me to him. He was taking part in a demonstration of combined sports at the White City and boxed three exhibition rounds daily. Not surprisingly, he had some difficulty finding sparring partners for, even just sparring with 'pillows' on his mitts, he must have taken a certain amount out of his opponents. His power was demonstrated when a behemoth described as the 'Heavyweight Champion of Jamaica' got into the ring with him. After a bit the 'Champion' started to stir things up and caught the real champion with a couple of heavy punches. Joe, who had been coasting gently along, peered at him in mild surprise, then let go two or three short snappy digs with either hand, at which the giant's frame shuddered as his legs buckled, and the champ relapsed into his absent-minded shuffle.

It was after this entertainment that I had the honour to introduce the brothers Bedser to the champion, whose eyes lit up on seeing them. 'That's a big fella,' he quipped, as the two brothers stood together, almost wholly identical. Afterwards I heard from Alec that he tried to interest them as boxers in his camp, but the twins, shrewd men, stuck to their cricket.

Dick still carried out occasional assignments for his paper, his last one being to interview a Polish ex-world champion of chess, then living in Hampstead. The formal interview complete, the champion indicated a chess board all set out, and asked Dick if he would like to play. Dick said it would be a great honour, and down they sat. The Master viewed Dick's opening gambit with considerable surprise, and the second he studied with obvious astonishment for a lengthy period before replying. Dick then moved another piece. 'Hey,' said his host, 'you can't move a castle in that direction.' 'I wouldn't know,' replied Dick, 'I've never played before.'

My remaining war days passed pleasantly, billeted in Kensington Palace Gardens. I found I had developed a certain allergy to old-fashioned bombs, but reckoned that with the buzz bombs one always had a sporting chance if, abandoning all dignity, one took a dive into the nearest basement. On one occasion, in 1944, I was at Lord's sitting on the players' balcony with Gubby Allen, who was captaining the Army against the RAF. The sinister rumble of another of Adolf's infernal machines was suddenly audible, and soon increased to a crescendo. Gubby pointed up at an adjacent thick cloud and, raising his voice, said, 'I reckon it's just in there.' There was an abrupt silence followed by a sinister whistle. The players threw themselves down and everyone who could sought shelter. The public could only sit and await the arrival of this monster in their midst. In the event it fell 200 yards short, but it made a fair concussion, and we felt a strong blast at that range. There was a slight pause, the crowd laughed in relief and Jack Robertson arose and knocked Bob Wyatt into the Father Time stand for six.

Dick Twining, who had a flair for extracting bizarre comedy from the most mundane situation, was standing in the Long Room beside a very short and immensely stout man truly rather higher in his prone position than when he was standing upright. After the bomb had passed, the members had arisen, and the laughter and chat had subsided Dick became aware of a sinister and regular 'tick-tock' from behind the table. On investigation he found it was his fat friend, who had 'dived' to the floor, and who was now see-sawing like a rocking stone on his enormous belly. The 'tick-tock' was the alternate tapping of the rim of his hat and the toes of his shoes on the parquet as he strove to arise. Dick said the bellow of laughter which greeted this spectacle may have dented the gentleman's feelings and delayed his rescue for a few moments, but it was a complete restorative for all the others present.

Lord's survived the war with a few bruises from the Luftwaffe, but Father Time had the indignity of being dragged from his position on top of the Grand Stand by the cable of an escaped barrage balloon. Sir Pelham Warner acted as Secretary to the club and ground he loved most in the world and, with the whole-hearted support of Mr Stanley Christopherson, President for the duration, performed prodigies in the face of wartime difficulties. Jimmy Cannon, head clerk, who had arrived as office boy when Disraeli was Prime Minister, was indefatigable, blaming every disaster not directly attributable to the Axis powers on 'them Surrey members' who were affiliated in wartime. Many cricketers, in various parts of the globe, must have dreamt, as Jack Stephenson of Essex did in the desert, that he had gone to Heaven and was playing at Lord's.

Towards the end of my stay at the Masonic Hospital I had been invited to Lord's for a Services' match, and was given a special dispensation by the chief surgeon. It was a laborious journey, as I was still on crutches, and my head was swathed in bandages, only my right eye being visible. As I mounted the pavilion steps I collided with a senior MCC member whom I knew well by sight from years past as he always sported a yellow waistcoat and a grey bowler. As we recoiled he surveyed my 'props' with mild astonishment. 'Had an accident, young fellow?' he queried. I knew I was back in my spiritual home.

# TWELVE

# Civvy Street to City Square

The first six weeks of 'freedom' I spent blissfully at Birnie, lazing, reading and breathing the good air. It was then time to return to London and address myself to the immediate problem of earning a living. The alternatives open to me were to return to my pre-war occupation with Ladbrokes and Seagers or to start up again with Hans and resuscitate Rhine Wines Ltd.

The choice was really made for me by Herbert Ross, who had taken a kindly interest in my affairs ever since I had been blown up, and was ready and willing to help Hans and myself restart. But there was an obstacle. On parting with Seagers Henry Horne had assigned his shares in our company to an associate which, strictly speaking, was a breach of our Articles of Association. Herbert was unwilling to move until we had rid ourselves of this encumbrance, and we were naturally reluctant to give a third of the profits to one who could not contribute to them. The shareholder, a very reasonable man, was helpful and accepted our modest offer of compensation without argument, so enabling us to re-establish the firm under the name of 'Walter S. Siegel, Ltd'. Herbert took over the available third of the shares and, in addition to this infusion of capital, gave us material help in the shape of supplies.

The scotch whisky trade was at that time in an interesting state. In 1939 a gallon of new whisky, known in the trade as 'new fillings', cost between 2/- a gallon for grain whisky to 4/6 for the finest malt. There was hardly any distilling during the war, so mature whisky in the broker's market had by 1947 reached the record price of 420/- a gallon in bond, which is to say before duty had been paid on it. Anyone who had stocks of whisky and the foresight to hang on to them saw their value increase by 150 times over these eight years. This prosperity naturally attracted some 'wide' practitioners to the trade, but the great bulk of these stocks were held by established traders.

Not unexpectedly there were some strange twists of fortune. Sam Coulter, Herbert's partner and close friend, died during the war before the price had peaked, but his holding of whisky, valued at £5000 before the war, realized £250,000, so that he died much richer than he ever lived. The tale went that when at the sale of his stock the price reached £10 a gallon a veteran of the trade fainted, and was revived with a glass of cold water. Because of the cure, rather than the malady, he was never quite the same again.

The most ironical of fortune's eccentricities befell an Invernesian family. The bachelor brother had a small business which he had built up for many years, buying new whisky with the profits and storing it away. This practice was greatly made possible by the frugality of the proprietor who lived in digs at 30/- a week, read the newspapers in the public library and, when he played golf, brought his own dram, a thimbleful of whisky drawn from a duty-free sample bottle. He died just after the war and the estate was due to go to his sister, of whom it was said her parsimony made her brother look like a spendthrift. Neighbours, knowing he had a drop of whisky, asked her what she expected to get. 'My,' she said, 'if I get twenty thousand pounds it will be far beyond my wildest dreams.' Herbert Ross and another major broker together bought the old man's whisky stock. The sum they paid was £745,000.

It may be realized from these examples how fortunate one was to be admitted to the trade at that point. We set up our office in two rooms in Billiter Street on the third floor. There was no lift, but our elevation had an unforeseen merit. When winter came in its grimmest form for years, and Mr Shinwell 'shed the load' (then a euphemism for switching everything off), we had to sit muffled in overcoats, but at least we had a little daylight. The troglodytes beneath us also sat muffled up, but they peered mole-like at their documents by the light of candles stuck in bottles, a drip at the end of their purple noses, but grateful to have a candle. The empty bottles must have struck a particularly poignant note for them, knowing that, by virtue of our trade, we above had the advantage here as well, in the shape of an occasional warming dram.

The wine trade was not without its problems. All supplies were strictly rationed, the allocation based on the amounts shipped in the three years prior to the war. This was not a profitable basis for us, as we had just started out, but we managed to get a few hogs-heads of Algerian wine and various odds and ends. The attitudes of individuals in the trade towards us, as returning with only a short pre-war history, varied considerably. Most were welcoming but, in several instances, we sensed resentment at the reappearance of a possible rival. The great thing was to find anything to sell, and the art of salesmanship was the avoidance of being trampled to death in the rush resulting from any sort of offer. We had a splendid champion in Colonel Ian Campbell, who personified the traditional Highland gentleman, as proud a title as man could have. He was an authority on claret, and a much respected figure in the trade. His brother had won a VC in 'Q' ships in the first war and his son, Lorne, had won a VC in the Argyll and Sutherland Highlanders in the second. Given the opportunity the Colonel would doubtless have done the same, but amongst many distinctions he did actually achieve was that of opening the innings with W.G. at the Crystal Palace on many occasions.

He was held in equally high esteem in his native Argyll where, amidst innumerable Campbells, he was known as Campbell of Airds. In such high esteem was he held, in fact, that he was invited to unveil a Macdonald War Memorial, which caused some surprise amongst the clansmen. The Minister who conducted the service, a good Macdonald, had no doubts as to why the Colonel had been chosen. 'You would be Campbell of Airds,' he said, which Colonel Ian acknowledged. The Minister explained he had known this must be so because a Campbell of Airds had saved some of the Mac-donalds after Campbell of Glen Lyon had perpetrated the Massacre of Glencoe which, after all, was only 300 years ago.

After my up-and-downer with the bomb there was no question of my playing serious first-class cricket again, and I resigned the captaincy of Middlesex early in October 1945. By a stroke of good luck Walter Robins was available and willing to do a couple of seasons as captain in order to get the club established again. He kindly asked me to play a few matches, partly to help out, as he was short-handed at first, and partly for old times' sake. I played about half-a-dozen games with great pleasure but to little effect, and then happily made way for younger and fitter men. My last wicket in county cricket was Maurice Leyland, caught by Jack

Robertson at Lord's. It cannot in the nature of things have been a very deadly ball and, Maurice also being fairly spent, it probably wasn't a very good shot; but I could not have finished in better company.

That my last home match for Middlesex was against Yorkshire had for me a particular significance. Every county had its attractions and I have wonderful memories of our matches against them, but to play against Yorkshire seemed to epitomize all the joys and tribulations that go to make up the game. It may strike some as a strange choice but for anyone who had the stomach for a keen battle, liked serious cricket and wanted a good belly laugh from time to time, it was a combination of all the pleasures I have described.

In the first place it was stimulating to see such a splendid cricket side in action, complete in every department, and imbued with a fiercely clannish spirit. Everyone was beautifully turned out, like the polished parts of a perfectly adjusted machine – which in fact it was – and all were characters, some on the grand scale, and not one without something to offer. It is not surprising that most of the good cricket stories come from the north of England, for from these characters flowed unbounded entertainment. There was much good wit and grand humour, some intended, some unconscious.

On the grand scale were Wilfred Rhodes and Emmott Robinson, of unfathomable knowledge, fanatical zeal for cricket and for Yorkshire, and gravely serious outlook. Their attitudes were illuminated by Wilfred's rebuke in later years, when coach at Harrow, to one of his impetuous young charges who hit several sixes in making a hundred. 'You doan't play this game for foon,' warned the Oracle. Emmott's underlying kindness of heart shone through his tough attitude to duty in his verdict on a very nervous amateur. 'Eeh,' said he, 'it's a reet shame that sooch a nice gentleman as Mr – should have to play cricket at all.'

There was the apt and occasionally ferocious wit of George Macaulay, whose interests were quick off-spinners and classical music. I quote a random example of a thousand sallies. When he threw his shoulder out he was taken to a local hospital where his roars of rage and pain attracted a visit from the matron. 'On the floor above, Mr Macaulay,' she said reproachfully, 'a young girl has just given birth to twins without a murmur.' 'Aye,' said

George, unimpressed. 'But have you tried putting 'em back?'

I thought I knew all the Macaulayisms until I had the inestimable pleasure of sitting next to Wilfred on his ninetieth birthday. He was blind, loquacious, and absorbingly interesting. He recalled taking the field in 1923 after reading about the disastrous fire which had completely destroyed Madame Tussaud's wax works. In Macaulay's two opening overs his slips Holmes, Sutcliffe and Kilner each dropped a sitter, at which the bowler addressed them from thirty yards away, 'When Madame Tussaud wants a set of bludy slips,' he bawled, 'I'll know where to find 'em.'

Of the apt good-natured wit of Maurice Leyland I have written earlier and would bracket with him Arthur Wood who, going in at the Oval when England were 770 for 6, came out when the score was 876 for 7. The plaudits of the members he gracefully acknowledged, modestly remarking, 'Ah was always woon for t'crisis.'

Finally, a treasured memory of making nought in the first innings for MCC against Yorkshire, and rashly boasting that I had never 'bagged 'em'. The elaborate courtesy with which I was received second innings was accompanied by polite enquiries as to whether I had ever previously made a pair, and observations that I now had a grand chance and a 'luvly morning for it'.

We had a glorious three minutes in which there were several massed choruses as all appealed whenever I missed the ball. My old Yorkshire friend and partner Bill Bowes, playing for MCC (no doubt reluctantly), did his best to run me out, but eventually I got four off the edge and a profound silence fell on the company. It was broken by another old friend, Ticker Mitchell. 'Mr Peebles,' he said, 'tha's spoilt bludy morning.'

But if the Yorkshiremen were a comprehensive entertainment in themselves there was character and fun wherever one turned. George Gunn, bored, asking the Leicester slips what shot they would like him to play to the next ball, and faithfully carrying out all request items. Phil Mead cajoled into bowling one very reluctant over by a desperate captain, and mortified when he took a wicket lest it should lead to further effort. The uncontrollable mirth of the Yorkshiremen when Wilfred was struck thrice into the Lord's pavilion by Frank Mann, and his infuriated, rhetorical question, 'What the bludy 'ell are you laffing at?' The first-class umpires' list, Reeves, Burrows, Skelding, George Brown (who got the new LBW law the wrong way round and caused widespread chaos), and a dozen others, the salt of wit and of the earth, a treasure house for the connoisseur. The eloquent martyrdom of O'Reilly when snicked for four, and the pungent speeches of Aussies on various subjects.

To anyone who should want to relish again the flavour of these times I commend the writings of Raymond Robertson-Glasgow, as fresh and vivid today as when he first delighted in the sayings and doings of Sammy Woods, or the captain of his prep school second XI. That he was always affectionately known as 'Crusoe' was due to his first meeting with one of the rich subjects he etched with kind and accurate pen. Charlie McGahey, another man of good will, returned to the Essex dressing-room having made a swift nought against Somerset. 'What happened?' asked his successor, scrambling to complete his arrangements. 'Bowled first ball by a bugger I thought was dead three hundred years ago,' said Charlie, 'Robinson Crusoe.'

At the beginning of August 1946 Ronny Stanyforth took an MCC team to Germany to play a few matches against various army formations in Germany, including the Army of the Rhine. In addition to Ronny there was a nice array of veterans with Gubby Allen, my brother-in-law Claude Taylor, and myself. Our opening batsmen Jack MacBryan and Dick Twining totalled 108 years between them, and did us proud. They usually provided a sound start but, what with the liberal Army hospitality and very hot weather, they were sooner or later liable to be blinded by sweat, having run like two-year-olds between the wickets.

Jack – who had been a prisoner of war thirty years before – had an eventful trip. A British officer had gone into a house in Germany not long before our arrival and, above the mantelpiece, had spotted a British officer's sword. On closer inspection he espied the initials 'J.C.W.MacB.' He requisitioned the sword, saying that he knew the owner, and later we had a small ceremony, when the finder restored the property to its original owner.

Whether it was in celebration of this, or just because he was determined to enjoy himself after the restrictions of post-war

England, Jack turned up late for a Mess dinner one evening. It was obvious that he had been enjoying himself and, beaming with goodwill, he sat himself down in one of the empty chairs. It was unoccupied because in the next seat was a strait-laced and not very popular general. MacBryan was undeterred, and embarked on what he doubtless regarded as the start of a beautiful friendship by enquiring, in old-fashioned terms, whether the general's sexual desires were being adequately met. The General managed a very wintry smile. 'I *am* a married man,' he said. 'No, no, no,' rejoined MacBryan, 'I didn't mean that – I meant rogering round the town.' After this brilliant opening conversation between the two rather faltered.

The tour was great fun as far as the cricket and the hospitality was concerned. The Army deservedly did better than those at home, as wine, liqueurs and beer were relatively plentiful and service rations were a good, robust diet. The two finest hotels in Hamburg, the Atlantic and the Four Seasons, had miraculously escaped destruction and were occupied by the forces, and, after some rough travel in a German troop-carrying bus and living in some fairly crowded billets, here we were duly lodged. The destruction about us was inevitably depressing, but we could only admire the way in which the inhabitants were already tackling the work of reconstruction.

At Hamburg we played on the beautiful polo ground at Kleinflotbek on the outskirts of the city on a tolerable turf wicket. The groundsman was a German who had swotted up MCC regulations, which he observed to the finest detail. When play started he would sit looking the other way until the end of the innings when he would rush on and address Ronny in German. Gubby, the great linguist, said he was saying '*mit der brosser*', and wanted to sweep the pitch, so Ronny would always reply '*Ya. Ya – mit der brosser.*' It wasn't till the end of the trip we learnt that what in fact he was saying was: '*mit der kleiner oder der grosser?*' and wanted to know which roller we required. Thus, whatever the state of the pitch, we always had the heavy roller.

Under Hans's competent direction the firm of Walter S. Siegel prospered. Having launched us into the whisky trade Herbert Ross maintained his interest, aiding us with supplies and giving us a shrewd word of guidance from time to time. We acquired the agencies for England of a number of distilleries, Fettercairn, Bladnoch, Auchentoshan and Bruichladdich, the last two good twisters for the Sassenach tongue. Although my parents had moved to the south in the early '50s I kept my connections with Speyside, and the highland distillers generally, and twice yearly would make the grand tour, going first for a few days to Herbert Ross in his house on Loch Long. Having done my business in the lowlands I would travel north where Ursula would often join me, and we would do our Highland tour, ending with a week in Sutherland with my cousin Hilda and her family. She had married Alan McCall, a Cameron Highlander who had captained Wellington at cricket, been taken prisoner at St Valery in 1940, and now farmed extensively with his brother. As we travelled I would visit all the distilleries with whom we dealt, which made for the very best of that time-honoured combination, business and pleasure.

Hans and, before him, his father, had done business with the Swedish State Monopoly for many years in German wines and, not long after the war, the connection was renewed when Gustaf Bergendal, the senior director, called at our office. He was in search of whisky, and through our Scottish connections we were able to supply a certain amount at a time when extra supplies were almost unobtainable. From this start we built up a very good business over the years, extending our operations to the neighbouring monopolies of Norway and Finland, and twice a year Hans and I would travel to Helsinki, Stockholm and Oslo. Acquaintanceships founded on business ripened into personal friendships, especially in Stockholm, where the Minister and the directors with their wives and families would entertain us in their homes, and we would ask them to dine with us in one or other of the many first-class restaurants in Stockholm.

At one party given by the Chairman of the Monopoly, who was also a Minister of the Crown, the host welcomed us with a speech in Swedish, his daughter giving us a running translation. She said that her father, on behalf of the King, was conferring on Hans and myself the Order of Vasa, a fine Swedish honour. We thought he must be joking, but it turned out to be perfectly serious and the reward had been awarded for our services to the Monopoly. To bestow on us such a distinction, besides giving us their valuable business, seemed the height of generosity. On returning home we were mildly discouraged to receive a letter from the appropriate department saying the insignia must not be worn in Britain except on occasions when Swedish royalty or their ambassador was present. An official explained apologetically that this prohibition was based on an edict of Elizabeth I who ordained that her dogs would only wear her collars. The restrictions have now been relaxed but, living in retirement in these informal times, there are few opportunities of displaying what is a very handsome decoration.

There was in our track another particularly agreeable combination of business and pleasure. Early in our return to the trade we had invited wine merchants in to taste our wares over a lunch-time sandwich, and found it a pleasant way of getting to know people, and getting them to know our wines. As the business prospered the lunches became more elaborate, eventually settling into a pattern of a cold three-course menu. With each course Hans would produce the appropriate wine, and usually round off the proceedings with something altogether exceptional, perhaps a *trockenbeeren auslese*. This, for the uninitiated, is a German wine made from grapes which have been allowed to over-ripen until they are full of rich, golden liquid, and the wine is then made from only the best grapes which are individually picked out of the bunch. The cost of such a process is enormous, and it is only possible in good vintage years, but the result is the highest expression of the vintner's art.

It was our practice to regard these occasions as strictly business, but presented in the most pleasant form possible. We would invite one guest outside the trade whom we considered would be of interest to the wine merchant or merchants present and, as between wine and sport there is a great affinity, our lunches had a strong cricket flavour. Hans had never played cricket, but was infinitely patient of the talk and came to be friendly with many eminent players. Many of them were appreciative of good wine, and conversed intelligently on the subject. He was delighted, for instance, when Richie Benaud remarked of a fine German wine of 1953 vintage that it was magnificent, but perhaps not as great as the '49, which he had tasted a couple of years previously.

Jack Hobbs modestly disclaimed any extensive knowledge, but was very fond of a glass of hock. When it was known he was coming to lunch there were broad hints from many vintners of his generation that they would like to come too, but our accommodation was limited. His presence was equally a special occasion for the hosts. There was about him until the last few months of his life a youthful air, enhanced by a lively sense of humour and, as a guest, he had but one failing – it was difficult to get him to talk about his own career, a subject everyone wanted to hear about. But when he had a glass or two of hock and a cigar, which he dearly loved, we would slyly guide him on to his active days, and the company would listen enthralled, putting in strategical questions when he threatened to turn to other subjects.

Don Bradman, his successor as the unquestioned greatest of his day, was an equally good guest in a different style. Characteristically he took a most intelligent interest in the wines, and got along splendidly with Hans, by dint of relevant and penetrating questions concerning their origins and the methods of vinification. There was again, of course, much competition to meet him, but again a necessary limitation of numbers which made for a nice cosy party on the occasions he came. Perhaps selfishly, the most enjoyable meeting from my point of view was on his last visit. Although he strove to maintain the 'incognito' under which he had arrived he was inundated with invitations to every sort of function so that, when I invited him to lunch, he asked that it should be an informal sandwich and a glass of wine between ourselves. This suited me very well and, Hans being abroad, Pip Jessel, a co-director, and the two of us had four hours of gentle but absorbing chat about all manner of things. Don was given some respite from his strenuous commitments and Pip, an ardent cricket-lover, had the time of his life.

We had many rewarding Australian guests. Ray Lindwall spent six months in the City of London learning about insurance, and found time to lunch with us a number of times. What struck all his fellow guests about this tremendous fast bowler was that he was such a warm, easy companion. Everyone liked him, and he was a great loss to our guest list when he returned to Australia. Richie Benaud was an old friend, as was Jack Fingleton, but it was dis-

3. Douglas Jardine in umpire's coat during a friendly match with Amersham C.C. on its centenary. Whatever his early reputation, he was always a good friend to me.

4. A box at Lord's. Bill O'Reilly is on my right, Jack Fingleton and Lord Birkett in the foreground. Mike Charlton takes a sandwich, Arthur Mailey examines a book and Ray Robinson surveys the company over Fingo's left shoulder.

15. With Learie Constantine and Eamon Andrews during a 'This is your Life' presentation to Sir Learie in 1963.

16. Family man. With Jane, Alastair and Mandy.

appointing that his side-kick Bill O'Reilly was always willing but never able to join us.

It was from a visiting Australian cricketer that Hans received one of the most sincere tributes a vintner could have made to his wares, and one which has kept him happy over the years. The wine was one of the finest German varieties, which I have previously described, and had reached its full grandeur. Its effect on the guest was gratifying. He took a sip and rolled it round his tongue. As he put his glass down a starry light came into his eye. 'Gee,' he said, 'it's a bloody shame you gotta piss this lot out again!'

There were numerous of my contemporaries nearby in the City. Walter Robins was at Lloyds, and Gubby, Greville Stevens and Tom Enthoven were on the Stock Exchange. When we were in Camomile Street we had Peter May as a next-door neighbour and, when we moved to St Mary Axe, were just across the road from him. 'Hopper' Read of Essex was a director of Blandy Brothers and so connected with our trade. Douglas Jardine came to the City at intervals and we saw quite a lot of him. He was a splendid guest with the agreeable habit of particularly addressing his remarks to anyone who seemed shy or left out of the conversation. This was consistent with the considerate trait in his make-up which I had discerned long at Old Trafford when having bowling trouble under his captaincy. Denis Compton represented a younger generation and Colin Cowdrey and Ted Dexter a succeeding cricket era. John Warr was at that time with Union Discount, not far away and a great addition at several good sessions. The only tee-totaller in our long batting order was 'Slasher' Mackay but, on the strength of our token glass of wine, was also a very agreeable guest.

Of many first-class conversationalists who entertained us over the years I would put Charles Cobham very high in my first eleven. In the first place he has a wide and catholic experience of life upon which to draw, having been a county captain, a Governor General of New Zealand, a director of a major industrial firm and a President of MCC. In all he has been a major success due not least to his capacity to understand and get along with all sorts and conditions of his fellow men without ever yielding an inch of his standards and beliefs, which must be the test of the complete man. For me his talk has the added attraction that he is an author-

ity on at least four of my pet subjects: cricket, steam engines, mari-
time disasters and Sherlock Holmes. In addition to being well-read
and a good historian he gives wonderfully life-like oral imitations
of a Model T Ford, a heavy lorry ascending a hill, and a Great
Western King at full cut-off slipping on a wet rail. He and Hans
had much to discuss as vintners – the keen amateur and the full-
time professional.

A particularly welcome guest was Mike Henderson who, as
managing director of John Haig, runs the village competition of
that name. It was when playing in a Sussex village-cum-country-
house match some years ago that I saw that Mike was the incoming batsman. As he passed me I said to him, 'Will you come and
lunch tomorrow?' He said he would, and took guard. The first
ball I bowled was a shooter which struck the sole of his boot and,
in answer to a general and raucous appeal, he was given out. As he
passed in the opposite direction he said, 'I'll be there at one o'clock
– and that was *not* out.' Both statements turned out to be accurate.

The sale of Walter S. Siegel Ltd to the Jessel Group took place
in 1972 and was conditional on Hans and I signing on for a further
period of service, in my case three years. Despite a certain amount
of ill-health leading to a slightly earlier retirement, this term passed
pleasantly, but saw much change. On 31 March 1975 Hans and
I parted officially after nigh on 40 years' business association.

# THIRTEEN

# For Better or for Worse

London was a lively place in the immediate post-war years. There was a lot of money about and, despite shortages of all sorts, and also Sir Stafford Cripps, the apostle of austerity, the restaurants, cabarets and night clubs did a roaring trade. It was at a dinner party at Claridges that I met Ursula, then Boxer, *née* Tulloh.

She came of an old Scots family but her mother had died very young and her father, a regular soldier, had been killed at the end of the Great War. She and her brother had been brought up by an uncle and aunt by marriage in the Border country. 'Uncle Bertie', her father's elder brother and guardian of the children, was a mixture of religious mania, stalwart Scots prejudice and eccentric grandeur on such a baronial scale that I listened spellbound to Ursula's tales of life in Lowland Scotland. She occasionally says that it was my fascination with Uncle Bertie which first kindled my interest in her.

His oddities may have been less funny to live with, especially on Sundays when no laughter was allowed, and only 'sacred reading' between an unending succession of devotions, starting with family prayers and ending with Evensong. A basically kind nature and a strong sense of duty could not outweigh a lack of understanding for children, and both Ursula and her brother escaped from this oppressive scene as soon as possible. She emigrated to Hong Kong, where she spent some wonderful years, and married a scholarly soldier. Soon afterwards, however, the Japs came to destroy everything. Her husband spent the war years in a POW camp, and war work took her to Java, Ceylon and India. In the long years of separation the marriage foundered.

I was now 39, and had never seriously thought of getting married. Before the war I never had enough money to support a wife and family and during it there were additional reasons for staying single.

Over the years I had always lived with a mistress for, despite a manse upbringing, I could never see that there was anything sinful in an arrangement which kept two people happy so long as it did not hurt anyone else. As most of my loves were women of maturity and experience who were without or had shed marital ties, this was usually the case, and most of our affairs were fairly lasting, ending happily by mutual consent.

My meeting with Ursula was entirely different. I was then of mature years and she had been through a divorce (another matter in which I could never see any harm), so we were two people with some knowledge of the world. Our romance was vastly happy but not the blind, delirious intoxication of first love. Very soon we both knew that this was 'it' and, despite the austerities all about us, had a wonderful courtship amidst a throng of friends returned from the ends of the earth and bent on making up for the wasted years. While we joined their parties and did much of our courting at the International Sportsman's Club some of our happiest times were our evenings at her flat in Knightsbridge. She had an electric frying-pan-cum-grill on which she cooked whale meat steaks, and I brought a small aperitif and a bottle of Algerian wine. Many people were scathing about the Algerian wine but, although it varied because of the wartime containers, it was basically very good. In all probability many of the scoffers had drunk the same wine under a fancy label and extolled its fine quality. We had one particularly good hogshead and kept enough of it for our own consumption. At any rate, it all went to make a cosy and, to current standards, Lucullan banquet, and we were immensely happy.

We got engaged in the spring of '47 and in June we were married in my father's church, where the sun shone for us on a scene ideal for a couple setting out together in life. We journeyed to Betty-hill, on the far north coast of Scotland. Ursula avers that I told her the climate was sub-tropical (owing to the Gulf stream), just like Hong Kong, but says that the only time she tried to wear a bikini an icy blast blew it half way to the Orkney Isles. Perhaps we both exaggerated. It was certainly fresh, but the sun shone for a week and we then journeyed down the West Highland coast, and through the glens to Invermoriston and Loch Ness. In the sunshine the scenery was incomparable, the clear blue sky brilliantly reflected on the waters. The astonishing intensity and variety of colour and the majesty of the mountains had an air of the Mediterranean, especially so in the bays and villages on the north-west coast. We had two days by Loch Ness but saw nothing strange, the monster at that time still being a 'beastie' known to the old Highland seers but undiscovered by Fleet Street.

We returned to London to a flat in Knightsbridge and, not long afterwards, I went to Holland on a cricket tour. Returning after a good trip on and off the field, I began to feel increasingly strange. Eventually the doctor was called and suspected meningitis but, as the polio epidemic was at its height, Ursula fearfully asked whether it might be that. The doctor said probably not, because if it was so I would be sick. At that moment I tottered from my bed and threw up. In the ambulance on the way to St George's hospital I had a lucid moment and my bride of a few months enquired if there was anything I wanted, fearing she was about to hear my last words. I said that there was a new book called *The History of the Highland Locomotive* and, having ruined the dramatic nature of the scene, passed out again. I was diagnosed as having polio and, after two or three anxious weeks, made a very good recovery.

Soon after I came out of hospital we sought some more permanent place to live and moved to a small house in Bedford Gardens on Camden Hill. It was one of four attractive Regency terraced houses, with a common wrought-iron balcony and canopy, the legend being that 'Prinny' caused them to be built for four of his former mistresses – surely a daring experiment. They were not easy to run, being three floors and a basement, with an old-fashioned coal-fired range and boiler, but we were blissfully happy in our first real home. Our neighbours were largely young marrieds, and it was a friendly and lively community.

The next year Ursula, although heavily pregnant, came with me on another cricket tour of Holland, this time with a Free Foresters side. Cricket in Holland is of good standard, played on well-made matting pitches on which the home side is a tough proposition. On this occasion they turned out a fast bowler, a great discovery made by a brewing member of the club for whom he worked as a drayman. He had a beautiful high action in the Maurice Tate mould, and the ball fairly whipped off the mat; but it seemed to me that, for a Dutchman, he was rather easily discouraged. When the tour was over he was convicted of murder which he had committed while a rum-runner during the war. He was given a long gaol sentence, so was unable to keep a contract he had made with (I believe) Ramsbottom, in the Lancashire League. They missed a very likely fast bowler.

The team was to fly home, but in view of Ursula's condition we thought it safer to go by sea. They had a smooth, uneventful flight but we struck a most tremendous gale, and Ursula, not a great sailor, was confined to a cabin which stank of fuel oil, as the ship pitched and rolled alarmingly. As least she was oblivious of the stench, being desperately ill. There was little I could do except be present and make her as comfortable as possible, and we had a harrowing trip which she bore with great courage. Eventually she arrived intact, or at least still in possession, wonderfully cheerful and, by the time we got on to the train, equal to a drop of brandy and ginger ale. I had a good whack myself to restore my nervous system.

Alastair, unaware of the hazard he had endured, arrived in St George's hospital two months later, on Trafalgar day, which is to say 21 October. When he was borne in for my inspection the Sister looked at him and looked at me, and laughed aloud. 'Well,' she said, 'there's no doubt whose son this is.' Even I could see there was an extraordinary likeness at that moment, which was again recognized a few months later. As Ursula was proudly wheeling him along in his pram she met Chester Wilmot, our friend and neighbour, who looked at the bairn and burst out laughing. 'Good God,' he said, 'Peebles in a bonnet.' It is fair to say that with time the likeness seems to have transferred to his mother.

The trip to Holland had been quite successful as George Newman, a considerate captain, had agreed that I would rest my shoulder by standing down in the second of three matches. It also proved to be the last time I was able to raise a modest gallop. Soon after our return I was playing squash with an old friend, Geoffrey Parker, a man of so many and such varied talents that it is worth briefly recalling them. He was an abdominal surgeon who had boxed middle-weight for Cambridge. He had acted sparring partner to

Joe Beckett, the reigning heavyweight champion, to speed him up, and to the immortal Jimmy Wilde to act as a punch-bag. He said the last assignment was remarkable in that occasionally Jimmy Wilde would say exactly how, where, and when he was going to hit him and always did so, whatever defence Geoffrey devised.

When war came Geoffrey was a prominent surgeon and, having worked round the clock during the Blitz in the east end, he went through the North African campaign with a front-line medical team. That done, his robust frame and serviceable knowledge of French were put to good use when he was dropped in amongst the Maquis. When he showed a taste and aptitude for guerilla fighting and it was suggested that he was supposed to save men not bump them off he replied that all his red-cross armband did was to provide a good target for snipers. During this period of his war service he spent ten of the most hair-raising minutes of anyone I ever met. Coming out of a shop disguised as a French workman he was with an Alsatian friend when they ran straight into the arms of a plain-clothes member of the Gestapo who immediately demanded their papers in, fortunately, execrable French. To their relief he returned them after a cursory examination but, at that moment, he was joined by two uniformed members who always patrolled thirty yards behind the plain-clothes man, and closed in if he accosted anyone. His duty discharged the leader now opened a general conversation, and the Alsatian kept switching into German. This took the pressure off Geoffrey as it pleased the policemen to hear their own tongue, but it also prolonged the interview. Fortunately no French Gestapo man appeared, for Geoffrey knew that a native Frenchman would immediately spot him as a foreigner, and he was keenly aware that in such an event the consequences could be horrible beyond imagination, for this was no gentleman's war. At length, after what seemed hours, their unwelcome acquaintances bade them a cheerful good morning and went on their way.

By the time of our game Geoffrey was back in practice, adding painting and a series of books to his other accomplishments. As we played he noticed that I could scarcely play at all on the back hand and, later, that I could no longer drink right-handed in any comfort. In answer to his questions I said that my shoulder had been X-rayed and manipulated, but no one seemed to know what was wrong with it, nor be able to help it. 'I know someone who will cure it,' he said and, a man of action, almost immediately introduced me to Osmonde Clarke, a friend and a famous orthopaedic surgeon.

Having gathered all the necessary evidence 'Knobby' Clarke said, 'I could manipulate your shoulder, which would do no good, but if you let me operate on it I will cure it.' This he did with complete success, the only trace being a faint pencil line which runs from my biceps to my shoulder blade. I did grumble to Parker that I had been told that it was only going to take three weeks in hospital, but no mention had been made of almost two years' hard work required to restore full movement. He made light of this, saying that orthopaeds had no sense of time.

Apparently I had a classic case of an occupational disability which befalls house-painters and googly bowlers, but in a severe form. I said I wished he had done this for me twenty years previously, but Knobby said that this type of surgery had not then been in vogue, and was one of the few benefits of war. It was late to restart as a cricketer, but ever since I have had a pain-free limb.

It may have been because I seemed accident-prone that about this time I was elected a Purchaser. The Purchasers was a club with strong cricketing affiliations which had been founded for those who at some time had 'bought it'. It numbered many distinguished members, one being Bill O'Reilly who was elected after the Oval Test Match of 1938 in which he had assisted Len Hutton to make 364. My own qualification was 'a long and disastrous way of life', which was unchallenged and certainly valid in my case, even if unspectacular. My proposer was Jack Harvey, of Bristol fame, and he was a King Purchaser which meant something really dramatic.

The scene of Jack's indiscretion was a Royal Warrant Holders dinner where the wine flowed in appropriate quantity so that most of the guests were ready to take advantage of the short interval before the speeches. Jack's party being unfamiliar with the geography could not find the gents and, with the speakers clearing their throats and the call of nature clear, crisis was at hand. Fortunately Jack found an unmarked door which led into an alleyway entirely suitable if not officially authorized for their purpose. Everything was going swimmingly (so to speak) when a bull's-eye suddenly illuminated the scene and a terrible voice said, 'Wot's all this 'ere?' Of the whole of London they had chosen the back wall of Bow Street Police Station. Their next 'By Appointment' was with the Justices, who upbraided them and fined them thirty bob.

The only other King Purchaser I knew was a stout-hearted citizen who emerged from another festive occasion held in his Pall Mall club to find that a heavy fog had fallen on the city. Seeing a parked taxi he asked the driver to take him to Half Moon Street. 'Not in this, Guv,' said the driver. 'Nonsense,' rejoined Stout Heart. 'I'll guide you there.' And after some discussion out they set, the guide marching 'breast forward' in the pale beam of the headlights, just like the old days of the red flag. On arrival he paid his dues as per the clock, plus a fat tip for his driver's co-operation. If the fare awoke 'a sadder and a wiser man' it is possible that the driver was also a shade thoughtful the following morn.

The family was completed in 1953 when Jane was born in King's College Hospital. She was brought into the world by John Peel, later Sir John Peel, who was a friend of Hans Siegel, and of whom I was to see a lot over the years. I have also a clear recollection of my first glimpse of our daughter. She had a slightly purplish face, bright red hair, and a nose that pointed straight up to Heaven whence she had come. It is also only fair to say in this case that her looks have also altered greatly over the years.

This addition meant that Bedford Gardens was now too small for us, and we had to consider a move. When consulted I said I would be willing to commute only if we could find a railway which ran Westwards from Liverpool Street, our office now being in Camomile Street. Ursula found the Amersham and Aylesbury line, and tracked it out to the Chalfonts. Having seen thirty different houses she found the right one eventually, and instantly loved it. She hauled me along straight away and, whilst the women went over the house and garden, a civilized owner and I made our contribution by talking cricket over a pink gin. So the matter was settled, and we have now been in the Chalfonts for over 20 years. Although we have seen much change, not always for the best, we have always felt we were most fortunate.

This was the first time in my adult life that I had ever lived outside a city, so that it made a sharp change in my well-established habits. Despite a good train service and a station within twelve minutes' walk, I have never taken kindly to commuting. On the other hand, I soon decided that I would not forego the advantages and pleasure of the country by returning to London. In any case, the situation was in many ways ideal for Ursula, and our young children, with golf, country walks, dogs, cats, geese and hamsters, were most fortunate.

One great boon for me was to have a workshop. All my days I have loved mechanical things and making models of them. Without the skills or the plant to fulfil a lifetime ambition to make a model locomotive, I did the next best thing and built a ship. The proto-type was the *Clan Ross*, a comely cargo liner, the third of her name. My mother, whilst still a Ross, had launched the first one in the '90s, so there was a certain tenuous family interest in the job as well. The enjoyment I got from this was immense but, what with five days in London and week-ends spent writing cricket, my career as a constructor became reduced to that of a handy-man. Perhaps it may burst forth again. Throughout the '50s my interest in cricket was as keen as ever. There were various social cricket functions for which I would array myself in flannels and bygone fineries, and thoroughly enjoy myself trundling a few spineless, guileless overs, and trying to scrape a few runs. The wine trade played a number of matches against some quite strong opposition and in the early post-war days I could justify my presence in the side. When, in one afternoon, I ran out two of our best customers, dropped a couple of catches off another, and broke a very precious bat which a fourth had kindly lent me, I felt that my usefulness as a player and an agent of commercial goodwill was on the wane.

For many years I had taken the field for the Authors *v* the Pub-lishers. Originally I had played for the other side when the fixture was the National Book League against the Authors, and on one occasion had taken the first eight wickets. Sydney Goldsack, our captain, was delighted and said if I got all ten it would be fine publicity for the League. As the batsman in possession was an office boy deputizing for his boss I said I thought I could do this, but he should be sure to instruct the bowler at the other end to bowl well wide of the off stump. To my astonishment he made a change of bowling and a small bespectacled man, despite my frantic gestures, attacked the office boy with a will. His fourth ball was very wide on the leg side, and struck the office boy; the umpire, apparently also making his first appearance in the middle, gave him out on a disgraceful appeal. The bowler was much taken aback when I expressed my views to Sydney in forceful terms, and Sydney couldn't think how it had happened.

My other memory of this match was of Charles Fry in one of his more eccentric moods in double terrai hat and smock with clerical collar, looking like something out of the Apostolic Church of Abyssinia. On introduction to Ursula to whom I was then engaged he burst into a learned dissertation on the scoring position past mid-on from the back foot. Perhaps seeing her blank incomprehension he snatched an umbrella from a stranger to clarify his point, precipitating the owner who happened to be leaning on it at the moment.

The fixture then became the Authors v the Publishers, and developed into a social annual occasion. The oratory supplied by a galaxy of distinguished guests vied and occasionally conflicted with the play, provided by a varied band of distinguished cricketers, ancient and modern, some of them famous authors. When gone far beyond even this modest standard I was allowed to take the field to see Lindwall and Miller bowl together for the last time in England. To get the best view of this historic occasion I cajoled the captain into letting me stand (nominally) at first slip, which really meant taking cover behind the ample figure of Vivian Jenkins, our wicket-keeper. My precautions were hardly necessary for Ray by then was not much quicker than myself. The technique, on the other hand, was a thing of beauty and a joy to behold. He would bowl a series of the most perfect late out-swingers, then suddenly cut the ball so that it literally broke the other way in the air. I was fearful that there would be widespread hernia amongst the Publishers as they vainly strove to follow this abrupt change of flight and direction.

It may have been in this match that we authors were captained by that delightful man, Edmund Blunden. He allowed me to bowl a few laborious overs and I was pleased and grateful when a Pub-

lisher struck a gentle skier to mid-on, where our leader had stationed himself. But regrettably the ball fell to earth on an unoccupied space for, weighed down by the cares of captaincy, he had
forgotten to change over with the rest of the field and so was still
stationed roughly at old-fashioned point.

In 1956 Amersham Cricket Club had its centenary, and I was
asked to bring a team to mark the event. Again our side was largely
at the veteran stage but, as they say, there's many a good tune
played on an old fiddle, and Jack Fingleton played a splendid
innings so that we held this strong club side to a draw. Stevens and
Jardine, the umpires, were comparatively local, as was Denis Compton from the next village, but our neighbours helped us to accommodate visitors from farther afield. We had as our guests Arthur
Morris and his wife, but we were aware that a tragic situation
had just arisen. Arthur had been warned that his young wife had
only a short time to live. She herself was happily unaware of this,
and a great addition to the general scene, while Arthur maintained
a wonderfully courageous attitude in concealing his knowledge
from her.

# FOURTEEN

# Gentlemen and Players of the Press

Since my original excursion into journalism with the *Evening Standard* I had written at intervals on a freelance basis. The *Standard* did not renew the contract, a decision which my brother said they would regret when 'their dripping vendors returned with armfuls of unsold copies'. But I had now got the taste for writing and enjoyed trying to put words together. I regretted the opportunities I had failed to take at school but despite these misgivings I persevered and wrote periodically for the *Sunday Times* and, largely by the courtesy of Max Aitken, for the *Express*. I also wrote a book, ambitiously entitled *How To Bowl*, for Chapman and Hall, who were the most kindly and long-suffering of publishers.

After the war I found a steady outlet for my writings in *Everybody's*. This was then a family-owned weekly, largely a re-hash of old stories, pieces of history and articles on every subject. It was soberly produced and well-written with a circulation of around a million – of which I was one regular and enthusiastic subscriber. It struck me that they might like cricket stories on the same reflective lines, so I sent one in. It was accepted, and from then on I wrote frequently for the paper until it was acquired by a large group who sought to modernize it and so robbed it of much of its character. Eventually, under the strain of a 'whizz kid' editor, it folded up altogether, much to the regret of its original supporters.

I then started to write short sketches of various scenes and characters which had caught my fancy for *Men Only*, still, in the '50s, a mildly risqué publication full of good stories on every subject of predominantly male interest. As these seemed to be popular I looked for a wider field which I found with the *Sunday Graphic*, a Kemsley paper. Player-writers were a much rarer species 25 years ago but, if I was nervous about my reception amongst the full-time professionals, I was soon reassured. My first assignment was to comment on the New Zealanders *v* Yorkshire match at Bradford, and everyone was both kind and helpful. When a leaky pen had covered me in ink Charles Bray, of Essex and the *Daily Herald*, observed that now I looked quite like a real newspaperman.

The *Sunday Graphic* was constantly changing editors, but the sports department remained unaffected under the guidance of an efficient, old-time sports editor, who must have dealt with a number of novices in his time. Late in the season he entrusted me with an important assignment. Paul Gallico was in London and was keen to see a cricket match, and I was asked to take him to the Oval to see the fourth Test against the New Zealanders. I felt I had some qualifications for the job as, during the war, I had introduced a number of Americans to the game of cricket. From hard experience I had learned that to take anyone, however intelligent, to a match without some previous tuition only led to confusion and exasperation. It had been the Peebles system to lunch with the student the previous day, and describe the rudiments of cricket with diagrams, and in simple baseball terms. If the guest knew baseball he would readily appreciate the subleties of spin and curve. In this case I was the guest, for Gallico said that, as he had his wife with him, he would like me to join them at the Savoy.

Anyone who had read *The Snow Goose* would, I imagine, see the author in his mind's eye as a gentle, sensitive and rather unworldly figure. Gallico turned out to be a robust New York ex-sports editor with slightly battered countenance which argued an honourable career in the ring. (In fact, his broken nose was a relic of sparring with Jack Dempsey.) He and his wife were most friendly, and we had an entertaining lunch. Not unexpectedly he grasped the basics of cricket clearly and rapidly, and soon was asking a number of pertinent questions. When the conversation turned to other matters I remarked that, to judge from *The Snow Goose,* he must know the East-Anglian countryside well, but he said no, he had never been there. He said he liked to write about a place before seeing it, in case it should not be as he imagined it, and he might be disappointed. One would surmise he has some telepathic power.

The next day we went to the Oval, and had a good view from the top of the stand. The play, as I had expected, was not enthralling. It was a series in which the Board of Control refused the

New Zealanders' request for an extra day on each of the three-day Tests, and it was said the New Zealanders then went out to show England that they couldn't be beaten in three days. In the beautiful summer of 1949 they made their point. We watched the England batsman hitting the ball into a deep-set field, whilst the disrupting art of the quick single seemed to have died with Hobbs and Sutcliffe.

Gallico was nonetheless absorbed, and his questions and comments were to the point, making for an interesting day for both of us. When he wrote afterwards it was in serious and informative vein, with a scrupulous avoidance of the dreary old jokes usually dragged from visiting Americans. He made but one unfavourable comparison with the merits of baseball. He said an Oval sausage roll was a poor thing compared to a Yankee Stadium hot dog, a claim which, with only half the evidence available, I would concede.

In 1953 Billy Griffith went to Lord's as Assistant Secretary, which left a vacancy on the *Sunday Times*. I was invited to fill it and accepted with pleasure and alacrity, for it was a much greater platform than the *Graphic* could ever be. Before going to see the editor, Harry Hodson, I took counsel with that sagacious and commonsensical man, Henry Longhurst, especially on the question of salary, always a delicate subject. 'Well,' said Henry, 'I would say it was a matter which you had considered, as doubtless they had too. You had come to the conclusion that the job was worth between x and y, and that half-way would be a fair figure.' Thus, when the question arose at the interview, I had not only got the figure, but also a tactful formula by which to voice it. I could see the relief on Harry Hodson's face at being spared a tedious and embarrassing discussion, as he turned to his assistant editor Pat Murphy and said, 'Oh, I think that would be all right, don't you?' I only wished I had started at y.

The *Sunday Times* was a rewarding newspaper for which to work, with Harry Hodson and Pat Murphy in the lead, and Ken Compton an undemonstrative but thoroughly competent sports editor. England won a series against Australia in 1953 for the first time since 1938, so there was plenty to write about, culminating in the deciding fifth Test Match at the Oval.

In the course of the years with the *Sunday Times* I covered a match almost every Saturday, and saw a series played by every nation of Test Match status. It was an eventful period in the cricket world, with considerable changes and occasional controversy, besides which I twice visited Australia, and also made one tour of the West Indies.

In writing about a cricket match I pursued a loose line which might be described as the 'absent friends' method. This was no more than imagining that, after the day's play, I was going to call on a group of friends who had not been present but who were generally interested in what had happened – some in the technicalities, some in the personalities, some in the historical associations and, from what I knew of all kinds of cricketers, a cosy bit of gossip, and a smile here and there. So in the space of a thousand words I would try to strike a balance to this end. This usually coincided with official policy but every writer has had disputes with sports editors and sub-editors at one time or another. There was for me the test case of the horse. During a Test Match at Leeds against South Africa I came on a mounted policeman in a secluded nook. The horse was peering at the game with such rapt attention that I enquired if he were fond of cricket. 'Aye,' said his rider, 'he likes the fast bowlers, but he gets fed oop with these slow woons.' I remarked that he must be a very intelligent beast. 'He's smarter than soom,' said his master contentedly. 'He hasn't paid to coom in.' This was cut out of the southern edition but duly printed in the northern edition, and seemed to go over so big with cricketers as well as horse lovers that I protested, and it was ordained that, in future, my whimsies should not be discouraged. I often seemed to get a quote from the Leeds constabulary as next year, on remarking that it wasn't much of a day, on officer mildly rebuked me, saying that on the previous day the sun had been 'very powerful'.

In the '60s Jack Fingleton started to make more visits to this country, and cover other series beside the Australian. It was a great privilege to be associated with him professionally on the *Sunday Times* for, with a complete and practical command of his subject, and a thorough training as a political journalist, he has always been in the forefront of cricket writers. We had always got along and, on this closer liaison, we became fast friends. As may be judged from his writing Fingo is a man of strong character, but was a most considerate and helpful 'cobber' with whom to work.

When I had started to write for the national press I had resigned from the Middlesex Committee on the grounds that it seemed to be impossible to be administrator one day and critic the next and still give unqualified loyalty to both sides. This did not alter the fact that I was a man of the 'Establishment'. Much of my life was centred on Lord's, where for years I had played, been a member of both MCC and Middlesex, and been on happy and friendly terms with everybody concerned in its existence. Successive Secretaries and their staffs had been more than helpful whenever I had called on their help and guidance in the many matters and problems of mutual interest which had arisen over this considerable period. My playing colleagues and close friends had attained positions of prominence in various roles in the management of both clubs, and this was also the case in most of the county cricketing centres which I visited.

The fact that I accepted so much hospitality, and was entrusted with so much confidential information and friendly gossip, presented no great embarrassment in the Kemsley days. The attitude of the *Sunday Times* was frankly pro-establishment and, if I could not divulge much of what I heard of the true facts of any situation, it would always give me a full perspective from which to argue a case. In such circumstances I naturally tended to be in accord with authority and, where I was critical of tactical matters such as selections, appointments and technicalities, this was accepted as fair comment. As I have said, I had early taken a great liking to the press box and found that I could skip between work desk and boardroom without arousing suspicion in either.

The arrival of the Thomson Group brought changes to the tone and attitude of the paper in general and to the sports side in particular. It was soon evident that, under the editorship of Harold Evans, the 'progressive' outlook and vivid phraseology of Michael Parkinson was the order of the day. The description of the MCC members 'snout-in-port' read strangely in the columns of the *Sunday Times,* although it doubtless conjured up delicious scenes of debauchery in some quarters, and maybe evoked a faint and envious nostalgia amongst the accused. I was not surprised therefore presently to receive a letter from the editor deploring the necessity for economies and suggesting a freelance arrangement. Apparently this was intended as notice of dismissal, but the writer's delicacy was such as to obscure his purpose, which led to a hiatus of some months. Eventually the Board intervened, and a generous settlement was made. We parted amicably, if without protestations of eternal friendship.

I much enjoyed the many different personalities in the press box, as fine a variety as one would expect with every newspaper represented on big occasions, ranging in political shade from the *Morning Star* to the *Daily Telegraph*. There were rivalries, feuds, enmities and prejudices, as in any other gathering of such differing views, but these were usually personal rather than political. In fact the few notorious dislikes seemed to belong among people in the same newspaper group. For my part I look back on much help and co-operation, and a great deal of good company and interesting talk. There was good fun and jest, from the astringent wit of Jim Kilburn to Clive Taylor's amusing drolleries. The nice acid tang in Alec Bannister's quips was accentuated by a gravelly drawl. Asked about the health of a colleague, whom the enquirer knew he cordially disliked, he replied, 'All right, I believe – between fits.' On a day when the cardinals in Rome were about to emit from the Vatican chimney the puff of smoke which tells the world it has a new pope we were sitting at Lord's. Suddenly the old power station chimney belched forth a solitary cloud of black smoke, causing the company much speculation. It was halted by Alec. 'Swanton,' he said, 'is the new pope.'

When time dragged, or it rained, *The Times* crossword was a great solace and Bowes, Kilburn and John Solon of the *Birmingham Post* were each and collectively shrewd performers. Once, during a South African series, my place was several times next to Frank Worrell, temporarily turned correspondent, who became an enthusiastic solver. Brian Chapman, if he had an idle hour, loved to while it away reminiscing about his native Leicestershire, which had some appeal for me after my days of Inverness and South Africa. My sister had also married into the county side.

With a Test series now part of every English season there is usually a fair contingent of overseas writers. The Australian tour brings a number of old friends headed by Ray Robinson, doyen of Australian cricket journalists. Keith Miller, Richie Benaud and Jack Fingleton also find their way to England more frequently, and are always a welcome addition to any press gathering. Not so long ago I had several meetings with Louis Duffus over from South Africa, and whom I had not seen since he had been attached to Percy Chapman's side in 1930/31. Cricket writers are good stayers.

Turning for the moment from writer to, as far as possible, objective reader of cricket writings, I would say that the general standard is remarkably high. Most contributors have a genuine love for their subject, which is a sound basis upon which to operate. There is also in their ranks a great amount of practical experience, a helpful factor in any commentator's qualifications, and here one must preserve a sense of proportion. It is an advantage for a writer to have a name as an international performer, because people will listen to what he says, knowing it has been founded on the most exacting personal and practical experience. But the value of what he says is dependent on many other qualities, of intelligence, memory, integrity and power of expression. What is important to the writer who commands these qualities is that he should have served some practical apprenticeship in order to have an understanding of the technical difficulties of the job and, importantly, enjoyed or suffered the mental joys or anguish. If he has dropped a dolly, or made a decision which has lost the needle match for the village, he is less likely to sit in lofty judgment of someone else who has done likewise in a Test Match. Many correspondents like Swanton, Kilburn, and Woodcock have been extremely capable cricketers. John Thicknesse was for three years in the Harrow side while many others who have not sported an England or Australian cap have figured in school, league or club cricket.

On the reverse side of the coin there are a large number of ex-Test Match players who write and talk good sound sense, and some like Fingleton, Benaud and Bill Bowes who are highly qualified professional journalists. If some old players have their opinions transcribed by a 'ghost' it ought to be clearly stated in the interests of all concerned. If a man has something to say there is no disgrace in a professional writer recording and clarifying his views; but to purport that he has actually written the script in his own words is a deception.

In the matter of cricket books I have decided tastes. Any work which is the genuine product of its author I am prepared to try, and that extends to cricketers who have told their stories to professional writers, provided this point is made clear. But I have already stated my objection to 'ghosting'. The book which appears under one man's name from another's hand strikes me as a deception which taints the whole work thereafter. This applies to all books on all subjects, one or two of which have appeared under very distinguished names in spheres other than cricket but, to common knowledge, are 'ghosted'.

As I have a taste for period cricket reading this is a prejudice I frequently have to swallow, for in years gone by it was an accepted practice. One of the great cricket classics is *The Jubilee Book of Cricket,* which is officially ascribed to Ranji, but is generally attributed to Charles Fry and, indeed, is very much in his style. Whatever its origins it is, to this day, grand reading and contains sound technical advice. Under Charles Fry's own name is a masterly work entitled *Batsmanship,* a complete analysis of the art which, it is said, he wrote in a long week-end under heavy pressure from the publishers. Recently I was given a copy of *W.G. Cricketing Reminiscences and Personal Recollections* published in 1899. The Doctor has never been notable as a man of letters, and the book  was in fact written by one Arthur Porritt, who received just £100 for his services – but *not* a signed copy from W.G. In this case it seems churlish to question the authenticity as the book is 524 pages, with over a hundred extremely good full page illustrations and beautifully bound, all for six bob. The price is not marked, but my estimate is based on the enormous atached list of other works available from James Bowden, the publisher. A striking if irrelevant feature of this list is the number of non-conformist Victorian clergymen who were given to writing 'powerful' novels. It is unlikely that W.G., thumbing through this appendix to his own book, was prompted to read them.

In 1922 Methuen published *The Art of Cricket* by Warwick Armstrong. Whether Warwick wrapped a wet towel round his enormous cranium and set to, I would doubt; the text is pedestrian but has a professional air. The book has a great attraction for two reasons; it is largely about his '21 side, and it contains several superb illustrations. The pictures of Ted MacDonald and Jack Gregory, the most photogenic of all fast bowlers, are about the best of their kind in my experience.

These illustrations made such an impression upon me that, although I had not seen them since reading the book as a boy, when I came to write a book of my own in 1963 I longed to include a few. It was unlikely that they were still available, since Sport and General Agency had lost the originals in the Blitz, so I turned to the publishers. A most courteous director of Methuen's, on whom I called, said they would be glad to help me if they could, but it was almost certain they could not. It was their practice to store illustrations in their vaults for a limited period after publication, and then destroy them to make space. This publication, he pointed out, had been forty years ago. At that I said my thanks and gave up the project.

Three weeks later the director telephoned me to say that they had searched the vaults and had found the complete set intact. My gratitude was made all the greater by the thought of the enormous amount of trouble this must have entailed, and I hoped they would be rewarded by the gratitude of others who would see these superb pictures. The 'others' turned out to be quite numerous, as the book went well, and the photographs have since been used again by various authors.

To students of 1921 *A Cricketer's Book* by Neville Cardus is required and compulsive reading. This is the thunderous vintage Cardus, tortured by England's disasters, bedazzled by the Australians' brilliant, awesome efficiency, and creating in cricket writing a completely new dramatic dimension. 'What conflict these Australians bring to the game with the beautiful name,' he cried with almost masochistic joy. It may be heretical but, for me, all subsequent Cardus is anti-climax. To the actual participant the romanticism never quite rings true. In a recent re-run of the Cardus interviews with John Arlott on television the author said that some reply given him by James Tyldesley was not in character, and so he had altered it in order to give it a more authentic ring. Here may well be the explanation of the player's doubts as expressed in the blunt words of Yorkshire 'Ticker' Mitchell. 'I think nowt to thy writings, Mr Cardus,' said he, 'they're too flowery.' It is fair to say that the critic was rebuked for this sally by Maurice Leyland, who observed that he knew 'nowt of such matters'. In after years Neville was inclined to apologize for the flamboyant passages of his earlier days, saying, 'That was the way we used to do it.' I would venture to say that it is the unrestrained emotion and exhuberance which sweeps the reader along – even if he smiles occasionally in the wrong places, as when Frank Woolley, seen as the 'graceful hunted creature', is in fact exchanging some extremely ungraceful words with Warwick Armstrong. But the general effect evokes the atmosphere of those cricketing times as nothing else I know.

Cricket, being a game subject to so many variables of weather, soil, light and character, apart from its infinite intrinsic variations, produces a wealth of curiosities. Its statistics in themselves are an unending fascination to the devotee, and it must be some measure of the game's scope that scores produced by eleven players can vary between nought and 1107. If further evidence of the violent fluctuation in cricket fortunes be required, it may be recalled that Victoria, the makers of that record score, were all out in the return match against New South Wales, a few weeks later, for 35. As one with a hearty appetite for useless and outlandish information, I find any reading on the more eccentric aspects of cricket wholly absorbing. My earliest and best source of these was a couple of articles published about the turn of the century in the *Strand Magazine*, of which we had bound copies covering many years. The articles were entitled 'Cricket Curiosities' and turned up some rich material, but unfortunately the volumes were sold in one of our moves many years ago. However, I still have a few numbers, the most treasured being that of 1895 carrying an interview with 'W.G.' in the season of his great Indian Summer.

*Wisden*, of course, is a ripe source to the seeker of the more eccentric happenings, and Gerald Brodribb has produced some very entertaining sidelights in *Next Man In*. The statisticians, such as the late Roy Webber and the present Irving Rosenwater, have unearthed every available statistic, but there must be room for a diligent researcher to put together all the mass of trivia and more consequential 'strange interludes' which add such spice to cricket talk and history. He will have one certain customer.

Cricket literature is now such a vast field that, apart from professional reviewers, there must be few who can keep abreast of the entire flow, especially in these times of inflation. For the last reason it is also less easy to enjoy the sister art of oratory as applied to cricket, but again it is pleasant, and occasionally highly entertaining, to consider the enormous flood of eloquence on the game that has poured forth over the years. Of such part of the flood as I have received the quality of the orators has varied as widely as the cricket scores I have quoted, and might appropriately be marked with the same range of figures, nought to 1107.

The late Lord Birkett is generally regarded as the most accomplished speaker regularly to have addressed cricket circles. He was doubtless equally appreciated by all sections of the community, but cricket was one of his first loves and he spoke of it with much feeling and understanding. One reason for his complete perfection he inadvertently demonstrated some years ago at an Authors v Publishers match, a function he was attending on that particular day as a guest with no intention of speaking. Despite his strenuous protests he was persuaded by the extremely persuasive captain of the Publishers, Sydney Goldsack, to 'say a few words'. He abandoned a very good lunch, called for a brandy and soda, and worked steadily through the interval. The speech was, as ever, a model and the delivery gave it an air of effortless spontaneity.

On the several occasions upon which I heard him, Charles Fry was, surprisingly, an indifferent speaker for the reason that usually he was patently unrehearsed. As he was also very lengthy, his addresses were inclined to become increasingly rambling. It was at a lunch in Sydney that Neville Cardus made the devastating reply to such a harangue in saying that for years they had known all about C. B. Fry, now they knew all about Fry B.C. This brought about a pause, if not a complete rift, in an old friendship.

Peter May also dealt firmly with a couple of over-generous orators at a dinner on the eve of his departure for Australia. Each took forty minutes in proposing and receiving the first toast of the evening and, when his time came, Peter with a good-natured smile observed that, if his first pair in Australia could stay in as long, he would have no complaints.

Earlier in this book I have mentioned Ronny Stanyforth, and I would still place him in the first flight, and as ideal as a captain of a cricket team. He was straightforward, imaginative and quietly humorous, while always apt and effective. But the greatest entertainer in my entire experience is John Warr, with a wonderful off-beat wit, and a delivery and timing precisely suited to these gifts. It is perhaps rash to quote him in a different medium, but I still treasure one passing remark made at a Cricket Writers' dinner to the Australians. 'Many of those present,' said he, 'seeing that the dinner was to be held in the Skinners Hall, had mistaken it for another Ladbrokes function.'

It was a matter of immense personal satisfaction when, in 1973, I was made Chairman of the Cricket Writers' Club and, as I had always been a part-timer, a signal honour. John Kay, as able an Hon. Sec. as he is a writer, ensured that any chairman batted on a very plumb wicket.

# FIFTEEN

# Down Under Twice

I had always believed in the truth of the saying that a cricket writer's education is never complete until he had seen a Test Match in Australia. Possibly to have played in one would have been equal qualification, but this I had not done. When the *Sunday Times* decided to send me to Australia to cover Len Hutton's tour it was a most welcome assignment and I accepted it with only one regret. We had just moved to Chalfont St Giles, and I would be parted from Ursula and the family for about six months. Because the children were so small she accepted the position philosophically and, at the end of September, drove me to Tilbury to join the *Orsova*, the latest addition to the Orient Line fleet, making her second voyage.

There had been a certain amount of controversy about Len Hutton's appointment as captain, on the grounds that as a leader he had not been markedly successful in the West Indies and, quaintly to modern ideas, that it was undesirable to have a professional captain on tour. These objections had been voted down, and the majority of cricketers were satisfied whilst the objectors were now resigned.

The voyage was pleasant rather than exciting. The *Orsova* was a beautiful ship, with what looked like a witch's hat crowning the funnel, giving her a distinctive appearance while protecting the passengers from fumes and sparks. The public rooms were all air-conditioned, something of an innovation and, by way of an experiment, seven cabins were included in the system. There was considerable doubt amongst my fellow travellers when I put in for one of these, but it proved a great success and in the heat of the Red Sea I had many applicants seeking to borrow it for a quiet, cool siesta.

The tour of 1954/55 was remarkable for a number of events, some wholly unforeseen. The series started with absolute disaster at Brisbane, and ended in complete triumph at Sydney. There was a lesser but equally successful transition in the individual career of Frank Tyson, who started as a somewhat unpredictable supporting member of the cast to finish the major figure of the tour. The young and untried Cowdrey proved himself a remarkably mature Test Match batsman, and Peter May enhanced his already established reputation. The saddest event was the end of Alec Bedser's great career, precipitated by a painful bout of shingles.

When, at Brisbane, Hutton had miscalculated the degree of help the pitch could afford his all seam attack and put Australia into bat, Tyson had bowled 29 eight-ball overs for 160 runs and one wicket. In the tropical heat a run of 37 yards or so was an exacting exercise and, periodically, Tyson had recuperated by cutting it to half-length. During these spells there seemed to be little if any loss of pace, and the whole performance looked more rhythmical and better controlled. When, on his next appearance against Victoria at Melbourne, he cut out the long run altogether and approached the wicket, in the happy words of *Wisden*, by 'beginning with six shuffling steps and finishing with ten deliberate raking strides', the result was six wickets for 68 runs. The transition had been effected.

Although England won the series by the handsome margin of 3 to 1, and had far the best of the drawn last match at Sydney, each game was hard fought. In their three defeats Australia at certain stages either held a distinct advantage or produced a sudden threat. The most nerve-wracking moment of all was the last innings of the fourth Test at Adelaide. The Test that would finally decide the series.

It was especially nerve-wracking for me because, before leaving England, I had been to Michael Gordon-Clark whose firm were agents for Glenlivet, the fairest distillery in all Scotland. Having consulted his charts, in response to my request for every drop he could spare us, he said he was sorry but two hogsheads (60-gallon casks) was our maximum ration. Then in a burst of patriotic fervour he added, 'But if you bring back the Ashes we might find you one more from some dark corner.' As this, a pearl beyond price, would probably have to be drawn from his own allocation, it would give

the series an added significance for both of us. I slaked my conscience by reflecting that his reward would be to rejoice at England's
triumph, whereas good pressmen are strictly non-partisan!

When England went in to make 97 on a still-perfect Adelaide
wicket all seemed to be decided and, apart from my 'non-partisan'
satisfaction at the prospect of England clinching the series, there
floated before my mind's eye a spectral oaken cask full of liquid
gold. This celestial vision was wildly disturbed when, in the first
over of the innings, Keith Miller knocked Bill Edrich's castle all
over Adelaide with a ferociously fast in-swinger. It lost focus
completely when he had Len Hutton and Colin Cowdrey both
beautifully caught in the slips from immensely fast balls which
moved sharply away off the pitch. With only 18 runs on the board
97 seemed an enormous score. Len, whose agony must have been
unbearable at the last of these disasters, was quoted as saying
at that point, 'They've done us – the buggers!' to be rallied by
Denis Compton observing that it was a fine thing to say when
he hadn't even been in.

Keith continued in this tremendous vein for another few overs,
but gradually he burnt out. For the first half-dozen overs it was
one of the most tremendous bursts of fast new ball bowling I have
ever seen. On retiring to extra cover he still had sufficient steam
left in him to make a brilliant catch when Peter May hit a hard,
low skimmer, but by that time the die was cast.

So the series was decided. For sustained excitement it had been
unsurpassed by any I had previously seen, and this was enhanced
by the astonishing reversal of fortunes after the upheaval of the
first Test Match.

The State matches were also interesting, the chief feature
to English eyes at that time being the uniformly perfect fielding.
Each State had a row of young, athletic slips of such ferocious
zeal that to snick the ball in amongst them was like tossing a bit
of meat into a den of hungry lions. General cricket standards were
high but, with only six teams competing, cricketers playing first-
class cricket (as against first-class cricketers) were scarce and their
appearances relatively infrequent. I pondered Douglas Jardine's
observation that Australia's first team was generally superb, but

the second XI was a long way behind, but I came to no definite
conclusion.

The Australian pitches were not as I had imagined them to be.
The old-timers of my youth played in days of plentiful Bulli and
Merry Creek soil, and their descriptions of the pitches made therefrom was of polished marble, in which one could see one's face
well enough to shave. This was certainly not the case in the mid-'50s
by which time the Australian pitches, in common with those elsewhere in the world, had slowed down and had a green and grassy
look. Perth was the first and the fastest wicket we saw on all our
travels. This general loss of pace was doubtless discounted by
the greater effect of the seam on the lusher surface, which also
helped to preserve the ball. In olden days it was said to be so
roughened in the course of a few overs that it had ears hanging
from it.

Len Hutton had every reason for satisfaction. Having survived
controversy in his own country, and early disaster on the tour, he
had steered his team home to the first win in Australia since 1933.
This he had done by a handsome margin, and with no more than the
day-to-day bickering inseparable from a Test Match series.

The social side of the tour was enjoyable and, for a newcomer,
interesting and instructive. The Aussies as a nation are warm-
hearted, friendly and hospitable. They are also clear-cut and frank
in their likes and dislikes, and fiercely loyal to Australia and its
institutions. Distinctions in class and status exist and, being theo-
retically non-existent, are the more subtle in consequence.

Australian clubs in the '50s were absolutely first-class, and probably still are. I was lucky in that from Adelaide on I was handed
from one to the other to live in the best possible circumstances
for a travelling grass-widower. At Perth, although I lived in a hotel,
I spent much time in the Weld Club, one of the most attractive and
old-fashioned – in the best sense of that term.

There were numerous official receptions and parties from which
one soon learnt that Australians are very fond of speeches if they
did not always listen to them with rapt attention. This impression
was confirmed when we were bidden to a large reception in the
Sydney Cricket Ground on our first arrival in New South Wales.
As the 300 guests drank the din of their conversation naturally

rose, and it was only by beating a thunderous tattoo with his gavel and bellowing long and loud that the Chairman was able to announce that Mr Sydney Smith, who managed the 1921 Australian side to England, would 'say a few words', ever a sinister form of introduction. Mr Smith said as many words as he could get into 38 minutes, but, as the conversationalists restarted as soon as he gave tongue I heard not one. Jim Swanton was luckier and heard two. They were 'Lord Hawke'.

For this loss I was more than compensated by meeting many survivors of the 1921 team, whom I had seen when 13 years old, and who remained to me the greatest cricketers in my lifetime. They were a splendid lot. There was Jack Gregory, for some the greatest cricketer of all time, 'Stork' Hendry, Johnny Taylor and Bert Oldfield. Tommy Andrews, whom I later sat next to at a dinner, was a most friendly man with an immense love of Britain. Arthur Mailey had, of course, accompanied us on circuit, giving forth shrewd comment, apt wit and pointed anecdote, all with dead-pan countenance. What his arrangements were with his papers no one quite knew, for his times of arrival in the press box were dependent on the attractions of his route leading to it. If the countryside offered a pleasing prospect he was liable to halt his dormobile and up with his easel, whilst the world went by wasting its time in hurry and worry.

To welcome us at Adelaide was 'Nip' Pellew, swiftest and surest of all outfields, and just about as good in any other position. He is on record as having dropped only two catches in England, both within the space of two minutes in the Lord's Test of 1921. When Arthur Mailey saw Nigel Haig coming into bat in this match he may, being Mailey, have had some telepathic message that Nigel was under orders from a distraught selection Committee – once again faced with disaster – to 'have a go'. At any rate, he said to Nip at mid-off, 'Drop back a bit; I think we've got a customer.' Nigel rushed at the first ball and hit a skimmer straight but high to mid-off, who got both hands to it but, to the astonishment of all present, dropped it. Even greater was their astonishment when exactly the same performance was enacted next ball.

Nigel profited but little from these lapses, being caught at the wicket off Jack Gregory for 3, but Nip remembered the incident

clearly. He said that he had jumped too soon for the first attempt
and too late at the second. He sent his best regards to the beneficiary, saying that it was very unlikely that he would ever again
perform the same service for him.

At Melbourne I made a point of seeking out Bert Ironmonger,
an interesting man and an unusual cricketer. Pat Hendren thought
he was the best slow-medium left-hander he had ever batted against
and, from his record, he was almost unplayable in his own country
when he got a helpful pitch. He was large and lumbering, a total
loss in the field or with the bat, and was generally regarded by
his colleagues as being far short of the Einstein level of intellect.
He also lacked about two-thirds of the index finger of his left hand.
The generally accepted explanation for this was that, when a tim-
ber worker and seeing a circular saw for the first time, he had ex-
perimentally thrust a finger into the blade, so losing the first section.
When an agitated foreman enquired what had happened he accompanied his explanation with a practical demonstration – which cost
him the second section. The stump left him he ground into the
seam of the ball and gave it such a tweak that Pat said you could
hear it buzz the entire length of its flight. Owing to a neat and
springy run-up he rejoiced in the nickname of 'Dainty'. There was
but one snag; many people thought he threw, and said that for
this reason he was never brought to England. Hearing I was going
to meet him Arthur Mailey said I had better prepare a monologue,
as there was unlikely to be much comment from the other side.

He had thinned down a lot from his playing days when we met
and seemed flattered that I should be interested in him. He had
grown loquacious with the passing of time and we had a splendid
exchange. He said he had never thrown, and it was all propaganda
to keep him away from England. We met several times after this,
on the Melbourne ground, and he always greeted me with great
warmth, and that was very flattering to me.

The most interesting view on his action came from Gubby Allen,
who had played against him in his prime, and had spent a whole
day observing him with close attention. His verdict was that in the
morning he threw two an (eight ball) over, between lunch and tea
he threw four, and after that, when tired, he threw the lot. Whatever
the truth of the matter it is certain that he acted in honesty and

good faith, and it is a pity we never saw him on English pitches.

We returned as we had come, on the *Orsova,* and I had the same air-conditioned cabin. This was a particularly good voyage largely by reason of the entertaining company aboard. At our table we had Jim Swanton, Alec and Eric Bedser and Johnny Woodcock. Prominent in the passenger list were the Lords McGowan and Nuffield who occasionally had a sort of Dutch auction concerning their hard start in life, each undercutting the other in recalling the harrowing poverty of his youth. The listeners were, however, able to restrain their tears without undue effort. The Lord McGowan I had known since dining with him when Nan, his daughter, was a deb and, what was more, he always knew me. He had a grand Scots humour and used to pull everyone's leg, including mine, with unerring touch. At Naples he went ashore with Betty George, the attractive wife of the governor of South Australia, and a Russian Princess, to be accosted at the foot of the gangway by a seller of strange and erotic postcards. 'My man,' said his lordship, 'as you see I already have one wife, and am trying out another. I cannot afford your dirty postcards.' The vendor was so shocked at this immoral way of life that he immediately broke off all business relations.

The good ship *Orsova* had time in hand, so the commodore was able to show us some of the beauties of the Mediterranean. Having sailed us around the Bay of Naples he sailed us inshore along the Spanish coast. I can remember sitting for several hours looking at this ruggedly beautiful, remote part of the world and thinking that if ever I wanted peace and quiet how wonderful it would be to have a cottage near one of the tiny fishing villages dotted along the coast. When I did in fact visit this part of the world it was scarcely for peace and quiet. What I had been looking at was the Costa del Sol, and the solitude and rustic tranquillity had given way to a solid strip of towering buildings, and the roar of a ceaseless flood of traffic.

A second trip to Australia to cover the 1958/9 tour was equally enjoyable, but in several ways much different. The whole season was overshadowed by the throwing controversy which, having simmered for the first half of the trip, burst into flame in mid-series, and led to much bitterness in both Australian and English camps.

All started on a happy and promising note. At Perth Alec Bedser and I stayed in the Weld Club, to which we had taken such a liking on our previous visit. It took a conscious pride in its solid, old-fashioned comforts and conservative traditions. The members recalled with pride how, during the war, they had made the American submarines honorary members and, with equal pride, would tell an illustrative tale. The admiral one day was brought a document by a commander for a signature, an operation he reckoned they could better complete with the help of a pink gin. When the document was produced it turned out to be an affidavit requiring an oath. 'Would they have a Bible in the Club?' asked the admiral. 'Well,' replied the commander, 'they might have the Old Testament – they wouldn't have the Noo.'

Alec and I lived in great comfort, dined well, and nightly had a bottle of the local red wine, which was very good indeed – especially at a bob a bottle. The evenings we frequently spent with a resident and friend of old, Berkley Fitzsimmons, who was six foot, eight inches tall and in his eighties, a descendent of the Clan Cameron. He had a tremendous store of Australian folk-lore and we both found his stories of early life in the outback enthralling.

The great excitement in Perth was the arrival of Norman O'Neill, Australia's newly discovered batsman who was the centre of a tremendous publicity campaign. Don Bradman had himself predicted a great future for him, an endorsement which redoubled the public's expectations, and he was now due to play for a Combined XI against the MCC following their drawn game with Western Australia.

He turned out to be a modest and personable young man, who seemed to take all the bally-hoo in his stride. On the afternoon of his arrival Alec Bedser and I bowled to him in a net, and had a nice private view of his talents. He was a powerful player with a model straight pick-up, and had a good duel with Alec – still, armed with a new ball, a formidable proposition. He met my gentle hack-like efforts with courtesy and restraint, and rewarded me next morning with a personal interview. I later learned that he had foregone breakfast in order to do so and had a pang of conscience, remembering what this meant to a lusty, fit young man.

In the match he upheld his reputation with a soundly-played 104 and was himself the recipient of a generous act. He proved to be a somewhat impetuous runner with a great turn of speed between the wickets and, when his partner, Kenny Mackay, just in double figures, played the ball into the gully he set off. There was obviously no run, and Kenny looked up to sight his partner three yards away. He looked sadly at gully already ball in hand and then went, to cross just as the bowler collected the ball at the far end. This was not the only altruistic gesture we were to see from this canny but generous cricketer in the course of our travels.

The seeds of the controversy concerning the legality of certain bowling actions had been laid before the MCC team had sailed. When the Australians had toured South Africa the previous season rumours reached Britain that Meckiff, a fast left-hander, had a most peculiar action which, unless modified, would lead to controversy in the future. Amongst these rumours was one to the effect that the South African umpires had made a clandestine agreement not to check him, believing this would have ruined the tour. These stories were noted but not taken too seriously at the time. A year later, by the time the MCC had reached Brisbane, they were convinced that every State had at least one bowler with a suspect action. These ran from a slight flex and bend in the arm to Jimmy Burke's blatant chuck, which I described at the time as being like a constable laying his truncheon on a very short offender's head. The last named was a merry little man who, aware that he was not blameless, made little claim to be a bowler at all. But Meckiff, who in some eyes was but a little more orthodox, was a highly dangerous proposition.

After the first Test there were many 'sair hearts' in the English camp, but May and Brown, although exasperated, maintained a stoic silence. The press were keenly aware that, in view of England's sad performance, any adverse comment on Meckiff would be regarded as a 'squeal', so were restrained in their comments. But when Meckiff cut loose at Melbourne and took six wickets for 38 runs in the second Test, Johnny Wardle, writing in the *Melbourne Herald*, did likewise. He denounced Meckiff in forthright terms as a 'chucker', and so set the atmosphere aflame. Both sides were sincere in their views but each suspected the other's motives and, in these heated circumstances, it was remarkable that the players and press maintained the fairly cordial relations they did.

The situation was worsened later in the series when Rorke was brought into the Australian side. A large, strong man, he added fuel to the row by dragging so far that he frequently delivered with his back foot over the popping crease, in addition to being, in the eyes of the visitors, another blatant chucker. Looking back, I have no doubt at all that Australia suffered at that time from a malaise of illegal actions so wide that honest men had come to regard these freaks as true bowling actions. I also believe that, when feelings cooled, responsible opinion in Australia realized that this had been the situation. It was indeed largely due to the weight of Australian influence that the offenders were driven out.

During the arguments I conceived a formula which came to be called the 'horizontal' law. It said that when the arm was shoulder high on the final swing it would be fully extended until the ball was released. I still consider this to be the most practical guidance the umpire can have, because it is impossible to define a throw in this context in terms sufficiently brief and succinct to be applied in practice. Meantime the question has not again arisen, largely because the search for suitable legislation focused sufficient weight on the problem to discourage any unorthodoxy. This in the Bard's words was to 'scotch the snake not kill it'.

On the social side it was again a delightful trip. I stayed once again in comfortable clubs where I enjoyed much good company. Jim Swanton and I spent many happy days staying with friends down at Frankstown, an attractive seaside resort about 25 miles from Melbourne. There I was routed out by the Lord Chief Justice, Sir William Owen, and made to play golf, being much the junior and quite the worst of the quartette. When the team went to Tasmania I had a fortnight's holiday staying in Adelaide with Sydney and Margaret Downer, and such was the general hospitality that I felt that I was an Adelaidian by acclaim.

Sir Robert Menzies appointed three umpires for his match with the MCC at Canberra — Jack Fingleton, Jim Swanton and myself. We each did a stint and I felt after mine that all players should be made to stand umpire for an innings, just to gain a little understanding of the difficulties of the job. My finest moment came when, with his connivance, I was able to no-ball Frank Tyson for throwing.

In the evening Sir Robert gave a dinner, and called upon all of his guests to get up and make a short speech. Lindsay Hassett, who was regarded as unofficial court jester to Sir Robert, heckled all the speakers but was so exuberant by the time my turn came that the host rebuked him. 'Peebles,' he said, 'is a noble town in Scotland, but Hassett is only a small village in Ireland.'

From this meeting I got to know Sir Robert well and greatly admired him. Whenever he came to Britain he would find time amid all his official engagements to have a private cricket dinner at the Savoy, to which he would invite a score or so of personal friends of whom I was lucky to be one. When he retired the guests changed their role with his and gave an annual dinner for him. The venue they changed to Lord's, but the company was un-altered.

He told me that, in days before I knew him, he had arranged one of those meetings to follow some important Commonwealth conference. He hoped to say his piece and get away in good time to change and receive his guests and, conveniently, the conference ended early. But Sir Winston detained him, saying, 'Now, Bob, we have some matters to discuss.' At that he launched into a majestic survey of world affairs gaining momentum and scaring to great heights as his listener glanced anxiously at the clock. At length Sir Robert was compelled to interrupt this tremendous oration. 'I am very sorry,' he said, 'but at this precise moment I have a dozen guests waiting for me at the Savoy.' Halted in full flow, Sir Winston's brow darkened ominously. 'This sounds very sherious,' he rumbled. Then a light came in his eye as he added, 'you *might* make the thirteenth at your own board.'

Recounting this, Sir Robert smiled affectionately and said, 'He never missed.'

# SIXTEEN

# Caribbean

A trip to the West Indies was for me an especially inviting prospect as it was one which had eluded me as a player. What with boyhood visions of pirates and blue water, conjured up by Conan Doyle's book of that title, *Captain Blood,* and other such works, the Carribean has a lasting aura of romantic beauty for most people. For cricketers, those who had toured had brought back tales of unbounded enthusiasm amongst the West Indians, which led to situations both comic and moving. It seemed that the view that no writer's education was complete without seeing a Test Match in Australia could well be extended to cover the West Indies as well.

To travel with Peter May's side of 1959/60 had the further attraction that, not only had one got to know many of the players from the previous year in Australia, but Walter Robins was to be its manager. Jim and Ann Swanton were going to make the trip and amongst the press were many old friends. In all it had the makings of a grand three months, but again I regretted the separation from Ursula and the family which kept her fully occupied at home. At the end of the day I could say that I had enjoyed myself, at times hugely, but at times I had reservations.

The team had gone by sea some time earlier than the bulk of the press who flew to Barbados via Gander just after Christmas. For many people Barbados is the most pleasant of the British West Indies. The people are agreeable and the climate is warm but, with a constant breeze, never uncomfortably so. It was not one of the spectacular islands, being completely flat, but the countryside is green and the seaside perfect for bathing in the clear blue sea which, like the climate, is ideal as to temperature. The whole island is about twenty miles square, and has produced more cricketers per square mile than any comparable area in the world.

This fertility in the cricket sense was soon evident when MCC was beaten by the Island by ten wickets in a high-scoring match, Nurse making 213 and Sobers 154. It was a rough start but the English morale, well established by May and Robins, was equal to the occasion, and the team was galvanized rather than discouraged. The Test Match which started three days later was an even draw, the scoring again being so high that only eight wickets fell in the making of over 1000 runs. The salient feature of the match was the extremely fast and mainly short-pitched bowling of Hall and Watson, countered by spirited English batting. Dexter at his most majestic made 136 not out and Barrington, by unflinching resolution, made 128.

To those who had not previously seen a cricket match in the West Indies the conditions and the crowd were as great a fascination as the play. The ground was filled to capacity – which means that every available tree and point of vantage within the range of human eyesight was occupied. The Barbados public is said to be staid by West Indian standards but, to visiting ears and eyes, there seemed to be an abundance of free comment and advice, and plenty of incident. There was a pleasant diversion with the arrival of 'King' Dyall, an elderly character with a taste in dress which made Liberace look drab. He usually managed a new outfit (said to be largely paid for by public subscription) for important occasions. For this match he wore his best each day, elegantly tailored suits in dazzling yellow, sky-blue, red and orange so that, even with his accessories of black Homburg and rolled umbrella, he would scarcely have passed for Foreign Office. He timed his entrance to a nicety and was greeted with deafening enthusiasm.

During my stay I had the honour to be driven across the island by Everton Weekes in his large red saloon, cheered by every passer-by we encountered. Years later I went to catch my homeward train at Liverpool Street Station to find the doors not yet open but, on arrival, the driver made such a graceful apology that there were no hard feelings. When it turned out that he came from Barbados I said the last Barbadian to drive me had been Everton Weekes. Had it been humanly possible I think he would have driven his train right up to my front door.

Travelling on to Trinidad we saw a very different public demonstration in the shape of a full-blown riot. England had batted well against another hostile barrage to make 382 and, on the Saturday, Trueman and Statham did a great day's work. The West Indian batting had an off day and at 98 Singh, a local lad, was run out and eight wickets were down. Discontent ran high and the rum ration had increased in direct ratio, especially in one densely populated spot behind the wire barrier. Suddenly out of this group a single bottle, glinting like a star shell, sailed on to the outfield, and the flood-gate burst. A shower of bottles followed the first, then the crowd rushed on as the umpires, very prudently, rushed off. The players found themselves in the centre of an excited yelling mass but, so far as they could understand, were assured the crowd wanted the umpires' blood, not theirs. They left the field without injury and the Prime Minister, the Governor and Learie Constantine all went bravely out and appealed for order. Learie had a moment's success when, with unerring hand, he caught a flying bottle, but otherwise the deputation was ineffective and retired.

When it was seen that the police were short-handed the fire brigade was sent for and provided a little comic relief when the hose burst and drenched the marksmen. The riot squad then arrived and, after a time, the rowdier elements were subdued. Having let off steam the crowd now wanted to see some more cricket, but the outfield was largely covered by patches of broken glass, and it was going to be a considerable job to dispose of it. The really tragic aspect of the day's events was the shame of the senior Trinidadians. One old Test Match player wept openly that his fellow countrymen could so affront a visiting team, and besmirch the good name of the island. But Walter Robins and Peter May once again proved a splendid combination. They assuaged bruised feelings, insisted that the match must continue on the Monday, and dealt with a sensitive local press with the tact which already had laid the foundations of mutual understanding. Virtue was rather more than its own reward for England won by 256 runs, and this match decided the Series.

Trinidad I remember as one of the world's most picturesque grounds, with a beautiful mountainous background as one looked out from pavilion or press box. When we were there, on each shoulder of the nearest mountain was one of those tropical trees which flower briefly, but with great brilliance. As these two were a vivid golden hue they looked like epaulettes, and further enhanced the scene. The donors of the splendid new score board, Messrs Coca Cola, had, understandably, put a large placard above it; but this was a small speck on a majestic background.

Jamaica provided another draw but a very good cricket match which ended fairly closely, the West Indies wanting thirty runs to win with four wickets in hand. My clearest memory of the match was that looking down out of the press box, straight up the wicket over a shortish boundary, one got a perfect view of Wes Hall in all his youthful zest. When the later batsmen came in he abandoned his bumping and bouncing to bowl a full length. This was a grand spectacle, with his tremendous approach and robust action producing such pace that later batsmen seldom picked up the line of his flight. Had I been his captain I would have advised him to bowl to this length at all times.

My other memory of the press box was that it was on the small side, so that, once this sizeable company of the press was seated, no one could get in or out. As I sat directly by the only door I acted as postmaster, caterer and sole contact with the outer world. Drinks and snacks I ordered for one and all from a charming coloured lady who came up from the bar below. Like many social benefactors I was subject to harsh criticism when anything went wrong, and one day I was roundly abused by the steaming, sweating workers because there appeared to be a glut of eatables and dearth of drink. Taxed with this my coloured lady friend consulted her notes and found that by mistake she had written 'cakes' instead of 'Cokes'. Of this she made light, laughing heartily and saying, with the intrusive Jamaican aspirate, that it was 'only a case of hay for a hoe' which, in a musical contralto, had the ring of an Elizabethan madrigal.

In Jamaica I spent a few days on the only sugar plantation I saw at close quarters and, expecting a scent of honey and marzipan, was struck by the unpleasant smell that pervaded the whole area round the processing plant.

Guyana, then British Guiana, was one of the happiest stays of the whole trip although it started with some sad news. Peter May had undergone an operation some time before the start of the tour for a non-malignant growth in his bowels and it was now given out that the wound had not healed properly, so that for some time he had suffered a good deal of pain. He was not a man to give in easily, but the stage had been reached where he could not carry on, and had to return home for further attention. For his peace of mind he was fortunate in having Colin Cowdrey to take over the captaincy, and a fine stout-hearted reserve batsman in Ramon Subba Row.

Walter, as manager, stayed in the 'big hoose' with Peter Gibbings who was managing director of one of the major sugar and rum companies. Just after Walter's arrival Peter's wife, Jeanette, had to leave on a trip to England, and I was invited to join the grass widowers' club. We had a glorious ten days looked after by Bacchus, Peter's cricket-loving factotum, butler, and Jeeves. He was delighted to have Walter in the house, and countered the fearsome threats of what England was going to do to his side with spirited forecasts of sweeping victory.

We had not had particularly encouraging reports from Georgetown as people said that, being below sea-level, it was humid and generally was not a very exciting place. These reports were entirely misleading for it turned out to be a fascinating city. When at one stage it had been a Dutch colony it was built round a system of canals which, when filled in by the succeeding British, made fine, wide streets. The architecture was also attractive, with wooden houses of gracious design and colour predominating. Gardens and streets were coloured by a profusion of tropical foliage, and the whole effect most pleasing. In the circumstances the climate did not strike one as being unpleasantly hot or humid.

Going back to Trinidad dormie one for the last Test, England won the toss and held the advantage until losing six wickets in their second innings for 146. This was not enough with a lead of only 45 on the first. The situation was remedied by a fine stand between Jim Parks and Mike Smith, who added 60 runs before the close of play. The problem then arose what to do on the last day if things went well. Walter, characteristically, wanted to declare early and make a game of it. Others, including myself, felt that having battled through a very tough series to the point of almost certain victory it was ill-advised to make any gallant gesture.

Parks and Smith went off at a good pace next morning and soon the question of the declaration became acute. Business had detained

Walter, but he had made his views clear with his customary force and, in his absence, Colin Cowdrey consulted me, knowing that I was very close to him. I said that I felt strongly that he should bat on, reinforcing my view by saying that in the same circumstances the West Indians would certainly not contemplate such a risk, and equally certainly they would not expect England to do so. What influence this had I do not know but, in the event, Colin took the safe line.

On arrival Walter was very cross to learn this. He was much troubled by high blood pressure at this moment and easily upset, and I was much concerned for him. Knowing him so well I felt I could help, so I asked him to come and have a walk with me, at which we spent about twenty minutes pacing up and down behind the stand. I repeated my arguments, and said that he had himself been largely responsible for the tremendous success of the trip, and it would be foolish and unnecessary to throw away the victory which would crown their efforts; the more so as it was against long odds when they had set out. All this gave him time to breathe, and presently I was able to tell him to take a couple of his pills and rejoice, which he did.

As it turned out everyone was happy and the West Indian press was most generous. It hadn't occurred to them that anyone might have declared before the game had been made safe.

Two days later I arrived at Heathrow and, having given my panama to a taxi driver who fancied it, prepared to resume my city bowler, which was in any case more appropriate to the weather.

# SEVENTEEN

# Sixty Glorious Years

From the time I was introduced to the 'glorious uncertainty' of cricket by the young woman who hit the tree to the present day is just about sixty years. For not one moment of any of those years has my love of cricket flagged nor has my interest – active, journalistic, or academic by turns – ever waned. Nothing has ever shaken my belief that it is the best of all ball games. Now, as an end to this book, I would, with the reader's indulgence, like to reflect on its various aspects and the changes over these sixty years as I see them.

I have already argued that, taking the '20s as a starting point, there have been no major inventions in the game. The googly was by then thoroughly understood, and countered. Many bowlers had completely mastered the arts of seam and swing, Maurice Tate to a degree never excelled. The bouncer had made its unwelcome appearance as a tactical and intimadatory weapon, which was to culminate in the uproar of 'bodyline'. In Jack Hobbs and Herbie Taylor of South Africa batting had reached a level as near perfection as man could achieve, while Charlie Macartney and Frank Woolley had produced every stroke to which a cricket bat could be applied. Tactics and field placings were thoroughly understood. Only in the general quality of fielding are standards undoubtedly higher in present times, especially in throwing from the deep (although the Australians of 1921 set a level of fielding never since excelled). The point is that the basic skills of the game had been crystallized over fifty years ago. It is an important one to bear in mind when times and records of younger and still developing sports are cited as evidence that cricket must have advanced to the same extent in the corresponding period.

This is not to deny that there have been enormous changes over this span, but they have been developments of trends rather than inventions or innovations. Many have been brought about more by circumstance than calculation, and not all have added to the attraction of the game, even where they have made for some advantage in efficiency. As might be expected in such a turbulent half-century cricket has suffered (and benefited) from the social pressures arising from a series of major upheavals. Surprisingly, the actual play has not been directly affected by the immense advances in mechanics and technology in other spheres – with one notable exception.

The greatest change in cricket as played today compared to cricket play in 1926 has been brought about not by cricketers but by chemists. Modern fertilizers have changed the nature of cricket in all the major cricket countries. The abundance of grass has led to the complete ascendancy of seam bowling and, as its logical extension, extreme pace. It is a rational development, for with a lasting shine of the ball and a lush surface seam bowling is not only economical but can produce spectacular results. But green, grassy wickets, so helpful to the seamer, are a deterrent to the spinner who looks for a puff of dust to provide him with the necessary friction. Cricket has gained efficiency in some respects, but has paid for this by the decline of one of its greatest attractions, which is the intrinsic fascination of spin and the variety it brings.

The loss involved in the decline of spin, especially wrist spin, is not confined just to the joy of watching a versatile craftsman but to the effect of his absence on the character of the game as a whole. The intelligent spinner of any type has many more resources at his command than the less flexible seamer. His permutations in variation of spin, flight and pace are infinite. The wrist spinner is also a gambler, and open to counter-attack. He is likely to get wickets or be hit freely and so injects incident and action into the proceedings. I believe that if a good slow leg-breaker was to appear today it would be surprising how many good players of seam bowling would be uneasy when faced with the high-flighted and well-spun ball of the Mailey or Freeman type.

The necessary action to bowl fast and accurately is given to comparatively few people but once this has been established the techniques of seam bowling are simple and easily acquired. The spinner has a much harder apprenticeship to serve and, until he has perfected his craft to a point beyond the capability of all but a few, his weapon is erratic and vulnerable compared to the consistency of even a moderate seamer. Now he is further discouraged, not only by chemically-prepared wickets but by other factors such as short boundaries, covered pitches and limited-over matches. I cannot foresee any great resurgence in this department, whatever artificial inducements may be offered to encourage it.

The other powerful influence on the tactics and technique of cricket during the period has proved to be the revision of the LBW law that was first introduced in 1935. This provided that a batsman could be given out when the ball pitched outside the off stump if the obstructing leg was in line between wicket and wicket. Under the old law a batsman could pad up to any ball pitching outside in complete safety, a form of protection which weighed heavily on the off-spinner, in-swinger and googly bowler. As a googly bowler myself – and considering the host of batsmen who, when legitimately deceived, had been saved by the accidental or deliberate intervention of a pad – I welcomed this revision to the law as plain justice. It was fair to the fast bowler of high arm action who previously had only a tiny margin upon which to pitch a good length, and hit the stumps as ordained under the old law. But those who, like myself, welcomed the change, can now see what was widely unforeseen at the time. The effect on bowlers was to place a great emphasis on the ball coming in to the bat rather than leaving it, so that in-swingers and in-slanters from the extreme width of the crease multiplied and off-spinners were – initially – given much encouragement (I say 'initially', for off-spinners have since withered under the malign influences which have militated against all spin). All this tended to throw the game towards the on-side until it was necessary to introduce undesirable artificialities, such as a limit on the number of fielders allowed on the leg-side.

The direct effect on batting was equally unfortunate. No longer could the batsman sit comfortably back on his stumps and pad up. He did the logical thing, and thrust his front leg out to meet the ball outside the line of wicket and wicket. Should he play and miss or just not play he was secure in the knowledge that even a slight misjudgment would not beset him, because no umpire can say with certainty what the ball would have done in the remaining three yards of its passage to the stumps. In short, if a batsman is hit on the front leg it is long odds against his being given out.

Admittedly the batsman under any law is more likely to be given out playing back than he is playing forward, but this probability has been increased out of all proportion under the present rule. Bob Wyatt, a clear thinker on cricket matters, has frequently pointed out the ill effects of this situation. The art of batsmanship is to play forward to the full-length ball, thus forcing the bowler to drop shorter until he is open to the many scoring strokes to be made off the back foot. A bowler then seeking redress throws the ball farther up, enabling the batsman to come forward and push or drive from the front foot. So the balance swings to and fro.

The modern batsman gets on to the front foot almost before the ball is bowled, and so encourages the bowler to pitch on a length which the uninhibited back-foot player would have attacked and harassed. The modern bowler, thus containing the batsman, is freed of the onus to pitch the ball farther up and of the consequences of a front-foot counter-attack. Anyone who wants confirmation of this objection has but to watch the average county batsman on his routine ploys. It is notable that great players when in command – as the West Indies recently demonstrated – can ignore the dangers of back play and, by exploiting it fully, reap a rich harvest.

It may well be asked what solution, if any, would be fair to all parties. Wyatt himself, supported by many good judges, says the answer is to go back to the old rule and widen the wicket. He hesitates on aesthetic grounds to advocate a fourth stump, which is a horrible thought to all traditionalists, but suggests the stumps might be made broader but elliptical. It is worth noting that Gubby Allen, with his vast experience of everything to do with cricket, is of the same way of thinking.

My own answer would be to go back to the old law, but offset the wickets so that the off stump at the bowler's end is in line with the striker's leg stump. The bowler would now, in the context of the LBW law, be bowling into a rectangle of (at present) nine inches wide and up to twenty yards long instead of into an acute triangle with its apex some distance in front of the popping crease. The fast bowler would have ample latitude to drop the ball on his good length mark and hit the stumps. The off-spinner could operate effectively from over the wicket, and would not be handicapped to any extent going round. The general effect on bowling would be to return the balance to the off-side and encourage the bowler, once again, to make the ball leave the bat. Should leg-spinners ever return to the scene they would find encouragement to attack the stumps.

The batsman would not be incommoded by the very slight alteration in the line of the ball delivered by a bowler of normal action. As often as not at net practice the bowling stump is moved about, as the bowlers wear the turf whilst at the less scarred batting end the stumps remain in their original position. I have never seen any batsman, given a new guard, notice any difference.

To pursue our comparison of the two eras, acknowledging the greatness of the present West Indian side we can compare them with the Australian side of 1921 to illustrate another aspect of the change. When Australia beat England in 1921 they scored at the rate of 56 runs per 100 balls. Even more remarkable was the fact that the beaten side managed a rate of 46. As no bowler's run was more than 20 yards and there was plenty of slow bowling, the over rate was alone 20 an hour, and it meant that the day ran to a lively tempo. In the case of the Australians the day opened with the enthralling spectacle of Gregory and McDonald, the most inspiring pair of fast bowlers of relatively modern times. Armstrong would then bring himself or Arthur Mailey on at one end and, according to wind and weather, ring the changes between the foursome. Occasionally Ryder or Hendry might deliver a few holding overs at fast-medium pace, but the quartette was usually more than equal to every occasion. Here was the ideal band, the superb but contrasting fast bowlers followed by two splendid spinners, who differed as widely as any two could and still both be classed as leg-spinners. The huge spin and frequent indiscretions in length and line by Mailey, and the mathematically accurate top-spinners of Armstrong were alike only in that both came from the back of the hand. To complete the scene they could have called on Charlie Macartney to bowl his slow left-handed spinners, but he had to wait until the following tour, when but one of the quartette remained, to get a regular bowl.

Now, as I write, English batting, as was the case in 1921, is being overwhelmed by fast bowling of a calibre at present unmatched amongst the native-born. The West Indians Roberts, Holding and Daniel are a superb trio of quite exceptional pace, and Holder a most useful man of less speed, but with more movement off the seam. To see the first few overs is an inspiring sight, especially when the bowlers aim at a sensible length to endanger the stumps rather than the batsman. But when the third performer is also a fast bowler it strikes one that two's company, three's a crowd. And when a fourth appears there is inevitable monotony about the scene, magnificent though the individuals may be. As each bowler runs around forty yards an over rate of 14 an hour is good going. If a spinner appears at all it is likely to be for a brief spell late in the day.

The pattern of play in a typical county or international match of the periods in question differs not because of any great disparity in the talent employed but because over the years the circumstances and the influences I have described have channelled them in certain clear directions. As a broad judgment I would concede that modern standards of efficiency have probably risen because of the great increase in the number of people who play cricket. However, as a spectacle, the game has lost much of its attraction. I am not, in what I have said above, considering one-day matches, which are a different world from three-day county matches and six-day Test Matches.

Many people blame one-day sponsored matches for a laxity in British batting techniques. This raises the whole question of sponsored competitions, and their impact on the game as a whole. By the '60s the entire organization of first-class cricket in Britain was threatened by financial collapse. Television had brought some money and a great number of new viewers to the game, but it seemed that many considered county cricket, in Dr Johnson's words, 'worth seeing, but not worth *going* to see'. At any rate, there was no dramatic rise in county gates. The combination of television and *one-day* matches was an immediate success, and the Gillette Cup, the John Player League, the Benson and Hedges competition and the John Haig village competition have all proved great successes. They have each brought money and encouragement to the game, and provided vast entertainment for the crowds who have turned out in numbers to see them.

Against these great benefits must be accepted less profitable features. Not being genuine cricket matches they tend to distort the true nature of the game. Presumably it is necessary to impose limitations of overs, restrictions on the length of bowlers' runs, and the amount of bowling any one man can do; but all these artificialities have side effects. As soon as time or the number of overs is limited a premium is put on stifling the batsman's scoring strokes instead of getting him out, and this is the negation of a bowler's first duty, and leads to a defensive attitude. The fielders retire from all attacking positions to fill the deep field. The batsman, if pinned down, has to resort to attempting suicidal and 'improbable' shots. It makes for brisk running between the wickets, but this frequently degenerates into recklessness. When the last few overs are due – as Sir Cyril Hawker, a very good cricketer and ex-President of MCC, recently said – one is faced with the most appalling succession of cross-batted mowing, cow-shots and slashes that ever disgraced a village pitch. If you allow a bowler only eight overs but permit batsmen to last the length of the innings it means, as Lyn Wellings so neatly put it, 'You allow Bradman to win a match but not O'Reilly.' Whatever the benefits of the one-day limited-over match may be, the development of these trends is not good training for the hard, exacting atmosphere of a modern Test Match.

I would underline the point that it is the restrictions that foster the evils of this type of cricket, not the fact that they are single-day matches. A genuine one-day cricket match can be a splendid game, and the element of time one of the more fascinating ingredients. When the captain of a successful batting side has to decide whether to bat on and make safe or declare and perhaps be defeated he has a ticklish problem on his hands, and can make or mar the day by the wisdom or otherwise of his decision; for time is one of the important elements in a genuine cricket match, and affects every manoeuvre.

No doubt experts in the fields of publicity and finance as well as cricket have worked the present formulae which have achieved their purpose. But if I were rich enough or (equally unlikely) entrusted with the funds to sponsor a competition I would have one-day matches as they were originally played – that is, to the rules without any strings or limitations. One hundred points would be awarded for a win, ten for every wicket taken. A draw would bring no profit to either side, except for the number of opposing wickets they had taken.

Between the two periods which I have compared lies a long, fertile period of gradual change and development. Its remarkable decade just before the war will ever be famous amongst cricketers as the Bradman era, for no individual since W.G. had so much influence on the game as The Don. On international cricket his impact was much greater than his illustrious predecessor. Apart from his supreme ability as a batsman, his astonishing physical and mental stamina meant that he could sustain a high rate of scoring over long periods, resulting in enormous scores achieved at record speed. So far as this provided his bowlers time as well as runs upon which to work, it gives some foundation to the saying that he was the first to show that batsmen could win matches as against the old cliché that bowlers did so.

Bradman had but one apparent flaw – previously remarked – his inability to adapt to slow, rain-soaked English pitches. These present few problems to the native English batsmen, but have always taken the visitor from sunny overseas countries some time to understand. Bradman apparently did not trouble to tackle the problem seriously, considering it to be so infrequent as to be trivial, and there can be no doubt that, had he applied himself, he must have conquered it as he did all other aspects of batsmanship. As he did not do so, however, he remains the greatest force of any cricket era, but must yield first place as the complete master batsman, to Jack Hobbs, in his own. This is a sweeping claim, but all who knew Hobbs from his early days to his mid-forties were agreed that, the greater the difficulties with which he and his colleagues were confronted, the more marked his superiority.

Towards the end of the era Denis Compton took up the running from Bradman, adding to the highest quality of batsmanship a jollity and generosity which occasionally, between the wickets, burst into broad comedy. Of the English batsmen of the past half century he must be the nearest rival to Hobbs and Bradman for admission to the immortals.

Having made these strictures of modern cricket I would as a

final and general judgment say that the game is in a healthier state
than ever before. Its finances now seem assured for some time to
come, which will enable its administrators to carry out the development necessary to meet the demands of its increasing public,
and the great number of young who want to learn to play it in
proper conditions. The number of active followers in overseas
countries is rapidly increasing, and may well soon be swollen by
the young of the emergent nations. Should the game ever take
root seriously in America its influence would indeed be world-
wide. If some of the present trends are not to the taste of the
older purist they seem to be to the satisfaction of the younger
generation, and it is they who will determine the future.

The truest testimony to cricket's unique character is measured
not so much by the numbers of its followers, which is now prodigious (although doubtless far outnumbered by soccer fans) but
in the spread of its adherents, socially, racially and in every other
way. It is only possible to surmise, but it would seem that this is
proportionally wider than any other sport, and has no limits to its
reaches ranging between Prince Phillip, an active cricketer as President of the premier club, and the little barefoot boys playing with
a petrol can for a wicket and a home-made bat, all over the Carribean.

The social structure of the '20s and '30s, although presumably
less strict than in Edwardian days, was still extremely formal. This
was naturally reflected in the realm of cricket, where the division
between amateur and professional was underlined by the amateur
being addressed by the professional as 'Mister', and referred to by
*Wisden* and *The Times* by the same title. Separate dressing-rooms
were the rule on all county grounds, and each party travelled
separately, to stay in different hotels. Viewed from the 1970s this
sounds impossibly feudal and wholly destructive of any 'team spirit'.
In practice that was entirely untrue. The vast majority of citizens
accepted the caste system as ordained by providence, although there
might be much latent discontent – which has since had full expression. Even the moderately successful professional cricketer was
better off in every respect compared to his counterpart in industry,
and generally accepted the social requirements of the era without
resentment. Whatever the formalities, the senior professionals were

major figures and treated with proper respect by captains, committees and the public, and regarded by the young amateurs with affection and awe. They had impeccable manners and strictly observed the code but they expected, and received, every courtesy and consideration in return.

By the later '30s there were signs that the rigid divisions were beginning to crumble. Hobbs, Woolley, Sutcliffe and their ilk had raised their profession to a status comparable with the stage and other entertainments. Wally Hammond turned amateur and almost immediately had become captain of England. On tour, Christian names were the rule and this was becoming prevalent in the county system. England teams now changed together in dressing-rooms.

Translated into human and personal terms, the cricketers who lived with this system were a happy, well-balanced and highly entertaining community. Doubtless every man thinks that his particular sphere of interest attracts people of special quality and character, but I am convinced that in the case of cricket this is true. The physical nature of the game would support this contention. It is the most subtle of the active ball games, and widest in its scope and variety, and certainly as susceptible to climatic influence as any other game. It contains all the psychological strains of golf, the nervous suspense, the call for firm decision under pressure – and with time to dither. Normally a reasonably safe game in the physical sense, it can be tough and dangerous. Anyone who doubts this can volunteer to open an innings against the Australian or West Indian fast bowlers, or put his hand to a nice full-blooded hit to mid-off on a keen April morning.

Having attracted good material, cricket seems to enhance it, and is as good a form of democracy as exists in the world of sport. I once said to a friend that cricket was the best type of trades union; he demurred, saying rather was it the best form of freemasonry – a timely correction, more than ever true today.

Looking back from this distance on a very large scene I sometimes try to assess my own small part in it. In the house in which we stayed on our first visit to London there was a book which purported to tell fortunes. In the first section there were various questions and the reader, having found the one applicable to the occasion, then went through a complicated process to find the answer to another section. My question was, 'Shall I fulfil my greatest ambition?' This was, of course, to bowl like Sydney Barnes, a pretty tall order. In due course I found the answer, and was snubbed. 'No,' said the prophet. 'The results would not be at all satisfactory.'

By the standards to which I aspired, and briefly glimpsed, I was a good might-have-been, or maybe a might-have-been great. Had I progressed from the stage I had reached when I went to the Faulkner School I sincerely believe that I might have made the top flight which Faulkner and other good judges so confidently predicted. When I altered my style to slow medium I think that, but for the breakdown of my shoulder, I would have reached the top in this line. But that is a large claim too.

My sudden descent from cricket's pinnacle was an appalling shock, but I was always buoyed up by the thought that the shoulder would mend and that I would return. When it became clear that this would never be so I had achieved a philosophical attitude and was happy and grateful in more modest successes. But still in my dreams I am, to my surprise, summoned to play for England

| | |
|---|---|
| 1908 | Born in Aberdeen. Two older sisters and one younger brother. |
| 1911-17 | Wick. Private school. |
| 1917 | Move to Uddingston on father's discharge from the Army. |
| 1919 | See first cricket match: Uddingston v Ferguslie. Uddingston lost. |
| 1920-25 | Glasgow Academy. Enter Bank of Scotland. In their cricket team for three years. |
| 1926 | Join Faulkner School of Cricket. |
| 1927-28 | Tour South Africa with MCC. |
| 1928 | Leave Faulkner for Nottingham. First match for Middlesex v Worcestershire at Lord's. |
| 1929 | Full season with Middlesex. Haig, Robins and self all take over 100 wickets. Go up to Brasenose College, Oxford. Intend to read Law. Ploughed in Law Pre-lims. |
| 1930 | Oxford Blue. Play for England v Australia fourth and fifth Tests. Get Bradman out for 14 at Manchester. Take six wickets in innings of 695 at Oval. |
| 1930-31 | Tour South Africa with MCC. Write on sport for *Evening Standard*. |
| 1931 | Play for England against New Zealand. Take thirteen wickets in two Tests. |
| 1932 | Join Ladbroke & Co. as apprentice bookmaker. |
| 1933-34 | Tour Canada, America and Bermuda with Sir J. Cahn. Take seventy wickets to Robins's ninety. |
| 1935 | Join Seager Evans and Co. as full-time member of staff. |
| 1936 | Tour Ceylon and Malaya with Sir J. Cahn. |
| 1937 | Found wine company with Hans Siegel. |
| 1937-38 | Tour India with Lord Tennyson. *Wisden* reports: 'Peebles was a failure.' |
| 1938 | Return to Middlesex as result of successful season in club cricket. Tour Holland with MCC. |
| 1939 | Captain Middlesex. Second place in County Championship. |
| 1939-46 | Army. |
| 1941 | Seriously injured during Blitz. |
| 1946 | Re-establish Walter S. Siegel Ltd. |

1947    Married Ursula Boxer (née Tulloh) in Birnie Parish Church.
        Contract polio.
1948    2 October Alistair born.
1949-53 *Sunday Graphic*. 26 March Jane born. Join *Sunday Times*.
1954    Move to Chalfont St Giles.
1954-55 Tour Australia for *Sunday Times*.
1958-59 Second tour of Australia.
1959-60 Tour West Indies for *Sunday Times*.
1966    Created Chevalier of the Royal Swedish Order of Vasa.
1970    Leave *Sunday Times*.
1972    Silver wedding 14 June. Walter S. Siegel Ltd. sold to Jessel
        Group.
1974    Retire from Walter S. Siegel Ltd.